Advance Praise for *Marathon War*

"Major General Jeff Schloesser has written a gripping account of his fifteen months commanding the 101st Airborne Division during the toughest days of America's long war in Afghanistan. Schloesser eloquently and candidly writes about being a senior commander at war, making decisions that likely will result in soldiers wounded and killed while simultaneously dealing with the political challenges of dealing with higher headquarters and senior echelons of the American, Afghan, and Pakistani governments. *Marathon War* is compelling and honest, telling the story of men and leaders in battle, the 'filth and gore,' the camaraderie, and the impact of soldiers' absence on the families left behind—including his own. Jeff Schloesser was a great commander. This book makes clear why."

—Robert M. Gates, Secretary of Defense, 2006–2011

"A deeply personal, powerfully insightful, and sometimes disturbingly candid account of command in combat by one of his generation's most thoughtful warrior-leaders. Jeff Schloesser captures the frustrating complexity of Afghanistan and the challenge of fighting America's longest war brilliantly. A must read for those who want to understand leadership in the toughest of environments."

—Stanley A. McChrystal – U.S. Army, GEN (Ret.),
Commander of US and ISAF forces in Afghanistan

"*Marathon War* transported me straight back to the year I spent learning to be a general officer from Major General Jeff Schloesser and his 101st Airborne team in Afghanistan. Jeff artfully recounts the story of people, places, and events to explore the challenges, complications, and responsibilities of leading counter insurgency operations on the other side of the world. You'll leave with a better understanding of both the choices and decisions that shaped our longest war and the human toll it took on the extraordinary men and women who fought it…and are still processing it."

—General Mike Holmes, USAF (ret.)

"If you truly want to understand the nature of wartime leadership; the heartache, the elation, the fear, the sense of frustration, and the great pride of leading America's men and women in combat, then you must read Jeff Schloesser's *Marathon War*. No one tells the story better."

—Admiral Bill McRaven, Former Commander,
U.S. Special Operations Command

"A lot has been written about Afghanistan, but Jeff Schloesser's *Marathon War* offers something different. The very personal reflections of a most thoughtful senior commander help us better understand the strategic context and consequences of America's longest war, but also offers insights into the incredible stories, tragic and heroic, of those involved. Jeff reminds us that, while politicians make the big decisions about war, it is soldiers and their families who bear the brunt of those decisions."

—General Carter F. Ham, U.S. Army retired, President and CEO of the Association of the United States Army, Former Commanding General, United States Africa Command

"*Marathon War* is a dramatic account by a unique leader. General Jeff Schloesser led our effort to develop the nation's first war plan for the global war on terror (GWOT). Incorporating all elements of national power, it was debated by the cabinet and approved personally by President George W. Bush. He then put on his cleats, jumped on the field, and executed it for fifteen hard and bloody months in Afghanistan. This book focuses on leadership at the tip of the spear. It is a fascinating and moving account of implementing grand strategy at the tactical level on the ground, where death and destruction are constant companions. It is a must read for those who labor in either vineyard, as well as a solid reminder for all that character is the *sine qua non* of effective leadership."

—Hon. John Scott Redd, VADM U.S. Navy (Ret.), Former Director, National Counterterrorism Center

"There have been several books written about leadership, and specifically leadership in combat, but Jeff Schloesser's *Marathon War* is an absolute must read to understand senior level command in war. It tells the riveting story of commanding for fifteen months in Regional Command-East, the most lethal region of Afghanistan. It masterfully provides the rich detail and insight into the trials and tribulations of how a senior leader must assimilate volumes of information, calculate risk to mission and risk to force, and ultimately make decisions that put men and women into harm's way. Despite having a dedicated staff and other subordinate commanders to provide their insight, their assessment of the intelligence, and despite innovations in technology and superior equipment, the ultimate decision rests with the commander. Jeff provides an intimate account of 'the interpersonal struggles' that senior leaders are challenged with in the most complex situations. Leaders in any profession who choose to be relevant need to read this account."

—John F. Campbell, General, US Army, (Retired), Former Army Vice Chief of Staff and Former Commander US and NATO Forces in Afghanistan

MARATHON WAR

LEADERSHIP IN COMBAT IN AFGHANISTAN
JEFFREY SCHLOESSER,
MAJOR GENERAL, US ARMY RETIRED

A KNOX PRESS BOOK
An Imprint of Permuted Press
ISBN: 978-1-68261-989-6
ISBN (eBook): 978-1-68261-990-2

Marathon War:
Leadership in Combat in Afghanistan
© 2021 by Jeffrey Schloesser, Major General, US Army Retired
All Rights Reserved

This is a work of nonfiction. All people, locations, events, and situations are portrayed to the best of the author's memory.

Permuted Press, LLC
New York • Nashville
permutedpress.com

Published in the United States of America
1 2 3 4 5 6 7 8 9 10

Dedicated to the soldiers, airmen, marines, sailors, Coast Guard, and defense and intelligence civilian professionals that labor, and sometimes fight, to keep our country free

CONTENTS

INTRODUCTION

"The will to do, the soul to dare."
Sir Walter Scott

For fifteen months—about 450 days and nights—I commanded the 101st Airborne Division's Combined Joint Task Force 101 (CJTF-101) in combat in eastern Afghanistan. It was a rare privilege: the most challenging and rewarding experience of my thirty-four years in uniform, and ultimately the cause of my retirement from the U.S. Army. With the preparations for combat, the actual deployment, and a short month after our return, I was a division commander for thirty-three months. That was unusually long, but these were unusual times.

War is the most brutal of human endeavors, and I have experienced enough war to know to take cover when politicians, poets, and armchair warriors speak extravagantly of patriotism and national honor. As they speak, I see the filth and gore. I smell the stomach-turning stench of burning flesh; I hear the sounds of incoming mortars and rockets. But I also think of those who lived and fought and cursed the heat, the bugs, the mountains, and the enemy. We fought a war too few Americans knew or cared much about, in a remote frontier populated by xenophobic tribesmen and cultivated city dwellers, both equally alien to our Western upbringing. We were not victims—we were volunteers—at war because our nation told us to go to war, but each of us with our own reasons for being there.

This is my story as Eagle 6, my call sign as the 101st Airborne Division commanding general. A lifelong runner, from the beginning of my command I viewed the 450 days and nights in command, in combat, much like the 26.2-mile race we call a marathon: an extraordinary challenge, requiring extensive and detailed training and preparation, and disciplined execution.

For most of my military life, I kept a daily journal. Each night I swept up the day's events and my thoughts, and deposited the lot into a small green notebook. This book is based on my notes and my memory and the historical record as best it is for such an ill-recorded endeavor in a faraway place.

My primary interest in exploring my past is most likely selfish: I buried many of these memories in deep locations of my mind, because they hurt so much. And yet at odd times they would come to the surface, and I would remember. As the pain eased with time, I realized my story—actually our story of the division and CJTF-101—was worthy of telling, and that it might be of direct utility for leaders and aspiring leaders, be they military or civilian. But in truth, I needed to tell the story to someone. Remembering, reflecting, and then writing about these events were helpful to me in settling this most rewarding but also most troubling phase of my life.

This is a book about senior-level command in war, focused on the interpersonal struggles to be an effective leader in the most challenging of circumstances, and written from my perspective as an American general with the prerogative and responsibility to command American and Allied troops at the tactical and operational levels of war. I was also a strategic leader. I explore the challenges of trying to competently lead when my decisions impacted the ultimate strategic outcome of our war from 2008 to 2009.

I hope the words I have written will be of some interest to those who fought this war or others before, or who seek to know of war and leadership in extreme circumstances as they prepare for what they cannot predict. More broadly, my intended audience is military and civilian national security professionals and business and civic leaders, as well as those seeking to understand leadership of the most challenging kind: that performed in war.

My story is essentially chronological: how we prepared, and then ex-ecuted our part of Operation Enduring Freedom. I use major events that impacted my command or me to draw general conclusions about warfare and leadership, as well as provide specific analysis of this Afghanistan War as I experienced it from 2008 to 2009, including its future course. I hope readers will find my experiences and thoughts on combat at the campaign level and leadership insightful, perhaps provocative, and that they will lead to self-analysis and growth. If, upon finishing this book, the reader is better prepared to lead in challenging circumstances, then I feel I will have been successful.

Ultimately, I write to honor those that died, but in dedication to the living: the soldiers, sailors, marines, airmen, and civilians of America, our allies, and their families that they left behind, as we journeyed to a most foreign of wars and fought with valor.

AFGHANISTAN AND REGIONAL COMMAND-EAST

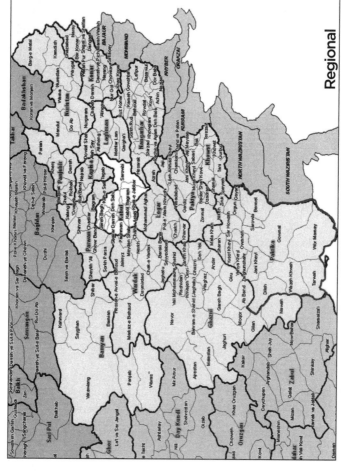

Map Page: Afghanistan, with Regional Command-East highlighted. Courtesy of CJTF-101, Operation Enduring Freedom.

PART

CHAPTER 1

"By failing to prepare, you are preparing to fail."
Benjamin Franklin

Sunday, April 27, 2008

I learned a big lesson of war seventeen days after assuming command of Regional Command (RC)-East and our Combined Joint Task Force 101 in Afghanistan.

We boarded my Black Hawk at 6:45 a.m. for the short flight from our headquarters at Bagram to Kabul. It was a beautiful, crisp morning, the sun already so bright that it hurt to look long at the brilliant blue sky. The tallest mountains surrounding the Shomali plain were still snowcapped, and the fields remained a dull brown, but spring was clearly right around the corner, and I was full of optimism.

It had been a busy early morning. At 4:00 a.m., a special operations task force attacked an insurgent stronghold in Tagab district, in eastern Kapisa Province, northeastern Afghanistan. The target was Haji Mawlawi, a leader in a growing suicide bomber network. Given my own background, I was personally a fan of special operations and this particular task force, but I was dubious when told early that morning the attack included six HIMARS missiles (our high-mobility artillery rocket system capable of firing well beyond the range of standard "tube" artillery), AC-130 gunship fires, and a bombing run by an F-15E all-weather strike fighter. That didn't sound like a precision strike using a minimum of firepower to me, especially with the target being a compound within a small village.

"We think we got him," I was told.

"Great. Civ casualties?"

"Six wounded, sir. We are still trying to sort them out. Some could be the Haji's foot soldiers."

I thought about the strike as we flew to Kabul. The special operations teams did not work for me, and reported to their own chain of command. As the land-owning battlespace commander, my troops and I were responsible for the overall outcome of the fighting and counterinsurgency campaign, but we often had to devote a lot of time and effort in consequence management from special operations conducted in our area of responsibility, our AOR. This attack was no different, and with all the munitions involved, it did not sound like a targeted precision strike to me. I was anxious to fly up to Tagab to see for myself.

First came my other duties. As RC-East commanding general, I commanded the largest of NATO's five regional commands in Afghanistan. The size of Pennsylvania, our area of operations included 450 miles of shared border between eastern Afghanistan and the Pakistan frontier. It was a stark, sometimes incredibly beautiful, sometimes harshly forbidding land. The Afghans who live there are a diverse lot, from sophisticated city dwellers in Nangarhar to the deeply suspicious xenophobic mountain dwellers of the Korengal Valley.

I also was the commanding general of CJTF-101, the combined joint task force formed around the 101st Airborne Division (Air Assault) headquarters and three brigades we had brought with us from our home base at Fort Campbell, Kentucky. We were part of Operation Enduring Freedom. It was seven years since 9/11 and the first U.S. and NATO forays into Afghanistan. Some said we had fought seven one-year wars since, and had learned little and accomplished even less. I did not believe that, after having sought the advice and lessons learned from my predecessors, studied what had worked and not worked for them, and made two previous trips to RC-East with my commanders and staff to see for myself.

Under my dual hats, I intended to conduct a vigorous counterinsurgency campaign augmented by an equally effective counterterrorism campaign to find, fix, and finish the Taliban, other insurgents, and al-Qaida. If they could not be convinced to stop fighting the legitimate government of Afghanistan, then they had to go. And we—the troops of RC-East and CJTF-101, as well as our partners in the special operations task forces, the U.S. Air Force (USAF), navy, and marine close air support aircraft that supported us all, our International Security Assistance Force (ISAF) allies, and increasingly the Afghan Army soldiers—would see to that.

Today was Afghan National Day, marking sixteen years since the Afghan mujahedeen captured Kabul from the Soviet-backed government. My job for the remainder of the morning was to attend a big, fancy military parade, make small talk with the senior Afghan and NATO leaders, and then get back to my own AOR, and Tagab, as soon as I could diplomatically do so.

In the helicopter with me was my command sergeant major, Vince Camacho, a tough infantryman from Saipan. Not a tall man but compact, strong as a mule, and just as determined, he was my battle buddy. We often traveled together on our daily battlefield circulation to our almost one hundred combat outposts and operating bases in our AOR.

Turk Maggi, my State Department political advisor (POLAD), was with us too. A former naval officer, Turk had an eye for the political dimension in Kabul and Brussels that I was still refining in myself, and I very much valued his sage, quiet advice. A big man, no longer quite as fit as in years prior, he had a ready smile and an infectious sense of humor. I'm sure the three of us made quite a trio to an outsider—Turk the civilian dressed in a tie and blue sport coat over his expansive frame, Vince the short but battle-hardened sergeant major, and me, the general, tall, skinny, and more inclined to smile than many of my peers.

To keep us out of trouble, we had my aide, Major Andy Beyer, my security detachment leader Chief Warrant Officer 2 Eric Clayton, and Vince's security man, Sergeant White. We had been told to leave our weapons behind in the helicopter. There had been several threats in recent intelligence reporting about potential attacks against President Karzai, who was to be presiding officer over the parade, and the Afghans were taking no chances. We were all to go through metal detectors before being allowed into the VIP section of the grandstands.

My team was also taking no chances. Andy and Eric had cooked up a way to smuggle a single 9-mm Beretta in a backpack, and I supported that. I did not know the Afghans or Afghanistan well enough yet to trust them in an ambiguous situation. I figured we could always make some excuse if the pistol were discovered.

The Black Hawk flared and landed in the landing zone (LZ). A waiting up-armored sport utility vehicle (SUV) manned by some of Chief Clayton's security team whisked us away, and minutes later we got out at the parade grounds, right across from the Eid Gah Mosque. It was an ordered scene, with lines of dignitaries queuing up to go through one of several metal detectors set up at the entrance to the grandstand. Almost midmorning, the sun beat down on the stone and sand, and beads of perspiration ran across Turk's brow as we waited to go through the detectors. I was pleased not to be in a coat and tie, and felt sorry for him.

How we got through the detectors with the pistol I don't know for certain. I thought that, like many things in Afghanistan, form reigned over content, and maybe the metal detector really didn't work or was not tuned right. But we were through it, and were ushered to our seats.

I smiled and waved at the U.S. ambassador, Bill Wood, who was chatting with Sir Sherard Cowper-Coles, the British ambassador to Kabul. The previous day, at Bill Wood's urging, I had picked up Cowper-Coles in Kabul. We had flown to Khost Province to visit U.S. troops, talk with our commanders, and see how we were doing COIN (counterinsurgency) in RC-East. A veteran diplomat with previous postings as UK ambassador to Israel and Saudi Arabia, as well as an amateur photographer with a professional's eye, I found Cowper-Coles to be engaging, witty in the dry, prototypical British diplomat manner one might expect of Kipling's era, and yet almost brutally honest about the political and military situation he saw in Afghanistan. As we flew him back to Kabul after the visit, it was clear I hadn't convinced him our counterinsurgency strategy was working.

My boss, ISAF Commander General Dan McNeill was near, and he flashed a short smile followed by a grimace. He did not like these events any better than I did, but we both knew it was our duty to be there, to be seen, and to soldier through the spectacle.

And what a spectacle it was. Arrayed on the parade grounds were numerous formations of Afghan troops, standing at parade rest on the hard-packed sand, oddly resplendent in their various parade uniforms. There were soldiers in dark green dress coats, white helmets, and white puttees; others in gray dress, pistol belts, and red berets; still others in desert camo and caps, with white gloves. All carried rifles or submachine guns. I wondered if any actually had ammunition. I doubted it. After three previous assassination attempts on Karzai, it would require stupendous folly—or enormous trust—to allow all these troops to stand in front of their president with loaded weapons.

We had great seats, and as the band played martial tunes, we sat down, those of us up front in the sun, those behind us sheltered by the stand's ceiling. My eyes drifted towards a huge billboard mounted to the side of the field: "Spinghar Vegetable Ghee." A clarified form of butter used regionally in cooking, ghee was an important foodstuff, but the garish sign standing incongruously next to the dignified parade field added to the vaguely exotic surroundings. I was a long way from Kansas.

In the background was the sprawling Kabul cityscape, accented by mountains in the distance. Kabul was growing at an unprecedented pace, with refugees, carpetbaggers, and patriots returning, and across the field was evidence of their return: new high-rise buildings, maybe a hotel or an apartment building, none of them yet fully complete. Kabul was a city under construction, with an ancient past and plans for a thriving and vibrant future. It just had to survive the "now."

As I mused, President Karzai mounted a camouflaged and highly polished HMMWV, a high-mobility multipurpose wheeled vehicle—we called them Humvee for short—outfitted with gleaming white wall tires and adorned by two small Afghan flags fixed to the front bumpers. He was dressed in his traditional dark gray coat, topped by a lighter gray Afghan karakul sheepskin cap. With his handsome yet somber face and impeccable dress, he looked every bit an Afghan president as he stood on the vehicle.

Behind him, and in a separate but equally decked out Humvee, stood Minister of Defense General Abdul Rahim Wardak. He was a former Afghan military officer turned mujahedeen resistance leader who fought the Soviets during the 1980s. Wardak was articulate, fluent in English, and savvy about the U.S. and European motivations and interests in his country. My wife Patty and I hosted the minister and his wife, a stunning and refined woman of noble Afghan heritage, at our home at Fort Campbell during their visit to the U.S. the year prior. I absolutely detested formal dinners and mandatory social events, but Wardak and his wife made the three-hour conversation and dinner pass quickly, with witty stories of Afghan history, its current challenges, and suggestions on how I could prepare my soldiers and myself for our deployment. From that night forward, and throughout my fifteen months of command in Afghanistan, I deeply respected Minister Wardak as an Afghan patriot and highly skilled defense minister.

Today I saw Wardak for the first time sporting a general's dark green formal uniform, heavy with colorful medals and gold braids. I felt he too, like General McNeill and myself, was uncomfortable on the parade field, but all of us were stoically doing our duty, while longing to get back to our real work running a war.

The two Humvees trooped the line, inspecting the Afghan formations, then pulled in front of the grandstand. After some speeches, Karzai and Wardak dismounted and took seats in the stands not far from my seat. We stood for the playing of the Afghan National Anthem. As the music started, a ceremonial artillery outfit started firing a salute, the cannon fire echoing across the field and into the stands. I counted the fire. A twenty-one-gun salute can seem inconceivably long when standing as a soldier in the hot sun, I remembered. *Almost over…*

"Boom!"

The shell landed about fifty meters in front of us, kicking up a dust cloud. Automatic weapons fire began immediately, some of it close. Camacho and I turned to each other: *Incoming.* Out on the field, the

Afghan troops dove to the ground, while others sprinted for the nearest cover. I did not see any try to return fire. I doubted they could tell where the fire was coming from. I couldn't. I didn't think they had any ammo anyway.

It was chaos in the stands. Karzai and Wardak were already gone, their security detail ever alert. Some diplomats were crouching behind the flimsy red upholstered metal chairs, as if the chairs could protect them. Others were low, crawling for better cover, and yet others were being hustled up and out of the stands. The fire was sporadic, not very well aimed, but it appeared that one or two Afghan dignitaries were down, and were quickly being surrounded by aides or security.

With Chief Clayton in the lead and White bringing up the trail, we ran up and out of the grandstand. Out of the corner of my eye, I saw a man trip and fall, or maybe he was shot, I could not tell. We ran to a stone wall. Clayton was talking on the radio and phone, and he told us to get over the wall. It would provide cover, and possibly allow us to make our way back to the street, where our armored SUV and the security team were moving in our direction.

Getting Turk over the wall wasn't easy or pretty, but the gunfire was a great motivator. In seconds we were huddled on the other side, smiling sheepishly. We knew we were not the target that day, and nothing we did was heroic in any way, but cheating death always feels good.

Once we were back safely in our Black Hawk and heading to Tagab, I pondered the whole thing. I assumed this was a Taliban attack, probably aimed at killing Karzai, but certainly sending a message to a broader audience, some in Washington, D.C., others in London, Brussels, Paris, Rome, Warsaw, Berlin, and Ankara, among even more capitals. The irony of the moment was inescapable. Today was to be a celebration and remembrance of the Mujahedeen victory over the Soviets, a victory shared by those who became Talibs as well as many in the current Karzai government. *If they could not find common ground on this day of remembrance,* I mused, *how can they ever come to a political settlement, and a laying down of arms?*

I was inwardly upset, disquieted. Six hours ago, I had felt positive, optimistic that while still a neophyte here in Afghanistan, I was learning fast, and that our plans, my plan, would be effective. *Maybe not.* What a difference six hours makes in war.

I jotted a few notes into my little green book, my daily journal. Anticipate the unexpected. Always. Focus on possibilities, not just probabilities. And plan for options, not just for what you think is likely, but also for what you think is not. Use every tool at your disposal. Andy and Eric were right. We did not use it, but I am glad we had had the Beretta.

On the way back from the parade, we did fly to Tagab, scene of the morning special ops task force strike. It was very clearly the most precise HIMARS targeting I could imagine. The Haji's building was almost destroyed and yet the homes immediately adjacent appeared undisturbed.

And we had killed the Haji.

A small victory.

CHAPTER 2

"Better to fight for something than to live for nothing."
General George S. Patton Jr.

Thursday, November 9, 2006

My "road to war" in Afghanistan actually began at Fort Campbell, Kentucky, on a cool morning in November 2006. The dawn was slow in coming, and I grabbed a mug of steaming hot coffee, stepped outside, and walked around our new home, the farmhouse. The long-standing residence of the 101st Airborne Division's commanding general, it had been built in 1833 as a cabin, and over the years had been transformed into a typical Southern farmhouse: white siding with a long open veranda in front, complete with several green rocking chairs. Situated on about ten acres near the front gate of the post, it was surrounded by plush green fields of grass and magnificent towering oaks. From two wooden columns on the front steps hung the American flag, and the flag of the Screaming Eagles—the 101st Airborne Division (Air Assault). I was to assume command of this historic division later that morning.

I sat down on the steps, sipped the coffee, and admired the yard. The grass was still green, and the early morning dew glistened in the sun. The oaks still had some leaves, and while no longer brilliant, the copper and faded yellow leaves were still beautiful.

Am I ready? I had spent thirty years in the army, and my career was one of those unusually diversified ones that defy categorization. I certainly wasn't the model general. Enlisting in the army in 1976 after graduating from the University of Kansas ("KU" to students and alums), I went to basic training at Fort Jackson, South Carolina. I still remember the old World War II barracks and the crusty drill sergeants, the open latrines that stripped away any sense of privacy, and my fellow trainees. It was post-Vietnam, and we were a motley group, poor white Southerners escaping the trailer park, skinny Puerto Ricans searching for a better life, and a handful of slightly older guys with college degrees. As for me, I was just following instinct. My dad was a career soldier, and as army brats, my brother Chris and I lived all over, sometimes on drab army posts, other times overseas. Moving every two or three years made for constant turbulence at home, but we made friends fast and learned to adapt quickly to new people and surroundings. After graduating KU in 1976, I wasn't sure what I wanted to do, but I knew for certain I did not want more school at that point, and certainly did not want to find myself trapped in some office job. The army beckoned, and I thought, *Why not?* It was only a three-year commitment, and by then I would have a better idea of what I wanted to do in life.

After basic training I headed to Fort Benning, Georgia, and Officer Candidate School (OCS). My father graduated OCS in 1959, and I was surprised to find myself in the same company and same barracks as he had shared. I wasn't a perfect candidate for sure, and most of the older guys with extensive enlisted time were far better at the barracks routine, the incessant drills, tactics, and the student leadership positions we served in. My best subject was physical fitness, and I mastered the weekly Sunday afternoon PT (physical training) tests. I scored well enough on all the other tests to be branched into the Army Corps of Engineers. When we graduated in March of 1977, my father and my fiancée, Patty Drysdale, pinned on the gold bars of a second lieutenant. I was green, but in excellent shape and ready to try my hand at leading real soldiers.

I married Patty two days later at the Fort Benning Catholic chapel. It was a simple white clapboard building that had seen many marriages, baptisms, and confirmations in its years. My buddies from OCS formed a saber arch that we passed through, grasping hands as we jumped into the waiting rental car, sabotaged by my brother Chris and unnamed OCS classmates with cheese on the engine block and shaving cream throughout the interior.

In the years to follow, Patty and I had two children, Ryan and Kelly, and tried hard to maintain a loving family. Moving frequently with too much time away in the field, on temporary duty, or on deployments made it a challenge, and Patty often had to be both mother and father. The kids grew up strong, independent, and wise in the ways of the world. Both were at Fort Campbell for the change of command. Ryan was an army captain, also an OCS graduate, and recently back from Ramadi, Iraq, where he had been a combat engineer platoon leader removing improvised explosive devices (IEDs), and had transferred to civil affairs. Our daughter Kelly became an army civilian public affairs intern after graduating from Loyola Marymount, and would soon head to Carlisle Barracks to become the deputy public affairs officer (PAO). I was proud of my children, extraordinarily so. And what I felt for Patty I could never fully express. Intelligent, caring, and compassionate, Patty had moved some twenty-five times during my career, constantly uprooting her own career as a speech pathologist and educator in favor of my latest job and requisite new duty posting. She was always there for our kids, and became a leader in her own right, volunteering to lead family readiness groups and help army spouses and kids in need. She was the foundation of our family.

Looking backward that morning, I was pleased but still a bit surprised that my career had led to division command. To call my career path "diverse" was an understatement.

My first duty station was at Baumholder, Germany, a large and fairly remote training base in Rhineland-Pfalz. I spent two years as a platoon leader in the 293rd Engineer Battalion (Combat Heavy), where I learned the basics of leadership. The U.S. Army in 1977 was still trying to recover from the Vietnam War, and we had drug issues, racial tension, and too many unmotivated soldiers. But we were constantly busy, building troop construction projects all around Germany during the summers, where it was just my twenty-five soldiers and I on temporary duty far away from the company headquarters, and where my noncommissioned officers, called NCOs or non-coms, and I were totally responsible for the outcome of the project. Like most things in the army, the noncommissioned officers ran the day-to-day operations of the outfit, including the actual construction of whatever we were building. During the rest of the year we would train, both in our secondary mission to fight as infantry, and also as combat engineers, with explosives of all types, laying minefields and doing hasty battlefield construction. I loved to blow up stuff, but found real satisfaction in small-unit combat training, and often wondered if I should have branched infantry. I volunteered my platoon for French Commando School, and reveled in the special, behind-enemy-lines training in the middle of a snowy German winter. During my third year in Germany, I was appointed the battalion-training officer.

I enjoyed the army, but knew the engineers weren't for me. Our battalion commander was Lieutenant Colonel Ted Stroup, a Vietnam vet and registered professional engineer. He encouraged me to stay in the army, even if it was in a different role. Disciplined, smart, and people-oriented, Colonel Stroup was my first mentor. I tried volunteering for Special Forces (SF), and was accepted to be a SF team executive officer at Bad Tölz, but the assignment officers at Frankfurt would have none of that. We were short engineer officers in Germany, and I was staying in the engineer battalion until my tour was over.

On a whim, I took the flight school aptitude test, passed it, and volunteered to fly army helicopters. At the time, the Corps of Engineers actually had a few of their own flight detachments, and so my branch approved. In the summer of 1980, Patty and I packed our things and left Germany, she tearfully. We had enjoyed Europe, traveled extensively, and Patty had a great job running the Baumholder Child Care Centers. It was the first of many, many forced career moves for her.

Flight school at Fort Rucker, Alabama, was challenging but rewarding, as I felt my flying skills improve on a daily basis. We flew the workhorse of the Vietnam War, the Bell UH-1 Huey. Our son Ryan was born right after I graduated and earned my wings, while I was learning to fly the big, twin rotor Boeing CH-47 Chinook. Two months later we packed again, bundled Ryan into a car seat, and drove to Fort Hood, Texas. I was a newly promoted captain, and was assigned to the only Chinook company at Fort Hood, within the 6th Cavalry Brigade (Air Combat). At the time, Chinook companies were the size of small battalions, with well over two hundred soldiers, and were commanded by majors, with captains and warrant officers filling the leadership and pilot positions. Over the three years in the 6th Cavalry, I was a flight platoon leader, company operations officer, and company executive officer. I worked hard on my flying skills, and made pilot in command early. Most of our senior warrant officers were Vietnam vets, and as warrant officers had repetitive flying positions which culminated in significant experience, I went to school on them. They taught my fellow captains and me how a twenty-ton, ungainly-looking cargo helicopter could be a powerful assault platform in combat.

In 1983 we moved back to Fort Belvoir, Virginia, so I could attend the Engineer Officer Advanced Course. I really enjoyed the outdoor classes, building Bailey bridges, learning to blow up large bridges, and things of that nature. I detested the classroom drudgery of road design and the like, and considered it my good fortune to be an army aviator.

During the course, I heard the army was looking for a couple of Chinook-qualified captains for a special assignment. Task Force 160 was a hush-hush aviation outfit at Fort Campbell, Kentucky, and they had a large Chinook company. Rumor had it they flew only at night, had the latest navigation equipment and heavy on-board weapons, and actually could land on ships out in the ocean. I was intrigued, and when they called me to come out for an assessment, I agreed.

The weeklong assessment was intended to weed out not only weak aviators but also those who could not handle heavy stress. We had too much to do in too short a time, and those who needed defined pathways were at a real disadvantage. The PT test and swim tests were unconventional, but I was in great shape and passed them easily. The night flights were really challenging, trying to fly the teeny MH-6 "Little Bird" and navigate with a map and stopwatch to remote, unlit landing zones (LZs) in the middle of the Kentucky and Tennessee woods. The standard was to touch down plus or minus thirty seconds from the planned landing time. I don't believe many of us made our times, and some never found their LZs.

At the end of the week, the assessment concluded with a formal board. We were in our army dress greens, appearing before the leaders of the outfit, including one or two of the senior warrants, who held the most important flight positions and were regarded as icons. They asked tough hypothetical questions, we answered as best we could, and then we were ushered out to await the board findings. When I got called back in, the task force commander looked grim, and he asked me what I would do if they told me I had failed. My heart sank, but I had already prepared my answer: "Sir, I will try again."

The colonel smiled, got up from behind the table, and said I had passed.

Welcome to the task force.

When I joined the task force, our existence was an open secret at Fort Campbell. We were the crazy dudes with our headquarters at Clarksville Base, a former sensitive storage site, with unusual aircraft that most people saw only as dark shadows passing overhead at night, and a no-notice mission that had all of us carrying beepers everywhere, including to bed. With a coded alert, we would assemble at the airfield, be met by large air force transports, load our aircraft and gear, and be gone. We could not tell our families where we were going or when we would return. We were a tough group of soldiers, and our families were tough too. We were Night Stalkers.

So we moved to Fort Campbell. One day I came back to the company headquarters after a noon run—the second PT session of the day, as I had started with a workout with my platoon in the early morning—and the company clerk said I needed to call the army vice chief of staff. The clerk was a bright young private first class with a wicked sense of humor, and I said something to the effect that I was born during the day, just not yesterday. About an hour later, he stuck his head in and said I really needed to make this call; a colonel named Ted Stroup wanted to person-ally talk to me.

Colonel Stroup? My former boss?

I called the number. The vice chief of staff's enlisted executive assis-tant answered. In a minute or two I was talking with Colonel Stroup. He told me that Vice Chief of Staff General Maxwell Thurman was seeking volunteers for a program, and that Personnel Command had sent them my name. Colonel Stroup, knowing me very well, had recommended the vice talk with me.

That day I spoke on the phone with General Thurman, and he gave me a concise but intriguing vision of the future: that American national interests would be intertwined in the Middle East for decades to come, that they would often be violent decades, and that the army and America needed warfighters, leaders, and commanders, who knew the people, the languages, and the terrain.

Was I interested?

Hell yes, I thought. I asked to be able to speak to Patty, and give him an answer in the morning.

Patty agreed that night that I would accept; what exactly that meant for us wasn't clear.

That call with General Thurman and Patty's acceptance to an un-known future changed our lives, and completely changed my military career.

Within months we were headed to Monterey, California, for a year of Arabic school. We spent a wonderful but linguistically challenging year at the Defense Language Institute in a new, untested program to teach commonly spoken Arabic to military officers and enlisted men and women. Our class was less than a handful, and sometimes we had as many instructors, all native speakers, as we did students, but we accom-plished a lot in less than twelve months.

Our daughter Kelly was born at Fort Ord Hospital that year, and forever became a California girl at heart and in disposition.

We packed up newborn Kelly at four weeks, our son Ryan, and drove our van from California to Virginia, where I spent the summer as an intern within the army strategic plans and policy shop in the Pentagon. In early fall of 1986, I began the two-year master's in foreign service program at Georgetown University. We had a very small but tight-knit group starting that year. One of our classmates was a fellow helicopter pilot: Abdullah Hussein, Jordanian prince and a Cobra attack helicopter pilot. He was as busy as all of us graduate students, articulate, and just a friendly person to talk worldviews with. Our class advisor was Madeleine Albright. She would become secretary of state. He would become a king. But we did not suspect that then.

The summer between my two years, I worked at the U.S. State Department. The friendships and understanding that I found after four or so months at State would be formative for my combat tours later, and have lasted my lifetime. General Thurman was subtly pushing me to experience relationships I would not have had, and still be in the running for higher-level command and maybe general officer, if I excelled. He told me to follow Major John Abizaid's career and accomplishments.

My next assignment after graduation from Georgetown took us not to the Middle East, but to Korea. I was selected for major, and I headed to command the 271st Aviation Company at Camp Humphreys, South Korea. It was a 220-soldier organization with sixteen Chinook helicopters, and a sensitive mission to support the Combined Unconventional Warfare Task Force in Korea.

Right up my alley. Back to flying, leading troops, and special operations.

It became clear after I reported that the command expected me to stay two years, and eventually Patty and the kids joined me in Korea. We rented two tiny apartments with a door in between in Anjung-ni, which I picked out because the hand-painted sign along the unpaved dirt road said "flush toilet."

Since I rented the rooms in a flurry of activity one Saturday before the family arrived, I didn't really notice the pig farm adjacent to the house, or the fact that the landlord and his wife used an outhouse in our front courtyard that drained directly into the rice field in front of the apartment. Patty and the kids found all that out soon enough.

On the positive side, in two years, I learned to lead and command over 220 soldiers in a very tough and active area of the world, constantly training and doing some "real world" sensitive missions, and spent six months as the battalion operations officer as well. General Thurman continued to keep a close watch, and had me meet him one morning during a visit for a thorough review of the strategic situation: Korea, the Middle East, the world. Patty taught school at Osan Air Base, Ryan earned a junior black belt in karate at the Korean Budokan, and Kelly developed a lifelong love for exotic travel and strange, even dangerous experiences. With her blonde, Goldilocks hair, she was kidnapped numerous times by local Koreans, only to be recovered as they posed for pictures with her.

In 1990, we moved to Fort Leavenworth, Kansas, for the Command and General Staff College. It was a bit of a homecoming: Patty was born and raised in Leavenworth, and both of us graduated from Leavenworth High School. When Saddam Hussein decided to invade Kuwait early in our academic year, several of us student officers with Arabic were certain we would be called away to war. I learned then the army is a big organization. My duty was to finish the staff college, which I did, but for sure I thought my career was finished as my peers in Task Force 160 went off to the Gulf War.

After graduation, we moved to Jordan for a year of advanced foreign area officer training, where we had a wonderful experience with the U.S. embassy and with the Jordanian and Palestinian people we came to know. I traveled extensively throughout the Middle East, usually alone, driving myself, stopping to talk with the locals, and getting the lay of the land. The family really enjoyed Jordan: Patty taught at the international school attended by both kids, and we had a blast exploring the ancient land of Jordan. To this day, Petra remains Patty's favorite spot on earth.

We reluctantly returned to the U.S., where I served as a senior major and junior lieutenant colonel at the Pentagon in Army Strategy, Plans, and Policy. I was selected for an aviation battalion command in 1993, and thought for certain we were headed back to Korea. But Colonel Doug Brown, commander of what had become the 160th Special Operations

Aviation Regiment (SOAR) called. Would I be interested in commanding 2nd Battalion, their Chinook battalion?

Yes sir!

Our 2nd Battalion, 160th SOAR Chinooks had the only air-to-air refueling army helicopter capability in the world at the time, and learning to get gas from a C-130 refueling plane in the middle of a dark night was physically and mentally the most demanding flying I had ever done. But the move back to the Night Stalkers and Fort Campbell was comforting to all of us in the Schloesser household. The unit and the Fort Campbell community were extremely close, they took care of their own, and the mission was important. And the troopers we carried—our "precious cargo"—were the finest counterterror forces in the world.

The two years of command in 2nd Battalion went by with lightning speed. We were fielding a new Chinook modified from the start for special operations, the MH-47E, and all of us had to become qualified in it. Problems in Haiti grew into an intervention, and one night we flew on board the aircraft carrier USS *America* offshore of Norfolk and sailed south, to Haiti. On board were most of the 160th's aircraft and pilots, maintainers and staff, along with the complete special operations team that made up our higher headquarters and those we supported. Our invasion was cancelled, even as we were sitting in the cockpits offshore of Haiti. The deployment turned into months of ship time, some flight support to those U.S. forces on shore, and a whole lot of "What are we here for?" We got back in the fall, and went immediately back to training for the next mission.

I left 2nd Battalion after two years in command to attend Senior Service College, the next level of schooling for military officers of my rank and experience. The unit gave me going-away plaques, one of which was the Night Stalker Creed:

> Service in the 160th is a calling only a few will answer, for the mission is constantly demanding and hard. And when the impossible has been accomplished, the only reward is another mission that no one else will try.

As a member of the Night Stalkers, I am a tested volunteer, seeking only to safeguard the honor and prestige of my country, by serving the elite Special Operations Soldiers of the United States. I pledge to maintain my body, mind and equipment in a constant state of readiness for I am a member of the fastest deployable Task Force in the world - ready to move at a moment's notice anytime, anywhere, arriving on target plus or minus 30 seconds.

I guard my unit's mission with secrecy, for my only true ally is the night and the element of surprise. My manner is that of the Special Operations Quiet Professional, secrecy is a way of life. In battle, I eagerly meet the enemy for I volunteered to be up front where the fighting is hard. I fear no foe's ability, nor underestimate his will to fight.

The mission and my precious cargo are my concern. I will never surrender. I will never leave a fallen comrade to fall into the hands of the enemy and under no circumstances will I ever embarrass my country.

Gallantly will I show the world and the elite forces I support that a Night Stalker is a specially selected and well-trained soldier.

I serve with the memory and pride of those who have gone before me for they loved to fight, fought to win and would rather die than quit.

Night Stalkers Don't Quit!

Patty and the kids and I headed north from Fort Campbell to Boston and the National Security Fellowship program at Harvard University. Stan McChrystal and Tim McHale were fellow students, both old friends. Stan was already selected for colonel and command, and was heading back to command the Ranger Regiment. In no time, the year was over, and we moved back to Fort Campbell, where I took command

21

of 1st Battalion of the 160th Special Operations Aviation Battalion in a ceremony outside the bunker at old Clarksville Base. It was the summer of 1997.

We had not even gotten completely out of boxes in our quarters when I was called for a one-on-one meeting with my commanding general. He told me that in addition to being selected for early promotion to colonel, I had been selected for brigade command. In Germany. I had to be there the next summer.

I was shocked. I thought I was in for two more years of commanding 1st Battalion, and we had just returned to Fort Campbell. Patty was teaching third grade at a Fort Campbell school, while Ryan was back on the high school soccer team, and planning to letter also in track and wrestling. He would be a senior the next year, and had hoped to spend the last two years in the same high school. At a family meeting that night, we told the kids, and gave them a choice. I could head to Germany the following year unaccompanied, and they and Patty could move off post into an apartment, and request to attend the on-post schools, so Ryan could graduate at Fort Campbell High School.

Ryan and Kelly voted for keeping the family together. We were going to Germany in eleven months.

Those eleven months passed by at a furious pace. We had a classified mission with a classified customer base using sensitive tactics and procedures, highly resourced, and with huge expectations of the leaders and aviators and maintainers. As General Pete Schoomaker would remind us: *To those much is given, much is expected.* We did our best to deliver.

After a short refresher course in German, Patty and the kids and I headed to Germany in May 1998. I assumed command of the 12th Aviation Brigade on a typical cool and cloudy early summer day at Wiesbaden Air Field.

We were supporting U.S. troop commitments to NATO's SFOR (stabilization force) in Bosnia-Herzegovina, training throughout Europe, and performing special missions like flying Vice President Al Gore to and from Chernobyl in the Ukraine. When President and Mrs. Clinton visited Ireland, we flew his support staff and the media around the country. In early 1999, the situation in Kosovo deteriorated, and we were alerted along with our Apache sister regiment, the 11th Attack Helicopter Regiment, to deploy to Tirana, Albania, as Task Force Hawk in support of Operation Allied Force, a NATO air war to bring Milošević to the negotiation table and remove Serb army units from Kosovo.

It took far longer than necessary to prepare, train, and finally deploy the task force that eventually landed at Tirana's airport and set up camp. There were several reasons: our Germany-based units were not trained or equipped to self-deploy their helicopters from Germany, through southern France, and down the entire length of Italy, to be armed for combat at Brindisi, and finally fly over the Adriatic Sea to Albania and be ready to fight that night. There were also the diplomatic clearances that moved at glacial speed, and resulted in our force waiting in a tent city outside Pisa, Italy, for the final "ok" to transit down the boot of Italy. And finally, there was four-star infighting and second-guessing that resulted in delays.

After we arrived in Albania, we flew almost every night, prepared to cross into Kosovo and destroy Serb tanks. But it was not to be—the force never received the ultimate go-ahead to launch the Apaches over the border. Instead, after a few months, Ambassador Holbrooke convinced Milošević to sign the Military Technical Agreement, and pull his Serb army out of Kosovo. I was told to take my task force of Black Hawks and Chinooks and a long-range surveillance outfit, augment it with a squadron of Apaches from the 11th Attack Helicopter Regiment, and fly to Skopje, Macedonia, where we set up operations supporting the Kosovo Force (KFOR), the NATO peacekeeping force. We did so for several more months, and redeployed to Germany in the fall.

When I got back to Germany, Ryan had graduated from Wiesbaden High School and was already back in the States, getting ready to start at William and Mary. I had missed much of his final year at home.

In early spring of 2000, I was quietly told that I was on the army brigadier general list. I was really surprised, having been a colonel for about twenty months or so. Patty and I guessed about what my next assignment might be, and where we would go. Just prior to my change of command at 12th Brigade, we were informed that I would be the chief of the Office of Military Cooperation, Kuwait (OMC-K). In spite of the danger zone pay, it was an accompanied position: Patty and Kelly would come to live in Kuwait City too.

We lived in a huge house of marble and concrete, decorated with faux French furniture with the gold trimmings so popular in that part of the Middle East. Our yard featured numerous date palm trees shading an outdoor pool surrounded by flowering bougainvillea. But our small walled complex was guarded by contract security guards, most of them Palestinian, and reporting to the U.S. embassy. There were constant terrorism alerts, and when the USS *Cole* was bombed in Yemen in December, the alert level pretty much pegged and stayed there until Patty and Kel left the next summer. I enjoyed working with Ambassador Jim Larocco, and my Central Command (CENTCOM) boss, General Tommy Franks, was always fascinating to watch in action during his many visits to Kuwait. Most of all, I enjoyed working with the Kuwaiti military leaders. Every week I met with the chief of the Kuwait Armed Forces, Lieutenant General Ali Al-Moumen, and his deputy, Kuwait Air Force Major General Fahad Al-Amir. With Operation Southern Watch (the U.S.-led operation to monitor and control Iraqi air space south of the thirty-second parallel), ongoing and routine missions to destroy Iraqi air defense units occurring on our immediate northern flank, it was a dynamic environment.

I learned about diplomacy, cross-cultural communications, and true coalition warfare. In hindsight, the coming war, a war quite different than America had participated in before, was evident enough. The World Trade Center bombing of 1993, Osama bin Laden's declaration of war against America in 1996, and the recent (October 2000) USS *Cole* bombing in Aden, Yemen, were all milestones along the way.

And then there was 9/11. I think all of us old enough to understand what happened that day will remember where we were when we first heard about the Twin Towers. I was in the OMC conference room, briefing the ambassador, when a staffer rushed in to tell us to come to a TV. We watched silently, and then we looked at each other, and we knew we were finally at war.

In a few weeks, I was told to report to the Pentagon's Joint Staff, and quickly flew back from Kuwait. I met with the J-5 (the director of the Joint Staff's strategic policy and planning shop), Lieutenant General John Abizaid. It had been many years since General Max Thurman advised me to follow then-Major Abizaid's career, and we had met and talked several times before. That day he told me I was going to start a new planning cell on the Joint Staff, to plan what was to be a global war on terrorism, the GWOT. I had no charter, so I was to write one and brief it in two days in the Tank, the designated meeting room of the Joint Chiefs of Staff and their deputies. I had no staff so I was to matrix joint staffers into my nascent organization. I had no offices, so I needed to get after that too.

The days, weeks, months, and years that followed were a whirlwind of activity to stand up the planning cell and actually get to substantive work. We worked from very early morning—the Joint Staff morning briefing started at 6:00 a.m.—until late each night, often seven days a week. Abizaid moved to be the director of the Joint Staff and Lieutenant General George Casey became the J-5 and my immediate boss. Soon the knives were out, as many on the Joint Staff resented a totally new outfit being brought in to build the strategy and advise the chairman and secretary of defense. Without the continued protection of Generals Abizaid and Casey, the office would have failed quickly.

Instead, we became the critical interface between the military staff and the civilian policy makers at the Office of the Secretary of Defense (OSD). I briefed our efforts and recommendations in the Tank often, and frequently briefed Chairman of the Joint Chiefs Air Force General Richard "Dick" Myers and Secretary Donald Rumsfeld. After over a year of coordination, in 2002 we published the National Military Strategic Plan for the Global War on Terrorism.

It was a hard slog, and when President Bush decided to invade Iraq in 2003, I pushed to be assigned to a deploying division. I was overjoyed to be nominated and accepted to be the assistant division commander of the 101st Airborne Division, commanded by Major General David Petraeus. I had a hard time getting out of the global war on terror group, which was now a fully established Joint Staff deputy directorate with a validated one-star chief, some twenty staffers, and our own offices.

In Iraq, the division had made fast progress and was already in Mosul when I joined it in June 2003. It was left to Patty to move herself and Kelly from Virginia to Fort Campbell.

Iraq started slowly. Initially it looked like we might redeploy home by the summer's end. Mosul was home to two million Sunni Iraqis that Saddam had sent up north to displace the Kurds in that region. The Sunnis had been the dominant sect since the British took over Iraq as a protectorate following World War I. After the coalition deposed Saddam, the Coalition Provisional Authority increasingly placed Kurds and Shia in positions of authority, a development deeply resented by the Sunni. Bad strategic decisions, including disbanding the Iraqi Army and forcing former Baath party members out of the government and schools, led to a low-level, then increasingly violent, insurgency.

On the night before the Fourth of July, insurgent mortar shells "walked" down the runway at Mosul Airfield, my headquarters for the logistics and aviation support to the division, and exploded in our Forward Area Refueling Point, wounding a couple of soldiers. I knew the nature of our occupation had changed. During this period, General John Abizaid became CENTCOM commander, responsible for much of the Middle East and Southwest Asia including both Iraq and Afghanistan. He made immediate changes and a positive impact in Iraq and our situation, which was a significant learning experience for me. However, the previous bad strategic decisions continued to plague those of us on the ground.

We fought against the insurgents that year and into the next, while trying to rebuild what Saddam had never really built: a functioning regional government not based on fear, an infrastructure that actually supplied power for more than a couple of hours a day, and an economy that was reopened to its neighbors. General Petraeus was in his element, and I learned daily from him about governance, the operational end of war fighting, and the necessity of a strong narrative that could be translated by the media and understood at home. Although the 101st succeeded in keeping violence to an acceptable level during its deployment, coalition units in Mosul in later years encountered persistent and rising resistance there, as well as in Tal Afar to the west.

We redeployed in March 2004. I had not seen Patty since May 2003, and she was beautiful. I was back home with my best friend.

I was transferred that summer back to the Pentagon. General Richard "Dick" Cody, a previous boss at the 160th Special Operations Aviation Regiment, a strong mentor, and newly appointed vice chief of staff of the army, needed an experienced army aviator to start a new organization within the army's operations and plans division. In July, I became the army staff's director of army aviation. It was a nascent organization, with two staffers, no offices, and no charter—a work in progress each day. We did have a superb report prepared by an ad hoc aviation task force led by Major General J. D. Thurman to follow as a road map. General Cody, one of two army aviation four-star generals (the other was General Doug Brown, former 160th Special Operations Aviation Regiment commander, and now the Special Operations combatant commander) was a superb, if demanding, boss. We worked on new force structure, aviation unit deployments for training and combat in Iraq and Afghanistan, aviation policy, and anything else that needed to move quickly.

Less than a year later, I was told to report to a nondescript federal office building a block or so from the White House for an interview. The Office of the Director of National Intelligence (ODNI) was in temporary digs, and was really just standing up.

I fought against this interview, asking the chief of staff of the army, General Peter Schoomaker, to weigh in. But Secretary Rumsfeld and Chairman Myers wanted me to at least talk to the ODNI team. I was ushered into a cramped office, where the newly appointed Principal Deputy General Mike Hayden and I had a cordial talk. He was a true gentleman, and asked if I was interested in taking a new position within the National Counterterrorism Center (NCTC) established in August 2004 by President Bush's executive order #13354, partially as a recommendation of the 9/11 Commission, and soon codified into law by the Intelligence Reform and Terrorism Prevention Act. As the prospective deputy director for strategic operational planning, I would stand up and lead the "all of government," multi-agency planning effort to coordinate and execute each and every department's contributions to our war on terror. If I took the job, I would work for the NCTC director and the ODNI director on a daily basis but by law would report for strategic operational planning to the president of the United States.

Was I interested?

No sir! My goal is to command an army division in combat.

About that time the door opened, and in walked Ambassador John Negroponte, the director of national intelligence. He sat down and we chatted. General Hayden told him I wasn't interested, and the ambassador smiled, nodded, and continued to talk about his job, and the challenges ahead for America. Al-Qaida seemed to be metastasizing, didn't I agree? How did I see our war? What would I do differently if I were in charge?

Soon I had grabbed a marker and was sketching on the office white board: who the enemy was, where they were, and what it would take to "win" a war when proven attrition of terrorist leaders was not sufficient. I got worked up, and was charting some thoughts on potential ways ahead when I caught Negroponte and Hayden exchanging a knowing smile. I shut up and sat down. We shook hands, and the ambassador said something to the effect that he thought I would be the right fit for this position.

In July 2005, I started at the National Counterterrorism Center, located in a state-of-the-art building in the woods near McLean and Tysons Corner, Virginia. I became the first deputy director, strategic operational planning. Unlike my other startups, I had a superb office, a small staff to build from, and a charter written into law by Congress.

Most of what we did was highly classified, but working initially with our acting Director John Brennan, and later for the director, retired Vice Admiral Scott Redd, was an honor and a learning experience that broadened my understanding of the interagency, the Executive Office of the President, the role of the CIA and ODNI, and so many other areas. The team we built, mostly from borrowed interagency officers, was top notch. We worked closely with the White House and the President's National Security Council counterterrorism office, and built relationships with Juan Zarate, Bill McRaven, Bob Harward, and Nick Rasmussen, among many highly dedicated presidential advisors. It took well over a year to coordinate, write, and publish our nation's first Strategic Operational Plan for the War on Terrorism, and somewhere along the tour I was promoted to major general.

I will never forget the day Admiral Redd and I drove over to the West Wing Situation Room to brief President Bush on the new plan, seeking his final approval. It was morning, but the president looked tired, probably having returned late the previous night from a trip, and he sipped steaming hot coffee as we got started. He grew more attentive by the minute; it may have been the strong coffee, but I believed he was actually beginning to hope that this plan, which we had been talking about for over a year, just might help in the war.

That morning he approved the plan. As we were getting up, Admiral Redd told the president I would be leaving soon. I had been nominated to command the 101st Airborne Division, and would depart NCTC in late October 2006.

I don't recall exactly what President Bush said to me, but I do recall kind, heartfelt words of thanks for the past year and a half, and wishing me luck on commanding such a famous outfit as the Screaming Eagles.

And so my crazy career path had taken me from combat engineer to army aviation to special operations aviation, and I learned Arabic and strategy along the way. We had lived in Germany, Korea, Jordan, and Kuwait. I had served in conflicts and peacekeeping in Haiti, Albania, Kosovo, and Iraq, and spent time in some twenty countries of the Middle East. Most important to me, I had learned to lead. Platoons. Companies. Battalions. Brigades. I'd served as a deputy division commander in the 101st Airborne in Iraq. I knew about Washington, the Pentagon, and the national security bureaucracy, culminating in this past job as deputy director at the National Counterterrorism Center.

Yes, I am as ready as I can be.

The sun crested the tops of the oaks, warming my face and causing me to squint. The coffee was cold. And it was time to go. I got up, stretching my legs, and grabbed the coffee mug.

"Time to get after it," I said out loud.

CHAPTER 3

"Proper preparation and planning prevents piss-poor performance."
Anonymous

2006–2008: Preparing for War

Unlike many of my fellow division commanders, I had adequate time to prepare before deploying to Afghanistan. When I took command from Major General Tom Turner that day in November 2006, the division had just returned from its second deployment to Iraq. A week later, we began the first of almost fifty battalion and brigade changes of command. We honored and farewelled commanders and staff from the past deployment and brought in new teams to prepare for future deployments. Thousands of soldiers would depart their units, headed to new posts or to transition back to civilian life, and we would bring in and train thousands more to take their place. It was a busy time as every unit in the division, which now included four brigade combat teams (BCTs), two combat aviation brigades (CABs), a sustainment brigade, and the 49th Quartermaster Group, shed their leadership and soldiers and rebuilt their units.

I saw preparation for combat as several endeavors undertaken near-simultaneously that resulted—ideally—in a cohesive organization ready to execute their mission in a combat zone. We had to first educate every soldier and leader, not always to the same degree, and to explain the five "Ws": who, what, when, where, and, most importantly, why. The basics of history, culture, terrain, and geopolitics of where we would fight were important to every soldier, and the higher one went, the more important the details. Squad leaders—staff sergeants—were entrusted with immense responsibilities in combat, and they needed as much of the education as a young platoon leader lieutenant.

At the same time, we had to begin our planning. There were so many overused clichés about planning: the World War II European theater's Commander General Dwight D. Eisenhower's that although "the plan is useless, planning is essential" or the nineteenth century's German Field Marshal Helmuth von Moltke's "No battle plan ever survives the first encounter with the enemy" are two that stand out. I grew up in the army admiring General George S. Patton's "A good plan violently executed now is better than a perfect plan executed next week." My own conception as a division and soon-to-be combined joint task force commander responsible for a very large area of operations, fourteen provinces totaling forty-eight thousand square miles, was to ensure we did the science—planning the logistics, unit movements, and the communications backbone—while also building a set of preliminary lines of operation that we could deviate from or branch off of during our deployment.

Of course, we had to know what we were planning for. First, we needed our ultimate objective: What were we trying to achieve? We were told the U.S. strategic goals were to ensure Afghanistan: (1) was a reliable, stable ally in the war on terrorism; (2) was moderate and democratic, with a thriving private sector; (3) would be capable of effectively governing its borders and territory; (4) and would be respectful of the rights of all of its citizens, including minorities and women. Next, we needed a strategy to give meaning and goals to our planning efforts. Trained as an army strategist, I believed in the simple but well-proven formula: means plus ways applied to achieve a feasible end state. The *means* were usually resources—soldiers, arms, equipment, logistics, communications—but also included provincial reconstruction teams (PRTs) and the U.S. interagency. The *ways* were the methods of war. In counterinsurgency, we usually spoke of lines of operations, and we decided early on that we would concentrate on a campaign to provide security for, connection to, and empowerment of local and regional Afghan governments, development projects to transform the environment, and a proactive approach to information operations to engage with our different audiences while actively countering enemy propaganda. Everything we did would be by, through, and with our Afghan military and security force partners. The *ways* became the CJTF-101 initial campaign plan. Finally, the *ends* mattered the most: we had to support the U.S. national and NATO strategic end states, and we decided on eight goals: (1) secure the Afghan people; (2) increase the Afghan/Pakistani border security and cooperation; (3) build Afghan governance at a district and provincial level; (4) improve Afghan rule of law; (5) support economic growth; (6) improve Afghan quality of life; (7) ensure our American public and international audiences received a fair and accurate understanding of the progress of the campaign; and last, but clearly not least, (8) help link the Afghan people to their own government. When wrapped together in one paragraph, our ways, means, and ends became our CJTF-101 mission.

While we were educating and planning, we trained, with multiple iterations on the same task to get it right, at the individual and unit level. Soldiers had to shoot their night optic-equipped M4s with skill at distance—every soldier a sniper—while knowing how to apply a tourniquet to amputations, including their own, give a detailed report on a wounded soldier's condition (referred to as a "nine line") to inbound medevac helicopters, and so much more. Units from fire team up had to know how to move to contact, react to ambush or indirect fire, and execute a small air assault with Black Hawks and Chinooks. They had to know how to conduct a meeting with local leaders called *shuras*, negotiate for everything, and gain a local elder's cooperation. At the training centers we would bring all the individual and unit training together; once considered a crucible event before 9/11 resulted in years of warfare, the training center deployments now were the last stage for graduate-level, force-on-force training, complete with civilians on the battlefield.

It was one thing to prepare our soldiers, quite another to prepare us commanders, our staff, and our sergeants major. We needed to understand how previous plans worked, or did not, and why. We needed to understand the role Pakistan plays in Afghanistan. We needed to develop a feel for the enemy, in all of his different manifestations. We needed to understand U.S. and NATO policy, and the role our coalition partners could and could not play in our area of responsibility. Most importantly, we needed a feel for Afghanistan itself: its terrain, its people, its cultures. We brought in successful commanders from previous Afghan deployments, and spent hours listening to and questioning them. We brought in former Ambassador Ron Neumann to better understand U.S. diplomacy in Afghanistan before 9/11, and asked author and former military intelligence officer Ralph Peters to challenge our thinking. We journeyed to the Pentagon, NSA, State Department, and the White House to understand how to embed our operational and tactical plans into the strategic. Finally, we made two site surveys [predeployment site surveys (PDSS)] to Afghanistan with our senior leaders, visiting the 82nd Airborne Division's CJTF-82 then commanding RC-East, meeting with Major General Dave "Rod" Rodriguez, and seeing with our own eyes the forward bases and outposts we would later command. A former West Point football player who was strong-willed and passionate about soldiers and soldiering, Rod was also a friend; we had been neighbors at Fort Campbell as battalion commanders, and our children had played together. I could not have had a better predecessor to follow.

The site surveys allowed the leadership of the incoming unit to see the terrain over which they would operate, meet senior commanders, interact with the outgoing unit they would replace, and talk with organizations they would support and be supported by. Of anything we did to prepare, I found the site survey the most important step in preparing myself for war.

It was during our first PDSS to Afghanistan in April 2007 that I met Colonel John "Mick" Nicholson. He was commanding Task Force Spartan, organized around his 3rd Brigade Combat Team, 10th Mountain Division. Sitting with my team in his plywood tactical operations center in Jalalabad, Nangarhar, Mick was composed, thoughtful, and forceful. Tall, ruggedly handsome, and more articulate than many of his peers, Mick caught and maintained our rapt attention as he sketched out his approach to waging counterinsurgency operations.

"We have to separate the local population from the enemy insurgents, giving the enemy options to either flee from Afghanistan, reconcile to the legitimate Afghan central government, be captured and detained, or be killed. Then we must achieve real positive effects with the people through adequate governance at the local and provincial levels, as well as in Kabul. Finally, we must transform the environment economically, providing roads, infrastructure, electricity, and education." Mick made no claim that this was an original strategy—it looked like a classic clear, hold, and build strategy adapted for the Afghan people—and in fact gave credit to retired Colonel Joe D. Celeski and an article called "Operationalizing COIN" that Celeski wrote after his own experiences. A former 3rd Special Forces Group commander, Celeski had served two tours as leader of Combined Joint Special Operations Task Force-Afghanistan during the early years of Operation Enduring Freedom.

Something else Mick said that day caught my attention: "The mountains and elevation change almost everything!"

Later that day I saw firsthand what he meant. We flew up the Kunar River and then west along the Pech River to Camp Blessing. We toured the fire base with Lieutenant Colonel Chris Cavoli, commander of 10th Mountain Division's 1st Battalion, 32nd Infantry, then flew north about twelve miles to the village of Aranas, and Combat Outpost Ranch House, located on the side of a mountain, almost near the summit. With the Black Hawk at a hover, lightly resting one main gear on the roof and the other wheel overhanging, we jumped out.

There was still ice and snow at Ranch House, and the climb up to the small base at the top required us to haul ourselves, weighed down with body armor, weapons, and ammo, along a steep narrow path. We used the ropes the squad had fixed along the pathway. With the added weight of all the gear, the elevation, and the overall fatigue of our too-busy PDSS, we were spent when we got to the top. We were in pretty good shape, but clearly not ready for life at Ranch House. For the next hour, the B Company, 1-32nd soldiers told us about operating there: how important platoon mortars had become, how difficult logistical resupply was, how challenging the weather and mountains were. It was truly sobering, and I jotted down several notes to myself to ratchet up our physical training back at Fort Campbell.

Just as armchair combat commanders focus on tactics to the detriment of logistics, I found that too many leaders did not spend enough effort or creativity in physical training, which in my mind was and still is the absolute bedrock of soldiering. There are clearly many military occupations that are desk-bound, be it in garrison or a combat zone, but most are not. And the sheer extravagant exertion that war requires over days, weeks, months, and sometimes years, means that to be a soldier, marine, airman, or sailor requires a level of fitness that most Americans normally don't achieve. So, when I got back to Fort Campbell, we increased our emphasis on daily, rigorous, and non-traditional physical fitness. We lived in the rolling hills and river lands of Kentucky and Tennessee, not in the mountains, but we had to use the former to prepare ourselves for the latter.

I would later bring Chris Cavoli to Fort Campbell after his return and before our own departure, where he spoke to our commanders and CSMs. He told us "fighting is a necessary but not sufficient component to winning" in eastern Afghanistan, and said "information operations was the main effort." He called it a campaign of persuasion: persuading the enemy to give up or get out, and persuading the locals to align with the legitimate government. He made good sense, and we went to school on Cavoli and Nicholson as we refined our own campaign plan.

But it was my own boss, U.S. Army Forces Command Commander General Dan McNeill, who got me really thinking about what we were about. At his January 8, 2007, change of command at Fort McPherson, Georgia, with General Charles "Hondo" Campbell, McNeill mused about his next job, which would be to command all NATO troops in Afghanistan. In his quiet yet emphatic way, McNeill said, "Generals will be blamed if we don't win this." Initially I thought, *Well of course;* that is what we sign up for as professional soldiers and especially as members of the general officer corps. It seemed self-evident. Our job was not to argue the political merits of policy, but to advise on strategy and especially the ways and means to a political and militarily feasible end state, a goal or series of goals in our own national interest and that of our allies. But as I became increasingly aware of the situation on the ground in Afghanistan, which was clearly worsening by mid-2007, the impact on Afghanistan of the "surge" in troops and resources to Iraq, and the overall sour political mood in Washington, I thought frequently about McNeill's words, which constituted a clear warning.

My father had served three tours over three separate years in Vietnam. I watched him return in 1967 full of optimism; by his return from the second tour in 1970 he had seen firsthand the Tet Offensive, and he was decidedly more somber. On his last tour, wrapping up the U.S. fighting force presence in 1973, he was pretty much tapped out.

"It's in their hands now," he told me, meaning the South Vietnamese.

When U.S. Congressional support ended in 1975 and the South Vietnamese military had to fight the North Vietnamese on very different terms than in the past, Dad was a realist, and foresaw the collapse. The North eschewed unconventional warfare to launch a conventional invasion spearheaded by tanks, heavy artillery, and improved Soviet air defense missiles to ward off defending helicopters and aircraft. The end came quickly as the Saigon government tried to defend everywhere rather than concentrate its forces at key points. The North had attempted something similar three years earlier in 1972, but they were defeated by South Vietnamese ground units aided by massive amounts of American airpower. In 1975, however, no U.S. warplanes were committed to aid our former allies. My father never forgave Congress or American politicians: he had led soldiers in combat and given three years of his life to South Vietnam, and he felt we as a nation walked away from it all. And who was blamed? Clearly the "generals" and the professional soldiers who made up the officer corps.

What if the politicians did the same thing in Afghanistan? There already seemed to me to be a ways-and-means mismatch with our national goals, but I was a seasoned military professional and had often been asked to accomplish a mission with fewer resources than I desired. But what if our politicians decided to abandon the war? My generation of generals, of soldiers, would be on the blame line.

★ ★ ★

As we prepared for war and our coming deployments, we dealt with the vestiges of the past deployments. The army had not prepared itself or its soldiers for the mounting issues of multiple combat tours. The suicide problem was almost incomprehensible. Soldiers came back from Iraq in 2006 to waiting families, girl- or boyfriends, and friends ready to renew relationships. And some came back to deserted apartments, empty checking accounts, and "Dear John" letters. Some missed the war, the emotional and physical rush of combat that was both terrifying and intoxicating.

In the 101st we had more suicides than we could have ever expected, sometimes more than one a week, sometimes in multiple tragedies such as when a soldier would shoot his wife, then kill himself. They shot themselves in the head with pistols, they shot themselves with rifles, hung themselves in closets and bathrooms, and overdosed on booze and pills. One soldier took his wife and two kids to see Santa, then killed himself with a handgun later that night. We had doctors, behavioral scientists, scholars, care workers—anyone we thought could help—advising us. The rest of the army was focused on us, and the army staff gave us access to resources. But we could not seem to get it under control.

I will never forget the weekend of December 1–2, 2007. That Saturday morning, I ran the Memphis Marathon, and Patty drove us back to Fort Campbell that afternoon. That night I got two calls: A young private was found dead in the barracks, an apparent victim of both drugs and alcohol overdose. He had survived a previous stabbing. Later that night, I got another call: another private was found dead, apparently from a fall from a bunk bed in the barracks, but clearly under the influence of booze and pills. I barely slept that night. Before the workday started early Monday, I was informed that another soldier, a young private first class, was found dead. He had hung himself.

How do we stop this madness?

That day, I called in every brigade commander and command sergeant major, my staff, and the hospital commander and his team, and we had a brutally blunt after-action review of all we had done and been trying to do. We admitted we were failing. I ordered them to mandate that soldiers who were being treated for pain, post-traumatic stress (PTS), or similar emotional and mental conditions not be allowed to drink alcohol. The commanders and CSMs were frustrated because, in most cases, they were not told when a soldier received drugs for injuries, and were not aware by policy when a soldier was being treated for PTS. There were clearly medical privacy issues, and the last thing I wanted was to reduce the number of soldiers seeking help. But we resolved to be even more active and intrusive in our soldiers' lives. It was the only way we saw to limit, if not stop, the madness.

In hindsight, we—and the army as a whole—were inadequately prepared for the combination of returning vets' mental anguish and physical problems, a medical system with a propensity to prescribe drugs for pain and then the abuse of those same drugs to self-medicate, and the well-meaning tendency to treat mental stress and suicidal ideation as something private between the soldier and his or her health-care provider. Commanders and leaders at all levels were initially cut out of the feedback loop from the docs and behavioral specialists: they did not know what was going on with their soldier, just that he or she had gone to the hospital, and they had no idea of the powerful pain and antidepressants prescribed. There were too few qualified psychologists or behavioral specialists at Fort Campbell, and we were late in realizing we could get many more, by engaging at very senior levels of the army leadership. Ultimately, I was personally briefing the army G1 (responsible for all personnel issues for the army) frequently and the vice chief periodically from Fort Campbell on our suicides, and they were pulling out all stops to help. Finally, there was one other issue: many of us professional soldiers just could not understand at the fundamental level *why* someone would commit suicide. I know I struggled to understand. And that limited our empathy, which in turn limited our creativity.

The three brigade combat teams headed to Iraq had very short dwell times back at Fort Campbell before redeploying, and we focused on getting them manned, trained, and equipped. Big Army gave us all the help we needed to rapidly acquire the latest weapons systems, and troopers and leaders spent hours on the range getting proficient with all the new gear. We also brought in sophisticated communications gear and the latest in command and control hardware and software, and trained on it all in multiple local exercises as well as at Fort Polk, Louisiana, at the Joint Readiness Training Center (JRTC), where every brigade combat team had its own several-week rotation. The Joint Readiness Training Center served as the light or non-mechanized infantry's counterpart to the more widely known National Training Center (NTC) where M1A1 Abrams and Bradley-equipped units sparred with a mechanized opposing force utilizing Soviet tactics and equipment. During this period both JRTC and NTC were transitioning from their decades-long focus on conventional conflict to scenarios resembling what soldiers encountered in Iraq and Afghanistan.

The brigade combat team was a powerful outfit, some three thousand soldiers or more, with its own reconnaissance, intelligence, engineer, artillery, and logistics capabilities. The JRTC exercises were the brigade's capstone exercises, and I went to Fort Polk for each one, trying to coach when it made sense. For the three units deploying to Iraq, they trained on an Iraq scenario, with Arab-American role players playing both insurgents and the local populace. None of the brigades were perfect, since in many cases they were still missing key leaders who would join them after the JRTC rotation but before they deployed, but they all did well enough. In just a few months' time, the units had returned from combat, changed all key leaders and staff and at least half of their soldiers, re-equipped, and trained as hard as possible. They could perform counterinsurgency at the platoon level, with companies coordinating and battalions and brigades resourcing, but that was about as much as we had time for. And then they were gone: colors cased on the parade field in front of their families and peers, goodbyes said, short farewell speeches made at Campbell Army

Airfield, and onto the contract flights bound for Germany and on to Kuwait and eventually Baghdad.

Our own training as a division headquarters for Afghanistan (along with the two combat aviation brigades, the 4th Brigade Combat Team, and the sustainment brigade), also occurred during this time, but intensified in August 2007 and continued until we deployed in March 2008. It wasn't until late August 2007 that my own command team, the two deputy division commanders, the division chief of staff, and the division command sergeant major were on board.

Brigadier General Mark Milley was the deputy commanding general for operations. Mark was a solidly built former hockey player from Massachusetts with an undergraduate degree from Princeton, a master's in international relations from Columbia, and impeccable infantryman credentials. He had served as Secretary of Defense Gates' military assistant. Bright, imaginative, and one of the quickest studies on the planet, he was as comfortable shooting the breeze with privates taking a smoke break at the rifle range as he was debating effective counterinsurgency campaigns in the West Wing of the White House. As the "O," he would help me command, control, and maneuver our units; help lead the counterinsurgent, combat-oriented parts of our campaign in eastern Afghanistan; and would ensure we were well coordinated and receiving the full effects of a broader, parallel counterterrorism campaign. Essentially, he would ensure CJTF-101 units were coordinated with my intent, while helping me synchronize our operations with our higher, adjacent, and allied commands. A very tough job.

My deputy commanding general for support was also from Massachusetts. Born in Quincy, Jim McConville was tall and personable, with a penetrating mind and dry sense of humor. Seriously smart, he was a U.S. Military Academy grad, had earned a master's in science in aerospace engineering from Georgia Institute of Technology, and had been a National Security Fellow at Harvard to boot. In a different era, he might have been a cowboy or horse cavalryman. Instead, he was one of the army's best aviation commanders, part air cavalry, part special operator, but 100 percent professional. Jim would ensure our support to the U.S., NATO, and coalition forces, and I also tasked him to overwatch aviation operations. Most importantly, he would be responsible for helping me plan and execute the "build" and governance part of the counterinsurgency strategy. And by the time he joined the team, I was certain his was the most challenging and most important part of our campaign.

Colonel Tom Vail became our 101st Airborne Division chief of staff after relinquishing command of the Currahees of the 4th Brigade Combat Team. Just back from his most recent combat tour in Iraq and nominated for the chief position by my predecessor Major General Tom Turner, I worried that Tom Vail might need a longer break before heading right back to war in a high-pressure job. After meeting with him and discussing his views of the division, training, and our upcoming deployment, I was reassured. A proud infantryman with vast combat experience as well as plenty of counterinsurgency time, Tom was articulate, savvy, and a bulldog who was perfect to run what would be a huge and highly diverse joint staff once we got to Bagram. The latter task challenged incoming division commanders, who not only left part of their own staff behind as a rear detachment at home station, but then also absorbed a large number of individual augmentees and small sections, many from the other services, for the duration of the deployment.

In early September 2007, I replaced outgoing Division Command Sergeant Major Frank Grippe, who was going on to serve as senior enlisted advisor to a three-star headquarters, with Command Sergeant Major Vince Camacho. Vince's many years working his way up the ranks as a light infantryman served as a foundation for what CSMs did best: teach, coach, mentor, and, when needed, supply that extra bit of motivation that might be missing. Vince was no diplomat for certain. He had some rough edges, but having served as CSM in both 2nd and 3rd Brigade Combat Teams of the 101st, I was confident he was the best man for the job.

We had our command team.

★ ★ ★

A series of joint and army-resourced exercises meant to prepare the division staff and myself allowed us to bring a slew of previous commanders and scholars to Fort Campbell. We hosted a conference in late August 2007 and brought Colonel H. R. McMaster to talk about his brigade's recent successful tour in Tal Afar, Iraq, and Colonel Mick Nicholson to give us his perspectives from his brigade's tour in RC-East, Afghanistan. H. R. was known throughout the army for his outspoken views on command and counterinsurgency, and he did not disappoint. He painted a somber picture of the current tension between Army transformation and counterinsurgency doctrine: "Army transformation and modernization efforts for the Future Combat System aim for certainty and centralization on the battlefield. Successful counterinsurgency must embrace uncertainty and completely decentralized operations."

Colonel Mick Nicholson, now "promotable" to brigadier general and serving on the Joint Staff, was equally compelling and yet disturbing. He told us, "The enemy will not defeat us in Afghanistan, but narcotics can." While we had met in Washington, D.C., with those agencies coordinating the counter-opium effort in Afghanistan, we would only play a supporting role once in RC-East. And yet the curtailing of poppy cultivation and the resultant opium trade was critical to the ultimate success of our own "people-oriented" campaign. I resolved to make staff and myself smarter on alternative farming, crop storage, and product-to-market strategies. I could imagine my 101st Airborne predecessors if they knew what I planned: "The Screaming Eagles have become farmers!"

Mick had another disturbing thought: "We have two enemies in Afghanistan: the terrorists and the thieves." The "terrorists" or enemy insurgents were a motley bunch of Afghan and Pakistani Taliban, al-Qaida, and the Haqqani cartel, as well as several smaller regionally based radical violent groups.

But "thieves?" I took this to mean the Afghans who, while not fighting the legitimate Karzai government and Afghan Army, were undermining its legitimacy and economy, and ultimately Afghan security and stability, through rampant corruption. Poppy growing and the narcotics trade were a tangible thing, with evident although complex and difficult solutions. But the "thievery" embedded in the very Afghan culture and persistent and insidious corruption that was deeply ingrained in the society, government, police, and business was a threat of an altogether different character and magnitude. Our combat units could fight, build, teach, govern if necessary, and yes, even be farmers. But we were not organized or trained to fight corruption so pervasive that it made up a significant part of everyday Afghan life. Yes, we could "clear" and "hold" and even "build," but if our campaign's ultimate success depended on a transformed environment for the people, then corruption, especially corruption with so much popular support, could be our undoing. After the conference, I drove back home that evening worried that Nicholson had pointed out a flaw in our evolving campaign plan. Maybe even a flaw in the overall U.S. and NATO strategy. In my mind, it wasn't that we had not planned for corruption or did not have institutions to promote good governance and ethical business; instead, it seemed to me to be ultimately out of our hands. Only the Afghans themselves could defeat this kind of thievery, and I was very unsure they were so inclined.

In November of 2007, we flew to Afghanistan for our second predeployment site survey. It had been a tough fighting season, and many of those we talked with warned us about the coming year. I went to Kabul to see the senior leadership first. At the U.S. embassy, I met Ambassador Bill Wood. With wire-rimmed spectacles, a receding hairline, a dark suit, and striped tie, the ambassador looked just like the foreign service officer and diplomat he was. I knew that he was also a tough negotiator, had been a strong proponent of aerial spraying against cocaine as ambassador to Colombia, and was not hesitant to salt his sentences with enough inventive swear words to make an infantryman proud. We chatted about the potential for aerial spraying in Nangarhar as a proof of principal, but he thought President Karzai would not support more widespread spraying. He was direct when we turned to the fighting. He told me the Taliban's spring offensive would be a real challenge for us. That was pretty much what my own staff had concluded early on in our planning process, so I wasn't surprised. The previous month CENTCOM released its own Afghanistan assessment, and it too was bleak: insurgent violence and presence was the highest it had been since the collapse of the Taliban in late 2001, and the insurgency was becoming more sustainable, expansive, and disruptive to NATO and our coalition attempts to improve social and economic well-being. Insurgent violence in 2007 would be higher than ever.

We next met with ISAF Commander General Dan McNeill in his small office at ISAF headquarters. I liked the blunt-talking North Carolinian. I had served under General McNeill for a short period when he commanded the Army Forces Command, and found him frank, opinionated, and deeply knowledgeable about Afghanistan and the Afghan leadership. He initially deployed to Afghanistan in May 2002 as commanding general of Combined Joint Task Force-180 for a year. During that period, McNeill conducted counterterrorist operations using a mix of conventional and special operations units, to prevent al-Qaida from regaining a foothold after its initial defeat. The Taliban, still licking its wounds after the initial American invasion, did not play a significant role during McNeill's first deployment. This was his second tour commanding coalition forces in Afghanistan, and he was witness to the growing enemy capabilities.

"Jeff, this will be an exciting April for you and your boys."

We talked about the problems of the coming transition: we were scheduled for our assumption of command of RC-East in April. Just when he thought the enemy would really pick up his game.

Our last stop was to speak with the senior American intelligence officer in Kabul. He echoed both Ambassador Wood and General McNeill: "Be prepared for April—there will be a real spring offensive this year."

I boarded the Black Hawk at Kabul Airport and headed back to Bagram. Nothing I heard surprised me. It was what the staff and I had planned for. But hearing it from the top U.S. leaders in the country back-to-back got my attention. I could expect no time after the transfer of authority from the outgoing CJTF-82 to my CJTF-101 to exercise the staff, or to ensure my command team was ready. This could not be like a foot race where we are straining to push off from the starting blocks. When we assumed responsibility, it had to be like a long-distance relay, with the 82nd and 101st staffs running at pace, and a smooth and speedy exchange of the leadership baton.

We spent the next several days visiting the various formations throughout RC-East. I met Colonel Charles "Chip" Preysler at his head-quarters at Forward Operating Base (FOB) Fenty, Jalalabad (sometimes called J-Bad), the largest city in Nangarhar Province. Preysler was com-mander of the 173rd Airborne Brigade Combat Team, Task Force (TF) Bayonet. Home-based in Vicenza, Italy, these "Sky Soldiers" were one of the army's most famous combat formations. The unit's soldiers had tough combat and counterinsurgency experience in Iraq and a previous tour in Afghanistan. Chip Preysler was one of the army's most experienced infan-try commanders in Afghanistan, having served as battalion commander in tough fighting in the Shah-i-Kot campaign of Operation Anaconda in March 2002 and later as the operations officer of CJTF-76 in 2005 to '06.

Chip greeted me on the tarmac at the airfield that split Forward Operating Base Fenty in half, and he led me into the plywood building that made up TF Bayonet's headquarters. A plain-talking midwesterner from Michigan, Chip had an easy smile and was comfortable leading troops. I liked him immediately. Originally intended to go to Iraq before being diverted to Afghanistan, the 173rd Airborne Brigade's tour of duty in Nuristan and Kunar Provinces had been an intense experience so far. The Vicenza-based paratroopers were located in the midst of what had been traditional safe havens for a wide array of militant groups. Preysler had positioned his available combat battalions along roughly northeast to southwest lines bisecting the brigade's area of operations in order to interdict Taliban supply lines running from Pakistan to the region around Kabul. In the northeast, Lieutenant Colonel Christopher D. Kolenda's 1st Squadron, 91st Cavalry (TF Saber) established a position at Operating Base Bostick. Lieutenant Colonel William B. Ostlund's 2nd Battalion, 503rd Infantry (TF Rock) established itself at Camp Blessing in the Pech River Valley in Kunar Province. Farther to the west, Lieutenant Colonel

Stephen J. Maranian's 4th Battalion, 319th Field Artillery (TF King) had been transformed into a hybrid organization composed of artillery and light infantry before being sent to Forward Operating Base Kalagush.

Chip and his staff told us about their campaign since arriving that spring. It was a tough fight, especially up in the Kunar and Pech River Valleys, and in the Korengal. They still embraced the clear-hold-build counterinsurgency concept, but did not have enough troops or resources to get it done. They had extremely long lines of communications, and several of their most remote outposts could only be resupplied by helicopters or airdrops. They rarely had enough intelligence, surveillance, and reconnaissance assets to locate the insurgents that traversed the Durand Line along the mountains delineating the border between eastern Afghanistan and Pakistan's frontier. The Durand Line was established by the British Empire in the nineteenth century to demarcate what was then Afghanistan and India, well before the founding of Pakistan. It generally followed a line of north-south mountains in our area of operations, and had not taken into account that it divided tribes and even families. It was still contested: the Afghan and Pakistani governments did not agree on exactly where the border was in some areas, and border arguments that sometimes resulted in violence were not unheard of. It would prove to be a continuing problem throughout our deployment. Robert Frost said something to the effect that "good fences make good neighbors." We could see that bad borders, or at least poorly conceived and not agreed-upon ones, made for bad relations between neighboring countries.

The brigade S-2 intelligence officer briefed that they were most concerned about corruption, poppy and narcotics, and the infiltration of insurgents from a relative safe haven in Pakistan. Chip specifically mentioned the influence, both positive and negative, of Nangarhar's Provincial Governor Gul Agha Sherzai. I added a note to self to learn more about Sherzai, and to meet with him soon after I took over.

I should have paid more attention to the corruption issue eighteen months earlier, when we had had the time to adapt our preparations.

THE DURAND LINE: Eastern Afghanistan and Pakistan's western frontier

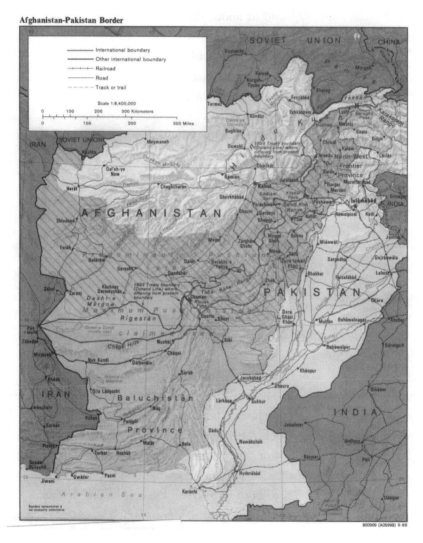

Courtesy of Central Intelligence Agency, Public Domain.

In March 2008, we were ready, and many of our units and staff were already en route or in Afghanistan, preparing for the passing of the baton in stride, just as I had thought about it during the last PDSS. On March

17, I flew down to CENTCOM headquarters at MacDill Air Force Base to receive my final guidance from CENTCOM Commander Admiral William "Fox" Fallon, and his deputy, Lieutenant General Martin "Marty" Dempsey. Usually comfortable with the brass, I approached this meeting with some trepidation. Admiral Fallon had been a four-star for as long as I had been a general officer (I was frocked to brigadier in 2000), was on his third four-star command, and had one of the keenest strategic minds in the country. He had a reputation of being brutally frank, could make a penetrating analysis sound like common sense, and was 100 percent comfortable voicing strong opinions, sometimes not in sync with the administration. All that was fine with me. But Fallon had recently gotten into hot water with the Bush administration for his off-hand comments about Iran in an article published in *Esquire* magazine. The previous week Fallon had submitted his resignation. I wasn't sure what I was walking into when I entered the admiral's expansive office that morning.

The admiral and General Dempsey greeted me at his office door. We made small talk as an assistant got us some hot coffee. Admiral Fallon quickly put me at ease. Warm, even cordial, he smiled when ruefully talking about the interview that led to his resignation. It was clear to me that while some in the administration wanted his head, he was leaving the service every bit his own man.

We discussed my upcoming command. Fallon gave a sweeping geopolitical review of the Pakistani/Afghan region and its primary players. I was listening hard and scribbling rough notes in my small green journal. This was a give-and-take at the strategic level that I had not experienced in my year-plus of preparation. He said I needed to get myself to Pakistan right away, as cooperation with and from Afghanistan's eastern neighbor was critical to achieving success with our counterinsurgency campaign in RC-East. He reviewed several Pakistani officers whom I would be meeting and working with. Then he moved on to the senior leaders in Afghanistan. President Karzai was a "skilled politician and deal cutter." Minister of Defense Wardak was "eloquent, but wanted a huge Afghan Army," not affordable. Afghan Chief of the Armed Forces

General Bismillah Khan Mohammadi, "General BK," was the "real deal," a strong and skilled leader with poor English. I would need to reach out to form a close relationship with him.

Admiral Fallon turned to our counterinsurgency strategy. I said I was concerned about the lack of troops in my AO, my area of operations. He said he did not think more U.S. or NATO/coalition troops were the ultimate answer. Instead, the Afghan Army and Air Corps and police needed to be better, probably bigger, and over time, they had to take on the bulk of fighting.

He told me to work hard on economic development in my sector. He saw four keys to improving the lot of the common Afghan, which would in turn bring them closer to their central government: roads, electricity, clean water, and agricultural development.

As I was leaving and we were standing at the office door shaking hands, he said, "Oh, and Jeff, the BTIF."

That's the Bagram Theater Internment Facility, the U.S.-run detainment facility that held high-level insurgents for interrogation, internment, and sometimes, release. And some, the high-value detainees, sometimes found themselves headed to Guantanamo.

"Sir?"

"I want it gone. Closed." He told me to get into the current BTIF right away and ensure it was running properly. He told me of plans to build a new facility, a state-of-the-art facility, which seemed to be languishing. He told me to take a personal interest in getting the new facility built on my watch.

On the flight back to Nashville and Fort Campbell that night, I had plenty to think about.

Eleven days later, it was time to depart. That morning I got up and drove to my favorite part of Fort Campbell, a wooded area with a trout stream running through and a circular five-mile road that almost never had traffic. I ran, thinking about the coming deployment, and also about my family. This would be yet another lengthy separation from them. The kids were fine, strong, and had their own lives. Patty too was strong, but I worried for her. She would be expected to be the smiling face at Fort

Campbell, as well as the backbone for the families and spouses left behind. She would be expected to attend memorials for fallen soldiers killed in Iraq and Afghanistan, weep with their loved ones, hug the newborn babies born with a father deployed, make small talk with local politicians, advise visiting senior military and national political delegations on how to help families, and generally hold it all together. I was confident in her; like me, she had been preparing for this role all of her adult life. But I worried nonetheless.

The day dragged on. Kelly, our daughter, was back at home for some medical tests, and we all tried to make small talk, but it was painful. Thankfully, the time came for me to go. I hugged Kelly, grabbed my pack, and Patty drove me the short distance to Division headquarters. I tried to put on a brave face as we hugged, but we both teared up. Lifting my kit, I hastily strode into the headquarters building, looking back for just a second, and gave her a short wave. I closed the door behind me.

CHAPTER 4

"I'm here to win."
General David McKiernan

Tuesday, June 3, 2008

It was a warm day in Kabul, the morning sun so bright that sunglasses did not help. I was in the stands on the ISAF headquarters grounds in Kabul, surrounded by fellow RC commanders from the south, north, west, and central regions, listening to President Karzai. A big Afghan fly buzzed around my face and I waved it away, which helped for seconds until it was back. The heat, Karzai's gentle and low voice, the lack of a decent night's sleep since I arrived in Afghanistan—they were my excuse, as I nearly dozed off.

It was an important day. It was the ISAF change of command, and General Dan McNeill would give up command to General David D. McKiernan. The speakers, President Karzai, NATO Joint Forces Command Brunssum Commander German General Egon Ramms, McNeill, and McKiernan, extolled the past accomplishments and set the goals for the next command. As usual, I could not wait for the ceremony's end. *What if this thing is attacked like the parade in April?* After all, President Karzai was right here, standing not fifty feet away. I'm certain many of those around me, all relatively senior in the NATO, diplomatic, or Afghan hierarchies, thought the same thing.

JEFFREY SCHLOESSER

Nothing happened. After the ceremony and a short reception, General McKiernan had his staff and subordinate commanders come into the ISAF conference room. It was a wood-paneled, windowless room, with framed maps of Afghanistan and symbols of NATO on the walls. I would spend plenty of time in the conference room, and in McKiernan's small office across the hallway, in the coming year.

"I will be here two years or more—longer than any previous commander," he started with. I was early into my own fifteen-month tour, surrounded by my NATO fellow commanders on six, nine, or twelve-month tours. I don't know whether I felt admiration for his commitment or just sorry for him. At that point of my tour, ISAF had yet to impress me; in fact, I usually departed the headquarters mildly unsettled by the slow pace, the "cappuccino in the garden" approach to strategy development, and somewhat disgruntled that each night the NATO staff got to enjoy a glass or two of wine in the leafy outdoor officers' club, while I had troops at the proverbial ends of the earth.

"I'm here to win." What followed was a lengthy examination of Afghan military history and cultural attributes, a dose of geography, and a levelheaded projection of strategic goals, with supporting ways and means. I took careful notes, not just so I could relay them to my own commanders and staff, but so I could personally ensure our CJTF-101 campaign plan supported the strategy of my new boss.

"What can you expect from me? The four Cs—commitment, candor, competence, and courage." And he said very clearly that he expected the same from us. On Pakistan: "We cannot be fully successful in Afghanistan unless we succeed in Pakistan."

What did that mean, succeed in Pakistan?

I wished he would detail that thought. He elaborated slightly: "Afghanistan and Pakistan are our area of operations." I already planned to devote significant time and energy to working with the Pakistani leadership and their army troops as well as the Frontier Corps, so I was pleased. "I want to energize our strategic comms." Strategic communications was the term used by the army to identify what information it needed to pass to both domestic and foreign audiences in order to explain what events happened and why things happened. In many cases, the ISAF strategic communications effort competed with its all-too-effective Taliban counterpart, so timely release of accurate information was important. Strategic comms was a critical, if sometimes unheralded, component of our own campaign plan. All good so far.

General McKiernan wrapped up by telling us he intended to spend the first thirty days traveling to all parts of Afghanistan to meet us on our own turf, meeting our junior leaders at their outposts, and talking with our Afghan military and government counterparts.

"I want to see what you are doing to support good governance and increase development, along with your security line of operation."

Until he completed his assessment, we should follow the current standing orders.

McKiernan was forceful, precise as he could be as the senior NATO commander in Afghanistan, and in spite of his thoughtful way of speaking, surprisingly energizing. And supremely concise. It was very clear McKiernan had done his homework; his comments about Afghanistan showed he had studied its history and had a good grasp of where we in ISAF stood in our counterinsurgency operations. His view of the very real importance of the Afghan-Pakistani border and security relationship closely matched my own. Finally, he seemed to be one who did not suffer fools, egoists, or spin artists. I had seen and worked with all of the above in my previous deployments, including with NATO, and hoped McKiernan could make a difference. I was resolved to help.

The issue was: Could the ISAF staff, as it was during that summer's day in 2008, actually help McKiernan? Did those officers, skilled in NATO politics but almost untrained in the type of irregular tactical combat that occurred outside of Kabul, have what he needed to *win* a war that was very different from their previous experience or training?

In hindsight, the task at hand was immense and difficult, even for the best-trained and combat-experienced commanders and staff. Our own AOR, Regional Command-East, was the size of a large state in the U.S., or just a tad smaller than Greece. The intelligence team told me that we had some four hundred different tribes among the seven to ten million population, who were mainly Pashtun, Hazara, and Tajik.

Along the entire 450-mile mountainous border with Pakistan, we had almost nightly rocket and mortar attacks, and the insurgents used the North-West Frontier Province and Federally Administered Tribal Areas (FATA) of Pakistan as safe havens and places to rearm and outfit. The two U.S. brigade combat teams in RC-East were aligned along the border, with Task Force Bayonet, the 173rd Airborne Regimental Combat Team (RCT) in the north from Nangarhar, Kunar, Nuristan, and Laghman. In late July, Colonel Chip Preysler would give up command of the area to Colonel John Spiszer and his 3rd BCT, 1st Infantry Division, Task Force Duke. John's incoming task force had about thirty-two hundred troops, some four hundred less than Task Force Bayonet. That was going in the wrong direction.

South of Nangarhar's Tora Bora Mountains lay Colonel Pete Johnson's area of responsibility for his 4th Brigade Combat Team, 101st Airborne Division: Khost and Paktika along the Pakistani border of North and South Waziristan; Paktiya, Logar, and Wardak to the west of Khost, stretching along Kabul's southern area, and finally Ghazni, south of Wardak. It was a huge area and the forces available were totally inadequate to secure the population across the vast territory. Pete and his troopers were also responsible for much of the three hundred miles of ring road (Highway 1) which connected Kabul to Kandahar, as well as the entire southern approach to Kabul. The 4th Brigade represented a substantial amount of the primary ground maneuver force for the upcoming Afghanistan rotation. Commanded by Colonel John P. "Pete" Johnson, it consisted of six organic units: Lieutenant Colonel Anthony DeMartino's 1st Battalion, 506th Infantry (TF Red Currahee); Lieutenant Colonel John Allred's 2nd Battalion, 506th Infantry (TF White Currahee); Lieutenant Colonel Tom W. O'Steen's 1st Squadron, 61st Cavalry (TF Panther); Lieutenant Colonel David J. Ell's 4th Battalion, 320th Field Artillery (TF Glory); Lieutenant Colonel Anthony K. "Kirk" Whitson's 801st Brigade Support Battalion (TF Mountaineer); and the 4th Special Troops Battalion (TF Strength).

Along the border we had small Afghan Border Police outposts. We worked together as much as possible, but they were outgunned by the insurgents and often had no mobility, no food, and no ammo due to a wretched Afghan resupply system. I was determined to work with the minister of interior to build the border patrol capabilities. In early summer of 2008, they were not much of a force to partner with.

The Afghan Army had two corps, the 201st headquartered in Kabul and 203rd in Gardez, stationed in our AOR. With three or four assigned brigades, the corps were smaller than a U.S. division on paper. In reality, many soldiers were habitually AWOL, or worse, and existed only as names on unit rosters, with their salaries going to corrupt officials. Add the uneven training and substandard outfitting and resupply, and the corps were still a work in progress in 2008. We partnered with the best units, and hoped to dramatically increase the numbers of direct partnerships by 2009.

The rest of my forces were even more constrained. In Kapisa, Bamyan, Parwan, and Panjshir, we would soon receive Colonel Scott Spellmon's Task Force Warrior, the 1st Maneuver Enhancement Brigade, scheduled for a July 10 transfer of authority with the ad hoc Task Force Cincinnatus. An extraordinarily rugged area even by Afghan standards, much of this area was dominated by the Hindu Kush Mountains. While the dramatic terrain and equally dramatic weather limited enemy insurgent movement in the area, it had the same impact on our own troops and efforts. One of the top five most violent districts in RC-East was in Kapisa, Tagab, a waypoint from Pakistan to Kabul. And if that was not enough, Bagram Airfield, headquarters for CJTF-101 and RC-East as well as the Air Force 455th Air Expeditionary Wing that supported all of Afghanistan, lay in the Shomali Plain, a fifty-mile-long and eighteen-mile-wide flat valley, ringed by the Hindu Kush to the north and west, the somewhat less imposing mountains of Kapisa to the east, and the capital city of Kabul to the south. This was all to be Spellmon's area of responsibility.

In the summer of 2008, we had a number of coalition forces that were NATO or allies assigned to RC-East: a New Zealand reconstruction team in Bamyan, a Turkish reconstruction team in Wardak, a Czech team in Logar, a small French OMLT in Kapisa, and a growing Polish presence in Ghazni.

The rest of the PRTs in the provinces were U.S.-led.

An Egyptian field hospital in Bagram and a small South Korean contingent added to our support capability.

We had plans with the French military and government to increase their troop strength up to a French battalion in Kapisa and a similar agreement with the Poles to build and support a small Polish brigade in Ghazni by the fall.

The special operations forces (SOF) task force based at Bagram had a good mix of coalition SOF troops, including some excellent Emirati Special Forces teams.

In addition to the 455th and its fighter and close air support aircraft, we had my own 101st Combat Aviation Brigade, with some 165 aircraft, including twenty-four Apache attack helicopters and thirty armed Kiowa Warrior OH-58Ds. For air assaults, lift, resupply, and general movement, we had thirty-eight UH-60L Black Hawks and twenty-eight CH-47F Chinooks. The twelve medevac Black Hawks were not enough to adequately support such a vast area and our one hundred outposts and FOBs, but they did miracles on a daily basis to try.

A rough count of total friendly forces in my area of responsibility was about twenty-five thousand in the summer of 2008. To secure a population of between seven to ten million (no one was certain) and to defeat an insurgency of seven to eleven thousand fighters—again it was anyone's guess exactly how many. The numbers weren't good.

But the insurgency was hardly a cohesive and united fighting force. We could identify a number of separate insurgent groups operating in our AOR: LeT (Lashkar-e-Taiba), Gulbuddin Hekmatyar's HiG (Hezb-e-Islami-Gulbuddin), TNSM (Tehreek-e-Nafaz-e-Shariat-e-Mohammadi), HIK/TBF (Hezb-i-Islami Khalis) led by Mulavi Younas Khalis, Baitullah Mehsud's TTiP (Tehrik-e-Taliban-i-Pakistan), Mullah Omar and the Afghan-oriented Taliban often referred to as the Quetta Shura Taliban, the Haqqani network inspired by Jalaluddin Haqqani and led by his son Siraj, and of course al-Qaida (AQ). Less frequently we could identify the IMU (Islamic Movement of Uzbekistan), JeM (Jaish-e-Mohammed), LeJ (Lashkar-e-Jhangvi), the IJU (Islamic Jihad Union), and Sipah-e-Sahaba.

We believed al-Qaida acted more as an inspiration than a true command and control headquarters, but were very much concerned that al-Qaida's global jihadist ideology was inspiring the groups to cooperate in broad jihadist objectives that included both sides of the Durand Line: defend the FATA, destabilize Islamabad, and defeat the government of Afghanistan and ISAF. We had begun to call this loose federation an "insurgent syndicate."

It was a gross oversimplification to attribute common objectives to each insurgent group, but broadly speaking in the summer of 2008, we saw the syndicate seeking to intimidate the local Afghan populace to reject the national and regional government, and they were using sustained suicide bombers and IED attacks to create fear and demonstrate the ineffectiveness of the government and ISAF to secure the people. They simultaneously were trying to limit ISAF, Afghan Army, and police freedom of movement, while attacking outposts and operating bases, usually with just enough force to harass, and from time to time, massing enough force to attempt to overrun our bases.

Given that RC-East was just one of five ISAF regions, it was easy to understand how the ISAF staff was overwhelmed.

CHAPTER 5

*"If you should cut them out of my dominions, they will never be
of any use to you or me. You will always be engaged in fighting or
other trouble with them, and they will always go on plundering."*
Abdur Rahman Khan, amir of Afghanistan

Tuesday, June 10, 2008

It was 9:00 p.m., and I was finally done with the day's planned activities. I was tired, and I looked balefully at my inbox. Paperwork, and these days, emails, didn't stop, even when at war, and it looked to be a few more hours to knock out the letters, awards, and reports that were neatly stacked by Sergeant First Class Gail Sims, my admin assistant.

I dreaded most the condolence letters, notes really, that I sent to the loved ones of all of our troopers killed under my command. I felt inadequate to such an important task, and frustratingly inarticulate. I tried to express the importance of their individual sacrifice to the next of kin with words, but in truth, I knew there were no words. No words to stop the pain. No words to explain why—why *my* husband, or wife, or son, or daughter. No words that could explain why this death helped us win a war like this, with no clear victory, and no clear end. But I tried, and regarded it as a solemn duty that I disliked, perhaps hated, but knew was my responsibility to do. I did my best.

Before I started on a note, I thought more about the day. Exactly three months prior, on April 10, Major General "Rod" Rodriguez and I had given short speeches, he reflecting on all his CJTF-82 had accomplished, and I assuring all that we would take up the baton and continue the campaign, and we had our transfer of authority (TOA) and command between units and unit commanders, at Bagram Air Base. Each and every day since had been packed with trips to combat outposts, to Kabul to meet with Afghan, coalition, and U.S. leaders, and a mind-numbing number of VIPs who came to Bagram to be briefed, to see the troops, and to see a little of the Afghan War. We oversaw the counterinsurgency campaign with early morning "stand-ups" and intelligence fusion meetings, routine decision briefs, evening combat operations update briefs that involved the entire staff, and broad guidance from me that the one-star deputy division commanders and chief of staff refined into mission command-type orders that would clearly convey what needed to be done, but gave subordinate commanders plenty of leeway on how they accomplished their missions. We operated on earned trust, constant battlefield checks to verify or better understand what was going on locally, and the very clear intent to maximize the effects not only of our own operations and extensive air support, but also the superb special operations forces in our AOR, our economic and agricultural activities, and maybe most importantly, our strategic communications.

I sighed, and turned to the first condolence letter. The direct line from the joint operations center (JOC) buzzed.

"Schloesser."

"Hey sir, we have something brewing down here and you need to come ASAP."

"The Paktika op? I thought H-hour was later tonight?"

"No sir, it's not Paktika. It's the Pakistani border, by Asadabad. And it looks bad."

"I'm coming now." I hastily walked out of the office, across the hallway, and into the JOC, Regional Command-East's command and control nerve center.

Brigadier General Mark Milley, the division and CJTF deputy commanding general for operations, was already there. The JOC night shift chief briefed us quickly, using a large map projected on one of the twenty or so screens on the wall.

"We have a pretty hot firefight going on east of A-bad right along the Afghan-Pak border near Nawa Pass, at Gora Paray. There are Pakistani Frontier Corps border posts involved, maybe two or three. It looks like insurgents are firing on friendlies from around or even from within the border posts." The Frontier Corps units were recruited from the fiercely independent Pashtun tribes living in the semi-autonomous Federally Administered Tribal Area (FATA) on the Pakistani side of Afghanistan's eastern border. Rather than permit Islamabad to permanently garrison the border with regular troops from outside the region, the tribes were provided with the authority, uniforms, arms, equipment, and pay necessary to form paramilitary units to perform that mission.

"Friendlies? What friendlies?" The area we were looking at on the map was a bad area, the Durand Line not well delineated for miles, and both the Afghans and Pakistanis claimed the high ground, which overlooked several mountain passes routinely used by smugglers and insurgents alike. We normally had no U.S. or coalition troops there, and if we did, I should have known about it.

"Sir, we think it's a paramilitary op, with some indig Afghan forces. We are trying to find out exactly now through ISAF as well as our liaisons. We are getting SA now—General Milley approved an ISR bird diversion." Essentially, we had U.S. paramilitary forces advising Afghan irregular forces in a fierce firefight with Pakistani Frontier troops, themselves more paramilitary than regulars. Milley had already diverted some of our scarce drone assets to survey the ongoing action.

"Air? Artillery in range? Apaches or KWs [OH-58D Kiowa Warrior armed reconnaissance helicopters]?"

"We moved the F-15Es and they will be on station momentarily. The CAOC is sending us a B-1B. They look to be there in a couple of minutes. They are our fastest response."

The CAOC was the Combined Air Operations Center at Al Udeid Air Base, Qatar, which coordinated the air war over Afghanistan and the entire region. The B-1B Lancer was a supersonic swept-wing bomber that could rapidly move into position to provide air support.

The Predator unmanned aerial vehicle redirected by General Milley soon arrived to provide us with real-time video of the situation. We could make out a small group most of the way up the mountain. They were clearly fixed by accurate small arms fire and likely rocket-propelled grenades (RPGs) from several high-ground locations. The situation looked grim from the drone feeds. It must have been dire on the ground.

As best we could tell, all of the friendlies were a few hundred meters from the border, on the Afghan side. But then again, the border here was contested, and both Pakistani and Afghan border posts were not well located on maps. We had less than good situational awareness, even with the Predator video feeds. We used our U.S. liaison team (LNO) in Islamabad to try to get the Pakistanis to help, but liaison was a slow process, and we did not have much time.

I assessed that the friendly ground force was in deep shit. We pushed to increase fires—air to ground, ground to ground—to help them.

The swing-wing B-1B bomber arrived overhead. I held deep respect for the aging platform developed by North American/Rockwell in 1974 as a low-altitude replacement for both the supersonic B-58 Hustler and venerable B-52 Stratofortress bombers. Although temporarily placed on hold until the stealth bomber could be produced, the air force began issuing a redesigned version designated as the B-1B to Strategic Air Command nuclear strike squadrons in 1986. At the end of the Cold War, the air force converted its one hundred-strong B-1B fleet into conventional delivery platforms. Fast, big, and technologically updated, it could achieve significant battlefield effects even in complex terrain: in plain speak, it held enough ordnance to accurately bomb the crap out of the enemy, even in mountains. Just one B1 could be a game changer in any ground battle.

The aircrew in the B-1B began a careful application of precision 250-pound JDAMs onto the insurgent positions. We watched the drone video, and clearly could see the explosions, the debris clouds, and the quick impact on the fighting. Small figures, the enemy, ran towards cover, some across the apparent border and back down the other side of the mountain, while others looked as if they disappeared while running, evidently into caves or fortified positions. As we continued the bombing, others just disappeared: you saw a handful of figures running, then a debris cloud, then nothing left.

I authorized hot pursuit, and so some who crossed back into Pakistan were engaged there, fairly close to the border, but within my authority to engage given the circumstances.

The B1 "Winchestered" (it was out of bombs) and we brought on other fires, until it was over. The friendlies got down the mountain, and we eventually got them out of the AO. The fight was over.

I knew I needed to get word immediately to my new boss, General McKiernan, as well as to our Afghan partners. I was also deeply worried about our nascent relationship with the Pakistani military and Frontier Corps. It looked to us like the insurgents were using the Frontier Corps border positions, likely with some level of Pakistani cooperation. I had no doubt we had killed plenty of insurgents that night, but was equally certain we had killed Pakistani Frontier Corpsmen too, complicit or not. And the Taliban would soon be working their strategic comms, crowing about U.S. and Afghans killed, Pakistanis wrongly targeted, and their victory on the Durand Line at Gora Paray.

The shit was about to hit the fan. I hurried back to my office to start making calls.

It was a long night. From our LNOs, we learned several Frontier Corps personnel had been killed and others wounded. No one could tell us how they got mixed into the middle of a hot firefight with insurgents attacking our friendlies. The Pakistanis were beside themselves, claiming we had purposely killed eleven of their Frontier Corps tribesmen and wounded thirteen more.

Very early the next morning, I had a call with the now acting CENTCOM Commander, Lieutenant General Martin Dempsey. We once had been peers, he a one-star directing the U.S. liaison to the Saudi

Arabian National Guard in Riyadh, while I was the one-star chief of the U.S. Office of Military Cooperation in Kuwait. We later served in Iraq at the same time, Dempsey commanding the 1st Armored Division, I serving as a deputy division commander in the 101st Airborne Division up in Mosul. I respected him immensely.

A true gentleman with a master's degree in English, Marty could also be blunt and plainspoken: *The fight the previous night had strategic impact. The chairman of the joint chiefs, Admiral Mullen, needed my assessment of what had happened and why, as well as what we were doing to mitigate the damage.*

Admiral Michael "Mike" Mullen was the chairman of the U.S. Joint Chiefs, the most senior officer in the U.S. Armed Forces, and advisor to the president. A former chief of naval operations, he was on his fourth consecutive four-star assignment. My report needed to be accurate, detailed, and quick.

The day was a blur of updates from staff to me, then to my NATO boss General McKiernan and my CENTCOM boss General Dempsey, who informed Admiral Mullen, as well as the Afghan leadership. We decided to declassify and publicly release portions of the Predator video feed to show how false the Taliban claims were. Meanwhile, in Islamabad, Pakistani Prime Minister Raza Gilani "vehemently condemned" our airstrikes, and Pakistani Army spokesman Major General Athar Abbas called our actions a "completely unprovoked and cowardly act" that "hit at the very basis of cooperation" in the war on terrorism.

In media releases, we did our best to drive our narrative of the border incident at Gora Paray. The Pakistani Taliban media machine ratcheted up its claims, stating that between sixty to one hundred of its fighters had repelled NATO and Afghan troops intent on setting up illegal military positions on Pakistani soil. Maulvi Umar, the Pakistani Taliban spokesman, claimed to have shot down a NATO helicopter as well as killed some forty NATO and Afghan troops, which was utter nonsense, as usual, but often believed by Taliban sympathizers and unsuspecting Afghans.

The stakes were high. The Afghan Donor Conference was to be held that week in Paris, with First Lady Laura Bush, fresh from her visit to Afghanistan the previous week, leading the U.S. delegation. The emphasis needed to be on building a stable Afghanistan, not on civilian or allied military casualties caused by U.S. and NATO strikes. We had to de-escalate the tensions as fast as we could. Mrs. Bush had her mission in Paris and we had ours in Bagram, but it was up to me to ensure the latter did not ruin the former.

Working closely with Minister Wardak, General McKiernan, the U.S. embassies in Kabul and Islamabad, and the director general for military operations (DGMO) for the Pakistani Army, we devised and announced a tripartite investigation, to be jointly led by U.S., Afghan, and Pakistani general officers, to investigate and report on the Gora Paray incident. It would be complicated, given the sensitive nature of the friendly force and the resultant need to keep them and their mission under wraps, but we felt it could be done.

The announcement of the joint investigation helped quiet the uproar almost immediately. The emphasis was on working together to understand what had happened and devise measures to prevent such incidents in the future.

In my headquarters, we had a less sanguine view. We knew what we saw on the video, we had the firsthand reports from the friendly forces, and we had experienced three months of almost nightly attacks along the Durand Line. Most of us felt the Frontier Corps had been complicit in the attacks, aiding the Taliban, and we were unrepentant about our actions.

As a learning point, I saw that no matter how proactive and transparent our information was, it could be trumped by the enemy broadcasting their "message" to the international and regional media faster than we could react. Speed did not represent the only issue, as the Taliban also proved more capable of putting their message in a cultural perspective familiar to their intended local audiences. Unsophisticated to the American soldier and commander but superbly "tuned" to the local and regional perceptions and mindset, the enemy were beating us in the information war.

One other point I learned was that joint investigations actually work. They serve to quickly defuse the situation, as long as they are transparent to all participants, and are supported with senior-level investigating officers of equal ranks from all relevant sides who have some skill in co-operation and military diplomacy. And when enabled, they uncover root causes that all sides can address and use to lessen the chances of exactly the same thing happening in the future.

CHAPTER 6

"If you lose patience, we will lose the war."
Major General Ahmad Shuja Pasha

Monday, June 16, 2008

Early Monday morning, Brigadier General Mark Milley, political advisor Turk Maggi, and our aides climbed into a UC-35 executive jet for the flight to Islamabad. It was a relatively short flight from Bagram, a bit longer than an hour, but it was like flying from one end of the continent to the other. Bagram was cool, very dry, and surrounded by tall mountains that still retained a bit of snow at their peaks. We flew over majestic mountains, the Tora Bora range below us, and then began a gentle descent into the lush, green Indus River Valley. As we deplaned, the heat and humidity hit us, and we were thankful to jump into an air-conditioned SUV for the ride to the U.S. embassy.

At the embassy we were met by Major General James "Ron" Helmly, the chief of the Office of the Defense Representative-Pakistan, ODR-P for short. We shared hot coffee in his cramped office. A senior general officer who had previously served as the three-star chief of the Army Reserve, then reverted to two-star for his current assignment, Helmly was characteristically blunt. Things in Pakistan were not good. The Pakistani government was incapable of governing and handling the security situation, and Helmly was equally negative about what he saw in the Pakistani Army, which historically served as the foundation of the Pakistan nation. We did not have nearly long enough to talk before we needed to trot upstairs.

U.S. Ambassador Anne Patterson was the quintessential professional senior foreign service officer, and one of a handful of our nation's finest diplomats. Small-framed, with piercing eyes and a formidable intellect, she possessed deep regional and international experience as well as a profound understanding of human weaknesses and strengths. I gave her my early assessment of the situation in Afghanistan, focusing on RC-East, and specifically updated her on the Gora Paray joint investigation and what we thought we knew about the cross-border incident that had occurred six days prior. I told her what I planned to discuss with our Pakistani hosts later that day. She agreed with my analysis and plans, and gave us a brief but very helpful insight into the current state of Pakistani affairs.

Brigadier General Milley, Turk, our aides, and I rode over to the Pakistani General Headquarters (GHQ) in a speeding convoy, with host nation police escort. The roads were jammed in the late morning with every vehicle known to mankind: speeding luxury cars competed with colorfully painted jitneys, along with donkey-drawn carts loaded with fruit and vegetables headed to the outdoor markets.

Major General Ahmad Shuja Pasha greeted us at the General Headquarters. Likely one of the most powerful army generals in Pakistan, Pasha's job as DGMO, director general of military operations, was part intelligence officer, part operations planner, and part senior advisor to the Pakistani Army's most senior leaders. His staff was planning newly pro-active and aggressive operations to begin in the Federally Administered Tribal Area, the FATA, soon. The FATA, a remote border region between northwestern Pakistan and our eastern Afghanistan border, was predominantly Pashtun, tribal, rural, and a safe haven for Pakistani Taliban. In the past, the Pakistanis were far more willing to target extremists seeking to usurp their authority in the Federally Administered Tribal Area or otherwise threaten the stability of the regime in Islamabad rather than the insurgent groups operating in Afghanistan.

This was my third meeting with the general. He had attended our April CJTF TOA ceremony and, in an office call with me, U.S. Chargé Bodde, and Major General Helmly, said that the Pakistani people no longer fully trusted their army, and that he regarded that as a major issue to overcome. He had quietly confided then that he intended to retire within two years. He sounded tired, defeated.

On May 19, Brigadier General Milley and Turk and I had once again visited Islamabad and Peshawar for our first formal meeting of CJTF-101 and the Pakistani military leadership. After discussions with the ambassador, station chief, and Helmly, we met at General Headquarters with the army vice chief of staff, Lieutenant General Muhammad Yousaf, and Major General Pasha. After a cordial welcome, we got down to a broad discussion of the situation on both sides of the border. I opened with what must have been a very undiplomatic, brutally frank description of what we—my staff, commanders, and I—saw as serious border incursions, happening all along our RC-East border with Pakistan but concentrated in the Nangarhar and Khost provinces. I said the army and Frontier Corps had to do more to stop the enemy from what seemed to be almost daily rocket, artillery, and mortar attacks on my outposts and those of the Afghans along the border.

Visibly angry—*I was clearly a new upstart in Afghanistan: How could I lecture them on their own country?*—General Pasha scolded me like I was a naughty schoolboy, and I pushed back. It was a rocky start, but in the end, Pasha gave us a face-saving out, which turned out to be brilliant in hindsight now. "General Schloesser, you have briefed us on what you and your staff see. Please return soon, and let our GHQ staff brief you on how we see the situation and what we intend to do about it."

We both were pretty hot, but it was a good idea, and I quickly agreed.

So, this time, I knew I had to approach General Pasha much differently if we were going to have the type of positive working relationship that could benefit our respective services and countries. I started by offering condolences for the loss of Pakistani lives at Gora Paray, without accusing the Frontier Corps of complicity with the insurgents. Pasha was equally magnanimous, stating that the purpose of the investigation needed to be to help us avoid such confrontations in the future, while allowing our cooperation along the border to move forward.

Pasha then led his staff through an agency-by-agency review of the security situation. It was clear that the Pakistani Army was not completely prepared for a series of major operations against the Pakistani Taliban on the frontier, and yet it was equally clear that they believed that some operations had to begin soonest, and that they needed our help. Using our nascent Border Coordination Center (BCC) at Torkham Gate in the famous Khyber Pass where U.S., Pakistani, and Afghan watch officers worked 24/7 to deconflict each others' operations, we would coordinate our operations to the west of the Durand Line while providing the anvil to the Pakistani Army hammer from the east. It was a request I could not turn down, and I was very much satisfied. The problem that remained to be solved, in hindsight, was that the Pakistani Army had been equipped and trained for conventional warfare against potential Indian opponents and as such was unfamiliar with counterinsurgency operations.

As we got ready to leave, General Pasha said something that still haunts me to this day.

"If you lose patience, we will lose the war."

It was a quiet flight in the cramped UC-35 back to Bagram. We almost always tried to grab a few minutes of rushed sleep when in the jet or Black Hawk, but that afternoon I think we all stayed awake, focused on the meeting. It could have dissolved into mutual accusations and denials centered on Gora Paray; instead, Pasha had truly helped us understand the military situation on their side, and most importantly, asked for our help. I was pleased, and determined to continue to build a productive personal relationship with the general, and between our staffs. But his warning bothered me. I had wanted to reply: *Don't worry about us Americans or NATO—we are here to win!* But I was not so certain. My own government saw Iraq and the surge there as the priority, and I was not at all sure we, as a government or a people, were in Afghanistan for the long haul. Did Pasha know us better than ourselves?

That night during our routine video teleconference with Secretary of Defense Robert Gates, I mentioned the positive meeting we had had with General Pasha. I also told him that we calculated that from January to May of this year, there had been a 40 percent increase in the level of violence in RC-East compared to 2007. It was pretty obvious to me that Admiral Fallon, the ambassador, General McNeill, the intelligence officers, and many others had been dead right: spring 2008 would be and was much more violent in my area of Afghanistan. And it was my job to turn that around, and soon.

The next day was a normal flurry of activity, but that evening at 9:00 p.m., I got a call from the JOC. A CH-47 Chinook, a twenty-five-ton tandem rotor helicopter that carried thirty or more troops, had crashed deep in the mountains of Kunar, west of Bari Kowt, not far from the Pakistan border, at 9,100 feet. Initial reports were that it had been attempting to insert a U.S. special operations team along with Afghan commandos, had hit a tree with a rotor blade, and crash-landed in a high ravine. The pilots had somehow managed to keep the aircraft intact. Three passengers were injured, none seriously. I had been a Chinook pilot since 1981, and was astounded from the reports. In most incidents like this, the aircraft tandem rotors intermeshed, some blades cutting through the fuselage, and any passengers, and the resultant forces jerked the forward and aft transmissions out of the aircraft. Usually the aircraft was totally destroyed, along with everyone in it. We were lucky.

We put a quick reaction force (QRF) on the site as fast as we could and helped extract the crew and "pax" (passengers). Our CJTF-101 Pathfinder Company had been trained for downed aircraft situations, even in contested or hostile areas like this, and they did a superb job of securing the site. I was confident they had enough firepower to hold until the next day, but we put up overhead air support. Colonel Jim Richardson, the 101st Combat Aviation Brigade commander, was away from Bagram, so I told his executive officer (XO) and staff that I reserved the right to decide whether we would try to extract the Chinook or destroy it, but needed their eyes-on and firsthand expert assessment, in the daylight, before I decided. I called my boss at ISAF, then my next boss at CENTCOM, and third boss back at the army, the Vice Chief of Staff General Dick Cody, who was one of the army's most high-time and experienced aviators, and passed on what I knew. I told them all I would make the decision to attempt to extract or destroy, in the morning. I think they all respected that I was the most senior Chinook aviator in the army, at least in rank, and would know what was feasible, and best. It was a short night, and I was restless.

CHAPTER 7

"You shall command more with years than with your weapons."
William Shakespeare, Othello

Wednesday, June 18, 2008

I was up at 5:00 a.m. as usual, and impatient to hear about the downed Chinook. The operations center told me the security situation remained stable, but the available intelligence indicated that insurgents and tribesmen in the area knew about the crash, and I did not think it would be long before they came to see what was left. The QRF, our Pathfinders, could hold off small enemy groups, and with air power and Apaches, could keep the site secure, but I wanted to make a decision and act on it before dark, before we had anyone else hurt. I was not one to reinforce failure. I normally cut my losses and moved on.

But first, I had to let Colonel Richardson's subordinates do what I asked of them: fly out to the crash site and assess it.

By 10:30 a.m., Lieutenant Colonel John Kline, Richardson's XO, and Lieutenant Colonel Tim Healy, the battalion commander whose CH-47 had crashed, were ready to brief me. They did not think we could extract the Chinook, and recommended we destroy it, to keep it from the enemy's hands and their propaganda machine. I had known both officers for years—John and I had served together in the 12th Aviation

Brigade, Tim and I in the 160th—and respected them both greatly. And yet I was not entirely convinced. I decided to personally assess the crash and the situation.

The flight from Bagram to Kunar took about forty-five minutes. I tried to sleep, but could not. This looked like I was second-guessing my own commanders, which is never good when you actually know and trust them, and yet, if I could figure out how to extract the aircraft, maybe by removing the engines and lifting them out separately, then I needed to do this. Or was I simply a cowboy, a division commander yearning to get into a tactical operation that would best be decided by a battalion commander and executed by a platoon leader and his soldiers?

We circled the crash site slowly, maintaining forward flight. At this altitude and weight, hovering wasn't a good idea. It was far more wooded than I had anticipated, the tall dark evergreens almost hiding the Chinook. It was really hard to get a good, unobstructed view, and I asked my command pilot, Dave Draper, if he thought he could get us on the ground. I could tell Chief Warrant Officer Eric Clayton, my security detachment chief, was not enthusiastic, but his young sergeants were smiling. Some action! They were always happiest when we were outside the wire.

Dave burned off a bit more fuel in circling and then dropped down a "hover hole" in the evergreens. It was rocky, no place to land, with a steep slope, and he put the right landing gear on the ground, held the aircraft steady, and the security detachment and I jumped out. Dave took off. We had just a few minutes available on the ground before he would need gas.

The Pathfinder first sergeant met us and we climbed down the rocky incline to the ravine and the Chinook. It took one good look and I knew there was no way to extract the aircraft without literally cutting it into pieces. The tall trees made a long-line helicopter extraction infeasible: it would take another Chinook to pull this one out, and it looked stuck in the rocks. The trees would need to be cut down, rocks moved, and the aircraft lightened. I made up my mind: we had to destroy it. Still I lingered, marveling at the crash, the crash site, and our good fortune. It was a miracle no one was killed.

It was midday, the sun was hot through the trees, and I could tell the Pathfinders were ready for a decision. The first sergeant looked at me. It wasn't every day his boys were sent to a nine-thousand-foot mountain, told to secure a Chinook from the enemy for twenty-four hours or more, and then had to watch over a lingering division commander to boot.

"You have thermites, right?" I already knew the answer.

"Yes sir, plenty to do the job."

"Blow it. Now."

"Yes sir!" The Pathfinders immediately started the process. They already had removed the secure equipment on board, so this was a relatively short but exacting process of getting the thermites emplaced in the right locations and ignited to achieve maximum destruction. Without getting anyone hurt. Without the enemy closing in before.

"Eagle 6, Mr. Draper says he needs to get gas, and he isn't leaving until you are aboard. We need to go."

I started my career as a combat engineer, still loved to blow things up, and had hoped to see this to the end. But I knew Dave was right. Reluctantly, I would have to miss the pyrotechnics. We scrambled back up the ravine, Dave came in for another single-gear hover hold, and we pushed ourselves aboard.

There were unclear reports of enemy or locals moving toward the crash site.

We flew to the outpost at Naray, refueled the Black Hawk, and flew back to the mountain. The Chinook was on fire, flames an orange red, the gray and black smoke from the burning aluminum and magnesium shooting skyward. Other aircraft would soon extract the Pathfinders, and they would go back to Bagram, to tell "I was there" stories and get some good chow and a bit of sleep, and wait for the next time.

That night I thought about the mission. Was it wise to ask my subordinates for their recommendation, then second-guess the recommendation they made, only to decide they were exactly right after I saw the situation with my own eyes? Sometimes a commander, or any leader, must lead from the front: first, in the literal sense, out where the danger is tangible, the options unclear, and the decisions have immediate impact on people. Secondly, a leader also needs to lead from the front in a more strategic sense: when the decisions will be second-guessed at every level up to the highest ranks, and when the ultimate responsibility *and* authority for success or failure merge. It is not right to make a subordinate *responsible* for an outcome without ensuring they have the *authority* to actually make and implement the ultimate decision. In the case of the crashed thirty-million-dollar Chinook that morning, the authority rested with me, and so I decided it was my responsibility to make the decision, and be held accountable. I was confident that I did the right thing.

Two days later, Friday, and I had slept in until 6:55 a.m. I felt guilty, but we had purposely designed this battle rhythm to ensure we could operate smartly for all fifteen months of our deployment. I had seen far too many staff, and commanders, slowly waste away in combat. They would get totally inadequate sleep, have absolutely no downtime, and get little physical training (PT), and over time the exhaustion took over. They were the ones with the thousand-yard stare, the mushy, almost drunken voice, and the all-too-slow, or worse, all-too-fast, decisions. So, on Fridays—the start of the Afghan weekend—and Sundays, we tried to schedule no internal meetings before noon. Combat ops of course went on as usual, as did the nearly daily visits to Bagram by American, NATO, and coalition senior leaders, congressional delegations (CODELs), and other VIPs.

That morning, we had no such visit and I snuck in a quick run around Bagram Airfield. At eight miles, it was perfect for me. A luxury, in fact. I usually ran every morning at 5:00 a.m. in the dark for part of the year, and only for about four miles or so. On Fridays, when schedules allowed, I indulged in a long run in the morning daylight. I found the runs peaceful, and usually did my best thinking during them.

On this particular Friday run, I decided that I had seen enough. It would soon be ninety days since our transfer of authority, and I had visited many of our combat outposts, been briefed by platoon, company, battalion, and brigade staff and commanders, and could see the impact our operations were having on the enemy, and their own impact on my troops. The casualty figures told the story: in the previous week, we had had thirteen troops killed in action (KIA), fifty-four wounded in action (WIA), and ten non-battle injuries (NBIs). We didn't do body counts of the enemy in our operations, but I knew that we (America, NATO, and our broader coalition) could not indefinitely sustain this level of friendly casualties.

I felt that we had the right campaign plan, and that our lines of operation—security, governance, development, and information—were appropriate for the time and place. But I had nowhere near enough resources to actually execute the plan: even with almost one hundred camps, outposts, and operating bases, I had too few troops on the ground in this vast area to impact both enemy and friendly. We had to find, fix, and finish the insurgents, or at least get them to flee or reconcile; we had to simultaneously ensure the locals were secure, link them to their governors and back to Kabul, and provide a better life: clean water, schools for boys and girls, at least some electricity, better crops than poppy, and roads to link it all together. We were not going to be able to accomplish all of this in a timely manner, or even within the patience of our home populations, without an increase in resources.

I was very much aware that Afghanistan was not America's priority at this time, and that my CENTCOM boss was overseeing and sending troops to support a very large Iraqi "surge." We in Afghanistan were expected to make do with what we had. But as a commander in combat, a leader of thousands who depended upon me, I felt a greater responsibility: to my troops on the ground and in the air risking their lives, to their families back home, and to the American people who actually desired us to win in Afghanistan and get back home.

I finished the run tired from the physical effort, but refreshed mentally. I knew what I must do.

★ ★ ★

A week later, on Saturday, June 28, I flew to Kabul to meet with General McKiernan. Brigadier General Mark Milley and Chief Colonel Tom Vail joined me. We briefed General McKiernan on our plan to pass responsibility and title as national support element (NSE) for all U.S. troops in Afghanistan from CJTF-101 to McKiernan himself, who would assume the title of commander of U.S. Forces Afghanistan in addition to his role as COMISAF (commander, International Security Assistance Force), the commander of all NATO and coalition forces. Long overdue, this would significantly streamline the often confusing command and control of U.S. Forces in the theater, and vastly improve the influence of the senior U.S. officer in command in Afghanistan where it was needed most: Washington, D.C.

There was some tension; no commander likes to give up responsibilities and I was no exception. My staff would also have to "chop" officers and NCOs to form the new U.S. Forces Afghanistan, and we would lose some key people, who would actually move to Kabul. But it was the right thing to do, and the staff and I needed to support it 100 percent. It was also not my biggest issue that day to discuss with General McKiernan.

After the formal brief on the NSE and his guidance, General McKiernan and I went to his office across the hallway from the conference room.

It had been a tough week. I had spent all day Saturday in Kandahar meeting with RC-South Commander Canadian Major General Marc Lessard and his team, checking on the U.S. troops in the area of operations, and discussing how to give RC-South an additional U.S. battalion task force that would come from my forces. It was clear RC-South was as short on resources as we were in the East. On Monday, I was in Kabul, meeting with three top Afghan government officials: Amrullah Saleh, director general of the National Directorate of Security, the Afghan equivalent of our CIA and FBI; Ghulam Popal, director general of the Independent Directorate of Local Governance; and Minister of Interior Ahmad Zarar. All of them indicated that this year was already much more violent than any they had seen since the NATO incursion, and that we needed to do more. On Wednesday, I pinned on Purple Hearts at our Bagram military hospital at 1:30 in the morning. At 5:00 a.m., we held a "ramp" ceremony for one of our fallen troops, who sadly was killed three weeks before the end of his tour. Later that morning, I visited our combat outposts at Gardez, Zormat, and Wilderness. At the latter, the company commander, Captain Tom Kilbride, told me of the fighting there the past two weeks. The insurgents, mainly Haqqani's outfit, had taken huge losses, but they were pressing still, and threatened our massive road-building project there, the Khost-Gardez (KG) Pass Road. That night we had an OH-58D Kiowa Warrior experience an engine failure in the mountains of the Watapur Valley. The pilots managed to auto-rotate with significant damage to the aircraft but minor injuries: it could have been far worse in that treacherous terrain. Within minutes, Alpha Company from TF Rock had both pilots and their aircraft secured.

On Thursday, I flew over the Hindu Kush to western Afghanistan to visit our Farah Provincial Reconstruction Team (PRT), where Commander Shoshana Chatfield, a Navy helicopter pilot, was doing a superb job leading a really remote site.

Commander Chatfield had previously commanded a helicopter sea combat squadron, and was tough as they come. I also knew she had a master's degree from Harvard and doctorate from San Diego, and was a quick study. I was impressed by her grasp of the tactical and strategic situation she was working in. Her PRT was co-located with the Special Forces Operational Detachment-Alpha (ODA: a twelve-man self-sufficient special operations team with its own training, communications, weapons, and medical experts) and a medical aid station on a dusty plain not too far from the Iranian border, and the white-hot sun and dirt and sand in the air made it inhospitable, but she and her team were making progress. There were troops in contact (TIC) during my visit, and a medevac Black Hawk brought in the wounded. We were in the aid station when they arrived: four WIAs, wounded in action. We said a hasty farewell to the doc and his team—they had work to do—but before we could depart the station, one of the soldiers died of wounds as Shoshana and I watched helplessly. The small aid station was no trauma center, but the doc and his team were trauma experts; they triaged each patient with a fervor for life—arms coated in the patient's blood, quietly tying off this part here, injecting this med there, and all along encouraging that soldier laid out in front of them: "Hang with me, dude! Think of your wife! You will see her soon! Hang with us!"

This wasn't the first time I had watched one of our troopers die while a medic or doc worked feverishly to keep them alive. Years before in Mosul, Iraq, after a mortar attack on the 101st Airborne Division headquarters, Division Commander Major General David Petraeus and I rushed outside to find one of our surgeons searching for a soldier's wound—amid blood pouring out from behind his chest body armor—and, too late, finding the tiny wound at the armpit, between the armor, where a small sliver of shrapnel had cut through the heart and ended that soldier's life. Then and now, the feeling of utter incapability to save one of my own, or even help in any meaningful way, was a bitter disappointment bordering on agony.

Later, as I boarded a small short takeoff and landing fixed-wing aircraft (STOL) to head back across the Hindu Kush to the east, I asked Commander Chatfield how I could help. She asked for at least another squad, about nine troopers, and some logistics specialists to help manage the dirt-strip airfield, as well as simple admin things like more phone lines. She was at the end of a very long line of communications, and I promised her I would do what I could.

I landed in Bagram to a duty status whereabouts unknown (DUSTWUN), a missing in action in progress. A CSTC-A convoy of the U.S. National Guardsmen had been ambushed in the Tangi Valley of Wardak. The situation was very unclear, compounded by the convoluted chain of command; these troopers did not work for my CJTF but were transiting through our area of operations. Nevertheless, we had American soldiers missing and unaccounted for. We airlifted a quick reaction force from the 506th Infantry, the Currahees, and helped move Afghan National Army troops into the sparsely patrolled area. Three soldiers and one Afghan interpreter were dead. One of the soldiers had been horrifically mutilated. The enemy had cut off the soldier's ears and forearms, among other abominations. We were dealing with jackals.

We piled on more troops and some special operators, and over the next several days Currahee 6, the call sign of 4th Brigade Combat Team Commander Colonel Pete Johnson, conducted battalion-sized search and destroy missions against the enemy in the area. We had no intent of holding and building in the Tangi Valley since our troop strength would not support that, but we eventually hunted down the ambushers, who were killed in a firefight.

A miserable week. So, when I had my private time with the ISAF commander, I did not beat around the bush.

"Sir, I have completed my assessment, and I believe we need more resources in RC-East: troops, surveillance, and reconnaissance, and close air support."

General McKiernan asked how many troops. My staff believed we needed another brigade combat team, some 3,500 troops, to really be successful, but I was cautious. I knew if I asked for too much, it could be too much too fast, and we would get nothing. With the surge in Iraq, the U.S. Army was hard-pressed to provide enough combat-capable units in Afghanistan, which was clearly not the priority effort.

"At least two battalion task forces, sir."

We discussed what types of surveillance and reconnaissance support worked best for us up in the East, with our high mountains dissected by fast-flowing rivers and streams and the hundreds of rat lines that followed ancient smuggling routes over the mountain chain that defined the Durand Line. Airborne ISR platforms, be they manned aircraft or drones such as the Shadow or Predator, were incredibly useful during actual combat operations: they provided "eyes in the sky" and allowed for fairly accurate monitoring and tracking of battles. But much more importantly, the right kind of platform, specially picked for the specific terrain and mission, could provide extraordinary insight *before* a battle, even preventing a battle in the first place. Picking the right kinds of platform for our very rough mountainous terrain was an art form.

McKiernan told me he agreed with my assessment and that he would support the request. We both knew this request would be unwelcome in Washington and elsewhere, and I left his office fully realizing that while I had his support, it was still my job to push this "request for forces" (RFF) within the U.S. military command structure, since I was still national support element commander for the U.S. forces.

I knew my CENTCOM boss, Lieutenant General Dempsey, was unconvinced that any additional troops were available this year. He told that to me himself in our frequent calls and emails. He was fighting on two fronts plus supporting a broader counterterror effort throughout his immense area of responsibility spanning the Middle East and Southwest Asia. My war was much more limited in scope and in relative importance to Washington at that time. To his credit, Dempsey did not block my request in the staff nor my own attempts to build support with his own superiors.

On Tuesday, July 1, we had our routine video teleconference with the secretary of defense and chairman. As usual, COMISAF, General McKiernan, led off the update, with the acting CENTCOM commander, Marty Dempsey, commenting when he felt appropriate. When it was my turn, I briefed the current large tactical operations in the Tangi Valley and KG Pass, as well as gave a short update on the joint investigation of the fight at Gora Paray. I did not mention my request for forces until the vice chairman, Admiral James Cartwright, asked about it. I could see the tension build, even through the sometimes fuzzy screen. I gave a concise assessment of the why, what, and how. I said it wasn't just troops we needed, but more ISR and close air support. General Dempsey stated there were no more troops to be had.

I don't recall anyone saying anything for some time. It was probably seconds, but it seemed much longer. I knew it was not my place to disagree with my CENTCOM boss in front of Secretary Gates and Chairman Mullen. I also knew it was my responsibility as Eagle 6, a commander in combat, to give frank, even brutally frank, assessments, and ask for the resources I thought we needed to fight with a reasonable chance of success. And that is what I intended to continue to do.

The chairman broke the silence. "Jeff, ask for what you need."

Secretary Gates agreed.

That broke the tension, and the discussion moved to my counterpart at the CSTC-A training command, Major General Bob Cone's update.

My mind wandered back to my command as Cone briefed. I jotted down in my green book, *Why is this so hard?*

Still, McKiernan and I had succeeded in gaining the secretary's and Admiral Mullen's support, and that was a major step forward.

Looking backward, the decision at the Chinook crash site and the decision to request more troops were remarkably alike in one fundamental sense. They were mine to make. I could have pushed the Chinook decision lower, and when I got the inevitable questioning from my bosses, told them I had delegated the responsibility and decision. I could have pushed the troop request higher, by just waiting and hoping General McKiernan would see what I saw and come to the same conclusions, but that could have taken months, and maybe he never would have seen it the way I did, since the view in Kabul was very different than what I saw in the almost daily visits to our outposts and forward operating bases. One was tactical (destroy or attempt to recover a massive helicopter in unfriendly territory) and the other strategic (admit we were not winning on a timeline the American people would support, and that we needed more soldiers and resources to have a reasonable chance of not losing); both had the potential to damage my bosses' assessment of my judgment, both would set a battlefield precedent, both would be subject to inevitable public scrutiny, and in both cases, I could have pushed the decision elsewhere, as if *it were not my responsibility.* I chose not to do so. Leaders lead, and knowing when (and having the moral courage) to "bet your bars," or at my level, "bet your stars," is really, really important.

CHAPTER 8

*"In Afghanistan, difficult missions were decided on
the basis of reconnaissance information."*
*The Russian General Staff, translated by Lester W.
Grau and Michael A. Gress,* The Soviet-Afghan War

Friday, July 4, 2008

The Fourth of July fell on a Friday, and I started the day with an eight-mile run around the airfield that morning. When I got back, the JOC staff told me we had received intelligence indicating that enemy insurgents were planning to disrupt our long-planned closure of Combat Outpost Bella. In fact, Bella was under threat of an imminent attack.

The COP was located next to a small hamlet named Bella directly on the Waygal River five miles from the district center at Wanat and ten miles north of TF Rock's headquarters at Camp Blessing. Bella had been established in 2006 by then Lieutenant Colonel Chris Cavoli and his 1st Battalion, 32nd Infantry. At the time, it seemed a useful location: it was between the district center at Wanat and the village of Aranas, which had the reputation as an insurgent waypoint. Cavoli had also established another combat outpost at Aranas roughly twelve miles north of Blessing, nicknamed the Ranch House, which I had visited during my predeployment site survey.

The village of Bella was small even by remote Afghan standards, with just a few stores and what passed as a local hotel anchoring a handful of homes, but it did have something Aranas and Wanat did not: a real medical clinic run by the humanitarian aid, non-governmental organization (NGO) called the International Medical Corps, with actual doctors and nurses present.

Ranch House was attacked in August 2007 and nearly overrun. Colonel Bill Ostlund closed it two months later and consolidated the platoon at COP Bella. Since then, Bella's relevance to our counterinsurgency campaign had diminished while its air-centric resupply increasingly disrupted other operations, and my predecessor Major General Rod Rodriguez began the planning to close the outpost and move the Bella forces south to the district center and village at Wanat. We wanted to close Bella and open a base at Wanat before we completed the transfer of authority between Colonel Chip Preysler's 173rd Brigade Combat Team and Colonel John Spiszer's incoming 3rd Brigade Combat Team, 1st Infantry Division, which had even fewer troops than the 173rd. This had long been an important priority for Lieutenant Colonel Bill Ostlund and his TF Rock, and I wanted to see it done.

Spiszer's three-thousand-plus task force consisted of Lieutenant Colonel Daniel S. Hurlbut's 2nd Battalion, 2nd Infantry (TF Ramrod); Lieutenant Colonel Brett Jenkinson's 1st Battalion, 26th Infantry (TF Blue Spader); Lieutenant Colonel James Markert's 6th Squadron, 4th Cavalry (TF Raider); the 1st Battalion, 6th Field Artillery (TF Centaur) led by Lieutenant Colonel Salvatore Petrovia; Lieutenant Colonel Patrick Daniel's 3rd Brigade Special Troops Battalion (TF Valiant); and Lieutenant Colonel Bradley A. White's 201st Brigade Support Battalion (TF Support). TF Duke also had assigned Lieutenant Colonel Stephen M. Radulski's 3rd Battalion, 103rd Armor from the Pennsylvania National Guard, which we deployed to Laghman Province.

Although the order of battle of the incoming brigade seemed impressive, Task Force Duke was a mechanized unit that left its tanks and infantry fighting vehicles at home station. As a result, it possessed far fewer trained dismounted infantry in comparison to the departing paratroopers. In addition, the mechanized soldiers were new to the theater, while the 173rd Airborne were the most battle-hardened and experienced troops we had.

The enemy always watched out for American efforts to close or reposition combat outposts, attempting to capitalize on the former by claiming they had forced the foreign troops to retreat while also seeking tactical advantage by attacking repositioned bases before their defenses were complete. I intended to close Bella and open Wanat while we still had Chip Preysler, Bill Ostlund, and the on-scene commander, Captain Matthew R. Myer of Company C, 2nd Battalion, 503rd Infantry, running the operation.

Captain Myer graduated from West Point a few months before 9/11, and had served an army at war ever since. Unexcitable and solid, he essentially had two infantry platoons and their Afghan National Army (ANA) counterparts to cover the entire Waygal Valley, which ideally would have been a battalion's area of operations if we had had sufficient troops. We didn't.

The day before, the enemy had mortared Bella, severely wounding one of our U.S. troopers. We had warned the villagers and the medical clinic of our impending departure, and the word had clearly gotten to the insurgents too. Our close air support dropped eleven laser-guided bombs (GBUs), and reports came in of fourteen enemy killed and nine wounded.

I ordered COP Bella reinforced immediately. TF Rock was already ahead of me: Captain Myer had requested reinforcement from Lieutenant Colonel Ostlund, who decided to move two additional infantry squads immediately from his B Company, Battle Company, to Myer. Brigadier General Milley was nearby, and the squads were airlifted in his Black Hawk helicopters.

"You are in for a fight," Milley told Myer. As the aircraft lifted off of Bella after delivering the troops, more mortar fire impacted Bella. We shifted ISR assets to overwatch the outpost, and placed Apache attack helicopters in support. And then we watched and waited. I wrote a note to myself that day that reflected my thinking: *Reinforce the COP, reduce the enemy (locate and kill), then move the COP to Wanat.*

It wasn't every day the insurgents came together in large enough formations to easily find, fix, and finish them, and I intended to take advantage of this opportunity.

It didn't quite work out the way I intended.

The enemy again began to shell Combat Outpost Bella, with one round of mortar fire hitting the camp and nine others hitting the village itself. Myer was ready. He located the enemy mortar firing position and sent two Apache gunships to attack. Two pickup trucks were spotted fleeing the mortar position, and the Apaches were cleared to engage. They did so, and killed several occupants. The injured were transported to Camp Blessing where they were treated. That is when word of civilian casualties reached me at Bagram. It looked as if the trucks held some of the civilian medical staff leaving the clinic at Bella, as well as some number of insurgents.

As we tried to get some clarity on what had happened, I called General McKiernan to let him know of the potential for civilian casualties.

It was soon apparent that the trucks had held both insurgents and civilians; it was not clear if the civilians were willingly aiding the enemy.

Over time, some of the civilians were interviewed and said several insurgents had hijacked them as they drove out of Bella. As the Taliban media machine went into high gear yet again, none of that was known for certain, and we—CJTF-101 and TF Rock—were accused of targeting and killing civilians.

We received intelligence reports about our response to their attack on Bella: the "situation was fucked." Six fighters were dead, ten wounded, and "two martyrs died in the trucks." Local insurgent leader Mullah Osman was injured and foot soldier Walid was "imperiled."

The mortar attacks at Bella stopped. In fact, there were no more attacks there. We closed the camp four days later.

Had we disrupted the enemy's plans, or merely delayed them?

On Sunday, July 6, a special operations task force executed a kinetic strike at 5:00 a.m. near the Tora Bora Mountains, south of Jalalabad in the Deh

Bala District of Nangarhar, killing over twenty insurgents according to first reports. As the day wore on, other reports poured in of civilian casualties from the strike. Locals were saying that the strike had hit an early morning wedding party, during a mass walk of the bride to the groom's village. We were already reeling from the potential civilian casualties from the COP Bella Apache engagement, and so I spent the day in the JOC and in my office working with the staff and talking to commanders via phone. There was still a great deal of uncertainty in both cases of what had actually happened on the ground, and I initiated investigations to figure it out. But we had a strategic communications nightmare on our hands; the enemy propaganda machine was cranking out that we deliberately targeted Afghan women and children, and President Karzai's increasing and very public denunciations of ISAF operations were, in my mind, aiding the enemy. My own boss, General McKiernan, was upset because Karzai beat him up daily on civilian casualties, Ambassador Wood wanted to see me soonest, and Minister of Defense Wardak wanted my investigation as quickly as possible.

That night around midnight two rockets exploded on Bagram, with no one hurt and no significant damage. Still, we huddled outside for a few hours in the dark, inside our overturned concrete culverts that served as shelters from rockets and mortars, until the all clear was sounded. If the enemy intended to pressure us, they were succeeding.

The next morning, a massive car bomb outside the Indian embassy killed 48 people and wounded 147, mostly local Afghan civilians. I flew to Kabul, and as we made our way by SUV from the airport to the U.S. embassy, security was tighter than usual, Afghan Army and police out at every corner, eyeing every vehicle with suspicion.

My meeting with Ambassador Bill Wood and DCM Chris Dell was tense. My troops and the special ops task force, who I did not command but supported, had to get control over the civilian casualties. The ambassador didn't mince words.

We drove over to the Defense Ministry headquarters. Normally exceptionally polite and diplomatic, Minister Wardak was blunt: The civilian deaths were "killing our government." The strategic ramifications were such that we were "putting the legitimacy of the government into question."

Karzai wanted a letter of apology from Secretary Gates. I told Wardak I didn't see that happening, but would inform my leadership of the request.

I talked afterward with General McKiernan. There was no doubt we at ISAF and Operation Enduring Freedom regretted the deaths of innocent civilians, and we were investigating both Bella and the special ops strike. But the secretary was not going to write an apology letter, that much was certain. At this point, I was having doubts as to President Karzai's motives: it seemed every time an Afghan civilian was mistakenly killed by U.S. or NATO airstrikes or soldiers, he would emphatically blame us, but when the Taliban deliberately targeted Afghan civilians, Karzai was silent. That had to be apparent back in Washington, D.C., as well, but at this stage I did not know what Secretary Gates really thought about the Afghan president. And no matter what, we had to work with Karzai.

Meanwhile, our operations continued. Preysler and Ostlund briefed Mark Milley that evening on the details of the Bella to Wanat move. They had already briefed me several days before on the concept of operations, which I approved. The enemy was likely to pressure the move one way or another, but we seemed to have disrupted the insurgents at Bella. Most likely enemy actions would be an ambush en route to Wanat, targeting the airlift helicopters, and probing indirect fires once we had troops on the ground at Wanat.

The plan was detailed and impressive. A U.S. engineer team from the 62nd Combat Engineer Battalion would augment First Lieutenant Jonathan Brostrom's 2nd Platoon of Chosen Company, as would an ANA platoon with three USMC advisors, a mortar section, and interpreters. The forty-five U.S. troopers and twenty-four ANA soldiers had both 120-mm and 60-mm mortars, and a TOW missile Humvee. The TOW had an Improved Target Acquisition System (ITAS) which included an advanced sensor and laser range finder, and the platoon would also bring a Long Range Advanced Scout Surveillance System (LRAS), used to find, identify, geo-locate, and ultimately target an enemy. They would have four up-armored Humvees, two of which mounted two .50-caliber (12.7-mm) machine guns while the other two mounted 40-mm M-19 automatic grenade launchers. The garrison would have priority of fires from the 155-mm artillery at Blessing and Asadabad (total of four howitzer "tubes"). They would also be supported by TF Rock's Low Level Voice Intercept (LLVI) teams (from 173rd's military intelligence company) operating the AN/MLQ-40 Prophet, which scanned the airwaves searching and homing in on enemy radio and cell phone signals. For an augmented platoon, this was significant firepower.

CJTF-101 would dedicate the single Predator allocated to RC-East and a communications intercept aircraft to overwatch the move and initial occupation. The staff allocated three full days of surveillance and reconnaissance support, which represented a very significant investment given our limited assets and the multitude of other ongoing operations throughout RC-East. Finally, Captain Myer himself would assume command of the operation at Wanat, which would initially be established as Kahler Vehicle Patrol Base, as the COP was being built (a vehicle patrol base was generally a simple affair: several military vehicles in a defensive perimeter, with concertina wire and maybe claymore mines for protection). It was named for Platoon Sergeant Matt Kahler, who had been killed by an Afghan security guard in January.

Milley found the briefing comprehensive and approved it. Operation Rock Move, the move from Bella and Blessing to Wanat, would begin in the morning.

CHAPTER 9

"Even though I walk through the valley of the
shadow of death, I will fear no evil..."
Psalm 23

Thursday, July 10, 2008

On Thursday, after early morning PT, I received a call from Ambassador Wood. A CODEL would visit us on July 19. We were very practiced by this time with CODELs, and did our best to describe our campaign plan and current status in a sit-down briefing led normally by me, then get the senators and congressmen out via helicopter to see the situation on the ground and talk with troops.

Ambassador Wood said there would be a twenty-five-person Secret Service advance team arriving several days beforehand.

This was no routine CODEL. Senator Jack Reed was leading a three-person CODEL to Afghanistan, accompanied by Senator Chuck Hagel and Senator Barack Obama, who was running for president of the United States.

I met as usual for our staff stand-up at 8:00 a.m., and got the wheels in motion to support the upcoming CODEL. It was strictly "close hold" and limited to those who needed to know.

Later that morning, I hosted the transfer of authority of TF Cincinnatus commanded by Colonel Jonathan Ives to TF Warrior commanded by Colonel Scott A. Spellmon. The outgoing task force led by Ives had a unique lineage, having been originally created by U.S. Army Forces Command using officers and non-commissioned officers stripped from the 23rd Chemical Battalion at Fort Lewis, Washington. When TF Cincinnatus mobilized on January 19, 2007, it received a complex non-standard mission. Its initial responsibilities were to oversee base operations for CJTF-82 installations. Fifteen days prior to starting that mission, Ives learned that his task force had been designated as the battlespace owner for five provinces encircling Kabul. As a battlespace owner, Ives gained responsibility for New Zealand's provincial reconstruction team in Bamyan, a Turkish one in Wardak, and American teams in Panjshir and Bagram. In order to create maneuver forces to patrol his area of operations, Ives pulled the security elements out of the Bagram reconstruction team along with military police from the division special troops battalion and whatever other qualified augmentees he could find. Despite leading a unit made up of odds and ends, Jonathan did a superb job of conducting development and governance support in the Bagram and Kapisa area of operations.

Spellmon's task force was composed of the newly formed Fort Polk, Louisiana-based, modular 1st Maneuver Enhancement Brigade. One of the first of its kind, the brigade consisted of the 46th Engineer Battalion, 519th Military Police Battalion, 88th Brigade Support Battalion, and the 83rd Chemical Battalion. However, the whole unit did not deploy to Afghanistan, as Spellmon's engineer and military police battalions had been sent to Iraq instead. Regardless, I now had a standing brigade-sized unit with a formal staff and assigned units in lieu of an ad hoc task force, so I hoped that TF Warrior would have more impact than its predecessors on what was turning out to be a very active local insurgency around Bagram Airfield.

Before noon I was in my Black Hawk headed to Kunar. At Bostick we picked up outgoing 1st Squadron, 91st Cavalry Commander Lieutenant Colonel Kolenda and incoming 6th Squadron, 4th Cavalry Commander Lieutenant Colonel Jim Markert and flew to Combat Outpost Lowell, then to Keating, where we were briefed by Captain Joe Hutto of Kolenda's squadron.

I had visited Combat Outpost Keating before, during my predeployment site survey. Located on a few acres of level land surrounded by steep, tall mountains in the Hindu Kush, and bordered on two sides by rushing river waters, Keating seemed to be a dubious location for an outpost. The rocky road that followed the Pech River to Keating was too dangerous for resupply convoys, and so everything was flown in by helicopter to a small, rocky spit in the river, which was connected by a narrow footbridge to the land and the camp. The troopers had done a great job to date of defending their turf as well as befriending the local hamlet and Afghan National Police contingent. Still, I jotted down in my notebook as we departed, *Keating—the ends of the earth!* and I added it to my mental list of bases we should close.

The next morning was Friday and I got in an eight-mile run around Bagram Airfield before my morning staff brief on a border incident the previous night. We had stopped it well short of anything like Gora Paray. Maybe our liaisons and the Khyber Border Coordination Center were learning how to de-escalate these cross-border incidents, I thought. Time would tell.

I flew out to Jalalabad and met with Chip Preysler as we waited for the arrival of the chairman of the Joint Chiefs, Admiral Mike Mullen. TF Bayonet was supporting a joint U.S./ANA operation in remote northeastern Nuristan at Barg-e Matal. The troops had run low on ammunition and supplies, and Chip told me we needed to resource the ANA troops with "ready-to-go" speedballs (emergency supplies that could be tossed from a hovering helicopter) of ammo and water that could be quickly airlifted into remote locations. I agreed.

Admiral Mullen arrived with a small team. It was a characteristically hot and exceptionally humid Nangarhar day, and all of us were sweating under our body armor as we boarded my Black Hawk, Mullen's staff in our flying spare UH-60, and headed north up the Kunar River, accompanied by two Apache gunships for security. Piloting one of the Apaches was Destiny 6, Colonel Jim Richardson, commander of the 101st Airborne Combat Aviation Brigade. A graduate of the University of South Carolina's first Reserve Officer Training Corps (ROTC) class in 1982, Jim was tall, a weight lifter in off-duty time, with an easy grin. He was also as tough as they come: he had earned a Distinguished Flying Cross for his leadership and actions in combat while in command of an Apache battalion in the early days of the invasion of Afghanistan. I knew of no one better suited to command this huge brigade with some 165 aircraft, which was larger than most countries' entire air forces.

We were going to the Korengal, the Valley of Death according to some writers, and I was taking no chances with the chairman on board. Hence the Apache armed escort.

The Korengal Valley was a relatively small valley by Hindu Kush standards, about six miles from its mouth at the Pech River to its southern extremity and just a few miles wide, but it was bordered by steep rock mountains, with tall evergreens, some of them highly valued Himalayan cedars. The Korengalis were xenophobic, insular, and distrusting of NATO, Americans, and their own fellow Afghans from outside the valley. Their dialect was a foreign language to most interpreters from other parts of Afghanistan.

Journalist Sebastian Junger had embedded with TF Rock's B Company, and his articles about the troopers in the Korengal published in *Vanity Fair* were hard-hitting, brutally vivid descriptions of small-unit counterinsurgency warfare in some of the most inhospitable terrain in the world. Korengal had become infamous, and B Company and its commander, Captain Dan Kearney, had become well known in the U.S., especially in the Pentagon. Colonel Chip Preysler was responsible for the most violent and dangerous region in RC-East, centered on Kunar and Nangarhar, and Lieutenant Colonel Bill Ostlund the most dangerous sector, the Pech. And Kearney commanded the Korengal, the most violent valley in Preysler and Ostlund's area of operations.

Dan's father, Lieutenant General Frank Kearney, was the SOCOM deputy commanding general at the time. Frank and I were special operations colleagues. In 1994, in an ill-fated training mission in the backwoods of Louisiana one dark night, my special ops Chinooks had navigated to a fast-rope LZ and then cleared one of Frank's Ranger platoons to exit the aircraft, ostensibly on target. The night was pitch-black, and my guys were off by fifty meters. The lead Ranger fast-roped into a tall tree and became caught by his equipment. The rest of the platoon came down the fast rope, hitting him, with most falling to the swampy ground below. Frank and I circled in a command and control helicopter, and I called in a medevac helicopter.

The lead Ranger died of his injuries. Many of his platoon members were injured, some badly. Fifty meters does not seem like a lot, but in combat it could mean life or death, or mission success or failure.

As we turned south of the Pech River and into the Korengal Valley, my pilot Dave reported that Vegas, a small outpost on the other side of the valley from Combat Outpost Korengal, was taking fire: troops in contact (TIC). A-10s were en route. We discussed the situation, and pushed the Apaches to help out. Colonel Richardson and team flew ahead and contacted the troops involved in the firefight. Hugging the opposite side of the valley, we made our way to Korengal Outpost.

I briefed the chairman on the situation and said I thought we could still land safely at Korengal. In the back of my mind, I thought that a small firefight on the opposite side of the valley would keep the local insurgents from attacking Korengal Outpost while we were there, which was a good thing. If the insurgents had known that the most senior uniformed officer in the United States military was visiting their valley, it might have been different.

If the chairman was anxious—after all, he was an admiral, not an infantryman—I could not sense it. I thought he was having the time of his life.

The Apaches engaged with their 30-mm chain gun and 2.75-inch rockets, joined by two A-10s with their awesome 30-mm GAU-8 cannon. We landed at the small landing zone halfway up the mountain, and hurried the chairman and his party up the hill and behind the worn

HESCO dirt- and rock-filled wire mesh defensive barriers that formed the perimeter of the outpost.

TF Rock Commander Lieutenant Colonel Bill Ostlund and Captain Kearney met us. Dan briefed the chairman and the rest of us on operations in the Korengal. He and his troops were fourteen days from handing over to TF Duke, and they knew the valley and its populace well, including the local insurgents and criminal gangs. Dan was composed and honest about what could be accomplished in the valley.

The non-commissioned officers lined up some of the troops and the chairman gave a short talk, thanking them for what they had accomplished in what had proven to be such a dangerous place. He pinned on awards, including a Silver Star on Captain Greg Ambrosia from A Company, a Bronze Star for Valor, and several Purple Hearts. I tracked the slowdown of the firefight across the valley. We called in the Black Hawks and soon we were speeding out of the Valley of Death.

I did not realize that Bill Ostlund could not get helicopter support to depart Korengal that day, and was stuck there overnight.

We flew out to the Pech River Valley, took a right onto the Kunar River, and flew south. Along the way I pointed out the camps, outposts, and passes over the Durand Line: Asadabad and Camp Wright, Joyce, Fortress, the Nawa Pass, and Gora Paray.

We entered the Khyber Pass and flew to Torkham Gate, the principal border crossing between Peshawar, on the Pakistani frontier, and Jalalabad, Afghanistan. After landing at the Khyber Border Coordination Center (BCC), we were briefed by U.S., Pakistani, and Afghan liaison officers about the BCC and its coordination and deconfliction mission. It was clearly a work in progress, a modern-looking coordination center under a massive Quonset hut with communications feeds to my CJTF operations center, the Afghan Defense Ministry, and certain key Pakistani units, as well as my liaison team embedded with the Pakistanis. It held promise to prevent or at least de-escalate incidents like Gora Paray.

Later that night after returning to Bagram, Admiral Mullen and I had a private meeting over dinner served in my office. I gave him my thoughts on the enemy situation and the continuing incidents all along our 450-mile border with Pakistan. We discussed civilian casualties and my issues with having to pick up the pieces after a special operations strike. We talked about the need and numbers for mine-resistant armored vehicles (MRAPs), which were finally and belatedly being fielded to Afghanistan to replace up-armored Humvees that had proved increasingly vulnerable to the latest improvised explosive devices being employed by the Taliban. We talked about my request for more troops and resources. He asked about my plans to ensure the staff and my deputies were able to withstand the rigor of a fifteen-month tour. He gave me his views on the upcoming CODEL and especially Senator Obama. It was a late night, but I gained a good deal of insight. I also came that night to greatly respect Admiral Mullen as a leader and a man. He was quiet, unassuming, articulate, and strategic, and he had warmth that many senior officials did not.

The chairman spent the night at Bagram, and left early the next day, Saturday, July 12.

At the morning stand-up meeting in my office that day, we quickly covered the night's combat activities. We received a "nothing significant to report" (NSTR) from TF Bayonet, the brigade headquarters, on Operation Rock Move; we had received negative reports on July 9, 10, and 11 as well. TF Bayonet also said that the Kahler/Wanat Outpost was 75 percent complete (years later as I wrote this book, Bill Ostlund told me this was inaccurate, and that TF Rock had never submitted such a report to TF Bayonet).

I was satisfied with the apparent progress of Rock Move. We had conducted three days of ISR coverage with our sole Predator line. We had to shift the Predator to troops in contact several times, but TF Bayonet did have it several hours each day to use—and we had received no indications of enemy movement or massing. Rock Move was a priority, albeit now our third priority, for surveillance and reconnaissance assets, and with no apparent enemy, the priority would shift quickly to other areas where we had much more enemy activity. They were badly needed elsewhere.

Saturday afternoon, I visited the Bagram Theater Internment Facility. Walking through the open bays divided into large detainee holding cells, I saw the various looks of the detainees as they stared at me. We had stripped off our names and rank from our uniforms, as was routine procedure, but with a small entourage leading me through the facility, the detainees clearly knew I was some sort of high-ranking person. I stared right back at them, and saw the various looks. I remember most the curiosity, wry amusement, and hatred on some faces. And a stoic resignation.

I felt we were doing as good a job as possible in our treatment of the detainees. Our guards and interrogation teams were professional, fair, and balanced. Our medical treatment team provided what was likely the best medical care most detainees had ever experienced. Still, the facility was old, from the Soviet occupation or before, and there was no good way to keep the irreconcilables from adversely impacting those that were fence-sitters, the "impressionables." In these surroundings, we were ensuring the ultimate radicalization of our detainees, even if some would be found to be innocent of enemy activity and released. I would need to push the engineers and contractors harder to get the new facility built sooner.

Overseeing a theater-level detainment facility for captured insurgents and terrorists was a distasteful but necessary part of my job. The special operations task forces had their own covert detainment operations and sites, and I had zero visibility into them. I had never seen one. At the strategic level, the U.S. maintained the Guantanamo Bay detainment facility for suspected and known terrorists, several of whom had been involved in supporting or planning 9/11. Iraq had Abu Ghraib to detain, vet, and ultimately hold those found to be guilty. And we had the Bagram Theater Internment Facility. But I thought Admiral Fallon was right, that the Bagram facility as it stood was a major problem, and that a new facility was very necessary: it was overdue. And in the meantime, I had to ensure we were treating those we detained humanely, within international standards for detained battlefield combatants or those suspected of aiding the enemy, and yet ensure we derived as much useful intelligence as we could from them. It was a fine and delicate line to walk.

At the early evening combat update brief, I was told again that there was nothing significant to report on Operation Rock Move. Around 7:30 p.m., I called COMISAF and updated him on several operations, including Rock Move. I thought it was going well.

CHAPTER 10

"Always employ outposts
Always utilize patrols
Always keep a reserve."
Field Marshal Erwin Rommel

Sunday, July 13, 2008

I t was early Sunday morning, and I planned a down day from my normal 5:00 a.m. run.

The operations center called and said I needed to come immediately. There was a significant enemy attack at Wanat, and we already had several casualties, including some killed in action.

The situation was dire. A force of what could be over a hundred insurgents had attacked before dawn, and they controlled the high ground around the outpost as well as the adjacent village. They had destroyed the TOW missile launcher, the mortars were out of commission, and the sole observation post (OP) called "Topside" had almost been overrun. The number of wounded and dead was unclear, but high.

Captain Myer was in command and reported via radio to Lieutenant Colonel Ostlund at Camp Blessing that "this was a Ranch House style attack," meaning the insurgents had massed a large number of fighters against the outpost. Matt called in 155-mm artillery support almost immediately, and after Ostlund was sure there were no friendly patrols outside the wire, the guns fired danger close. The CJTF operations center had already positioned a B-1B bomber overhead, and it began dropping five-hundred-pound GBU-38 bombs north of the Wanat Outpost to attempt to seal off the battlefield. About forty minutes had elapsed since the initial volley of rocket-propelled grenades destroyed the TOW and started the attack. Bone, the call sign of the B-1B, was effective in isolating the battlefield and preventing more insurgents from moving into or out of the area, but could not drop ordnance close enough to OP Topside or the main outpost to destroy the main attacking force.

WANAT AND COMBAT OUTPOST KAHLER (VPB)

Photo courtesy of the U.S. Army.

Task Force Out Front, the 101st Airborne Division's 2nd Squadron, 17th Cavalry based at Forward Operating Base Fenty at Jalalabad and supporting TF Bayonet, launched its aerial quick reaction force, two Apache gunships and two medevac Black Hawks. They had been alerted about five minutes after Myer's initial call to TF Rock headquarters. It was the Apache team's shift change, but they and the medevac helicopters were en route twenty-three minutes after their alert. It was forty miles from Fenty to Wanat.

They flew directly to Blessing, arriving twenty-nine minutes after takeoff. The medevac aircraft stayed at Blessing to loiter until the battlefield could be stabilized, and after the air space was cleared to allow the supporting artillery to strike enemy targets without fear of hitting an orbiting aircraft, the Apaches flew directly to Wanat.

The Apache gunships (whose call signs "Hedgerow 50 and 53" honored the 101st Airborne Division World War II fight in the dense bocage of Normandy) arrived over Wanat roughly one hour after the start of the attack. Hedgerow 50 used its 30-mm cannon just north of Topside in an overgrown area that the friendly aerial or artillery fire had been unable to hit, making it dead space for the defenders. Wingman Hedgerow 53 fired into the eastern-side dead space adjacent to Topside. Both runs and many subsequent runs were very close to Topside, but were accurate and seemingly effective.

Thirty minutes later, around 6:00 a.m., Chosen Company's 1st Platoon, acting as a quick reaction force, arrived at Wanat, after a hell-bound forty-five-minute convoy from Camp Blessing. Led by First Lieutenant Aaron Thurman and Sergeant First Class William Stockard and joined by Chosen First Sergeant Scott Beeson, the quick reaction force immediately assessed the situation and began a coordinated response at Topside, as well as clearing operations against insurgents in the village.

But Bone, the B-1B bomber, the Apaches, and the 1st Platoon QRF were all too late to save nine soldiers who died that morning.

Landing at 5:52 a.m. during the still ongoing firefight, Dustoff 35 (the call sign of one of the medical evacuation helicopters) carried out five wounded, followed by Dust-Off 36, which carried out four wounded. Soon two more medevac helos, Dustoff 34 and Profit 71, joined the evacuation. At the end of the day, the medevac crews pulled out sixteen Americans and four ANA soldiers from Wanat, in the midst of incredibly challenging battlefield conditions. There is no doubt in my mind they saved several lives.

Ostlund reinforced Wanat throughout the day, adding a second ground quick reaction force of six Humvees carrying a rifle platoon and scout section commanded by Company A Commander Captain Dave Nelson, which arrived in six Humvees around 8:20 a.m., and that afternoon another platoon from Kearney's Company B led by 3rd platoon's First Lieutenant Mike Moad and Sergeant First Class Dave Barberet (who had also led the Bella reinforcement days earlier). Captain Nelson assigned Moad's platoon to secure Topside and the area around it. They took a hard look at Topside, where most of the American fatalities had occurred, before deciding to evacuate it. They wanted higher ground, better dominating observation, and distance from the dead space. By evening, they had evacuated Topside and established a new observation post 150 meters to the east on higher terrain.

Throughout the day, the staff and I in the operations center seized each detail as it flowed in from TF Bayonet's brigade headquarters. We had shifted intelligence, surveillance, and reconnaissance assets back over to Wanat, and could get some feel for the firefight as it petered out over the morning, as the Apaches, the quick reaction forces, Bone plus follow-on close air support provided by F-15E and A-10 flights, and the 155-mm artillery did their respective jobs.

By mid-morning, I felt I needed a better understanding of what was happening. Brigadier General Mark Milley and I talked it over, and I decided to send him out to Jalalabad to see Colonel Preysler, and if it made sense, to continue on to Ostlund's headquarters at Camp Blessing, about five miles from Wanat. I did not want the division leadership or staff to run a company-platoon level operation, but I did want more information on what was happening and what we needed to do and decide at the CJTF level.

Milley took his two Black Hawks and flew first to Jalalabad, talked with Chip Preysler, and then went on to Camp Blessing. After talks with Ostlund and the TF Rock staff, Milley gave both me and our staff a series of combat updates that were very useful during the day.

One of the alarming reports was that it appeared the local villagers had abandoned the village before the attack, probably the night before, and it appeared that the local Afghan National Police (ANP) at Wanat might have aided in the attack.

We decided to pile on more troops, specifically to do a complete house-by-house search of the entirety of Wanat, and to try to exploit as much intelligence as we could glean, and rapidly. Working with the Combined Joint Special Operations Task Force (CJSOTF), a multinational task force of special operations troops from several services, such as army, navy, air force, and Marine Corps at Bagram, we flew in an Afghan Army Commando unit advised by a U.S. Special Forces team. We added an AC-130 gunship. By night, the Predator was effective in locating the enemy in small groups in the surrounding wooded mountains, and we engaged them. The next day, as small probes and skirmishes continued, we added a 101st Airborne Pathfinder platoon to work the high ground above Wanat. Captain Myer continued to command the ground forces, now numbering about two hundred U.S. and Afghan troops, but Ostlund sent his operations officer, Major Scott Himes, to Wanat in the afternoon of July 13 to establish a battalion tactical command post to assist in overall coordination of assets.

The ANA commandos swept the entire village and nearby countryside, searching about one hundred buildings, homes, and structures. At the Waygal District Center, which was also the local police force headquarters, they found a large number of recently fired weapons, ammo, and RPGs. The enemy had used the center as a key firing position, and expended brass was everywhere. The search clearly showed that the enemy had used the entire village to mount and sustain the attack, and that the villagers and police had helped them, and may have even participated.

That night I wrestled in my mind with what to do in Wanat. We would pursue the enemy and destroy them if we could find them—that much was clear. My instinct was to find, fix, and finish the attackers, then find the village elders and police leaders and arrest them, as well as the district leaders, including the governor. These were tactical decisions, and they were much easier. But I faced the hard choice of reinforcing our failed attempt to win over the local people (clearly we had not) or withdrawing from Wanat. I asked the staff for options, and asked Preysler for his assessment by midday the following day. I could not continue to maintain the large force and surveillance and reconnaissance resources at Wanat for long. They were needed elsewhere in my area of responsibility. Badly.

Very late that night, I went to Bagram hospital and met with the troopers who had been medevacked from Wanat. Those who could talk did so. They were dazed, proud of the heroic defense, pissed off that the enemy had killed nine of their comrades, and most wanted nothing more than to be patched up and sent back to their platoon and Wanat. I pinned fifteen Purple Hearts on those there, and spoke to them all about the importance of what they had done that day. My words must have seemed small, totally inadequate to express the heartbreak of the loss, or the magnitude of their heroism.

At 4:30 a.m. on July 14, almost exactly twenty-four hours since the enemy attacked Wanat Outpost, we held a ramp ceremony for the nine soldiers killed: Sergio Abad, Jonathan Ayers, Jason Bogar, Jonathan Brostrom, Israel Garcia, Jason Hovater, Matt Phillips, Pruitt Rainey, and Gunnar Zwilling. It was still dark, and under the airfield lights the colors—the U.S. flag, the CJTF flag, and that of the 173rd Brigade Combat Team and 2nd Battalion, 503rd Infantry—were marched into place. Humvee after Humvee drove through the main street of Bagram, each carrying one metal case, a coffin really, each with an American flag draped and secured over the case. The street was lined with soldiers and civilians, hundreds of grieving people, perhaps thousands, who watched quietly as the vehicles passed by out to the airfield concrete ramp.

Assembled under the airfield ramp lights stood the CJTF-101 command, including Generals Milley and McConville, Command Sergeant Major Camacho, and myself, and the leadership of the 173rd BCT and Task Force Rock.

Fellow soldiers unloaded the remains, Sergeant Major Camacho and I led the commanders to a position just short of the nine coffins, and the chaplain said the 23rd Psalm. Bagpipes played "Amazing Grace." We filed past the coffins, spending a minute or two in prayer at each case, carefully placing our commander's coin on the American flag, on top of the case. The coffins were loaded onto the waiting U.S. Air Force plane. Before the sun was up, they would be gone.

The ramp ceremony was our way, the warrior's way, to honor our fallen, and to say farewell to fallen comrades. It also reassured the living that what we were about in this foreign land was honorable, and would not be forgotten by those who shared in the experience.

It was still too early in our fifteen-month deployment to be numb, and I wasn't. The loss was heartbreaking, and that these brave men had survived many—too many—battles in Afghanistan, only to be killed in the final battle, just ten days shy of redeployment, haunted me. These nine troopers were my ultimate responsibility, as were all the soldiers in the CJTF, and the feeling of loss would remain with me for life.

Later on the 14th, the CJTF staff and Chip Preysler gave me their four options and recommendations. We were already doing option one, attacking the enemy, but they had effectively dispersed and I knew would soon be impossible to track or locate. The other options were to hold what we had with the forces we could muster, or conduct a battlefield handoff to Colonel John Spiszer's units that were replacing TF Bayonet. Or we could withdraw: abandon Wanat Outpost, and consolidate at Camp Blessing, and then do the battle handoff between the two units.

I asked Preysler to give me each of the commander's recommendations, from Captain Myer, Lieutenant Colonel Ostlund, and his own. I also wanted an assessment from my staff and my deputy commanding general for operations, Mark Milley.

The commanders and the operations team recommended a tactical withdrawal from Wanat. My J2 intelligence team was of a different mind, stating we needed some kind of presence in the Waygal Valley to block the insurgents' ratlines, their maze of secret trails transiting from Pakistan throughout Afghanistan.

I needed to think on two levels, both tactical and strategic. At the tactical level, company Commander Myer's thoughts made great sense to me. He said that the human component and physical terrain requirements had changed so significantly from our plans that Wanat Outpost was no longer tenable without a major relocation of the outpost away from the unfriendly population center, a consequent major increase in the number of friendly troops to protect it, and a huge effort to flush out the complicit villagers and police. He, Ostlund, and Preysler all felt we clearly did not have the resources to do this, and the follow-on unit from John Spiszer's brigade combat team was even smaller.

I thought they were right, and I didn't agree with my own J2 team that the cost-benefit ratio to maintain a blocking position on the enemy ratline at Wanat was worth the effort. I doubted we would achieve any positive effects with the Wanat district population, and I felt that our forces at Camp Blessing could maintain a periodic patrolling presence in the Waygal Valley that would disrupt, but not totally end, the insurgents' use of the valley.

Strategically, I was certain the enemy media machine would crank into high gear about defeating us at Wanat if I decided to pull out. I figured our own media would dwell on the pullout, deeming it a defeat for U.S. and Afghan forces.

I talked with my own staff as well as General Milley and Sergeant Major Camacho into the evening. After one final call with Chip Preysler, I made up my mind. I was responsible for outcomes, and I could see no positive outcome for our counterinsurgency operations by reinforcing Wanat Outpost or moving to a higher ground and then adding more troops. Every day and night would be a struggle against a hostile population in our midst. That made no sense to me at this far outpost.

I was also responsible for perceptions, and knew that they had a very real impact on all the audiences I cared about: the enemy, my own troops and NATO, and the U.S. public. We would have to be proactive in our narrative and get ahead of the enemy in telling what had happened and why we were withdrawing.

It was almost 11:00 p.m. when I called my boss General McKiernan and told him we would withdraw our forces from Wanat to Camp Blessing. To his credit, he didn't try to second-guess my decision. We both knew we were in for plenty of Monday morning quarterbacking from national defense pundits, politicians, and other concerned citizens. The next day, July 15, 2008, we withdrew from Wanat Outpost.

In the days, weeks, months, and years that have passed since the attack and defense of Combat Outpost Kahler, there has seldom been a day that I have not thought about Wanat. Few battles in America's experience in Afghanistan have been as bloody, as heroic, as controversial. The day of the battle we began formal investigations, the first Army Regulation 15-6 investigation (a commander-directed investigation under the Uniform Code of Military Justice) by the 173rd BCT. I would later initiate a second 15-6 investigation by my own CJTF-101; a third formal investigation was conducted by Central Command, and then a fourth and final review by the U.S. Army in 2010.

A definitive account of the battle and the events leading up to it was published by the staff of the U.S. Army Combat Studies Institute: *Wanat: Combat Action in Afghanistan, 2008*. Much later, Gregg Zoroya's superbly detailed *The Chosen Few* tells the story of the attack and the lead-up to the attack with exquisite attention to the human story. The U.S. Army Command and General Staff College at Fort Leavenworth, Kansas, developed a virtual tour of the Wanat battlefield and produced a virtual "staff ride" to illustrate learning points.

So, I approached the writing of my own analysis with trepidation. After all, I am hardly a dispassionate observer or trained historian, nor was I physically on the ground at Wanat during the battle. And yet I believe that just as what happened before, during, and after the attack was my ultimate responsibility, I therefore have the responsibility to provide my own thoughts.

Up front, I believe the heroism displayed on the battlefield by the defenders of Combat Outpost Kahler was extraordinary and uncommon. Sergeant Ryan Pitts earned the Medal of Honor, fourteen defenders earned the Silver Star, our nation's third-highest award for battlefield heroism, and sixteen earned the Bronze Star for Valor. Two army aviators earned Distinguished Flying Crosses. I have no doubt that subsequent reviews based on still-emerging eyewitness accounts may result in the upgrade of some awards. What went right at Kahler that morning was that seasoned, battle-hardened, close-knit, and ultimately highly professional soldiers overcame one of the most well planned and executed insurgent attacks of this Afghan war, fighting off a force estimated to have been between 150 and 300 insurgents over the duration of the battle. I am convinced this fight will long be remembered for the personal bravery and sheer determination of the leaders, including company Commander Captain Matt Myer, Platoon Leader First Lieutenant Jonathan Brostrom, who was killed defending Topside after fearlessly running the gauntlet of enemy direct fires between the main outpost and the observation post, and Platoon Sergeant David Dzwik, as well as every squad and team leader, including those of the quick reaction forces that came to their relief. The soldiers and three marines who fought off the enemy that day were extraordinary, doing what was necessary to prevent being overrun by a numerically superior force, in brutal, no-holds-barred close combat the likes of which most professional soldiers never see in a long and honorable career of soldiering.

From my viewpoint as the CJTF and Regional Command-East commander, and as professionals who study, plan, and conduct our nation's wars, we must also examine what went wrong on that day and the time preceding, with the desire to help prevent a future Wanat.

Fundamentally, I, and most of the commanders below my level, underestimated the enemy. To cut to the chase, the Battle of Wanat occurred because a major insurgent force was able to maneuver in small groups over tens of miles of mountainous, rocky, wooded terrain in radio listening silence, without our awareness, in spite of significant allocated and utilized surveillance and reconnaissance assets, over a period of a handful of days. That the enemy fought at Wanat as well as they did is a completely different subject; that they maneuvered into battle positions surrounding Kahler and Topside without discovery is significant. How did that happen?

We underestimated both the enemy's intent and capabilities. In Operation Rock Move, the closure of Combat Outpost Bella and movement to and establishment of Combat Outpost Kahler were my biggest concerns. The enemy had shown an ability to mass and attack Bella many times, and the previous attack at Ranch House demonstrated the ability to close on and threaten to overrun an outpost. I was concerned the air-centric Combat Outpost Bella would be attacked when we were extracting our forces, when the large Chinook helicopters were most vulnerable, on the ground loading troops. I truly thought the enemy intended to attack us as we departed Bella, and to destroy the extraction helicopters. A second but lesser worry was an ambush of the convoy from Bella to Wanat. After the July 4 Apache attacks near Bella, I believed we had disrupted the insurgents, potentially so significantly that no attacks against Bella would be possible.

I also did not believe a massed attack against Combat Outpost Kahler was the enemy's intent. From experience in the area, Ostlund's units had seen a pattern where new outposts were probed over a period of many days or weeks before the enemy was confident enough to attack in any significant way. We studied the enemy's most likely reaction to our establishment of a base at Wanat, and we concluded probing attacks and harassment fires would occur during the establishment of the base. A full-scale major attack was not considered likely. It was only later, in reading the investigations, I learned that Ostlund's battalion intelligence officer, Captain Benjamin Pry, warned of that very thing.

In hindsight, it was clear I did not apply my first lesson of this deployment: expect the unexpected. Focus on what is *possible*.

We also underestimated the enemy's capabilities. We had seen very few sustained massed insurgent attacks of a well-armed, strongly defended, even if not completely constructed, combat outpost. We had combat in RC-East each and every day, sometimes indirect fires, sometimes an IED covered by direct fires, sometimes complex ambushes, and sometimes full-fledged attacks against established outposts and forward operating bases. Many of the attacks were poorly planned and sometimes badly executed, and the enemy demonstrated a tendency to chatter on the radio as they maneuvered, allowing us to triangulate their signals and cross-cue a sensor, and maybe permit a shooter to engage. I did not think a battalion-sized insurgent force could infiltrate through the mountains north, west, and east of Wanat in total silence and without us knowing beforehand. In doing so, they demonstrated a capability that surprised all of us, and thereby achieved tactical surprise.

How do I think they did it? Why did our surveillance and reconnaissance assets not pick up the enemy movement? I think the insurgents infiltrated in relatively small groups, using the complex terrain of ravines and rocky, wooded slopes to mask their movements from the Predator EO/IR (electro-optical and infrared day and night cameras) sensor above looking for hot spots, and using radio listening silence. Most likely they used multiple infiltration routes from several directions, avoided the main trails, and did not carry weapons, but instead used cached weapons and ammunition.

They were very successful. Later I would learn that human intelligence reports from battalion-level sources indicated the enemy wanted to mass for an attack at Wanat, but these did not make it to the CJTF J-2 as far as I am aware. On the evening of July 12, a soldier at Kahler on ITAS (the thermal sensor) duty spotted about fifteen men walking along the slopes well above the village of Wanat, and alerted his shift leader, but ultimately the men were not engaged, nor was a wider alert given. In hindsight, I believe the pressure to avoid civilian casualties that we felt at all levels of command made us very conservative in positive identification and targeting of enemy forces. This is not an excuse, but it did impact our operations.

Should we have attempted to establish an outpost at Wanat in the first place? The withdrawal from exposed and air-centric bases north of Blessing had been planned since the attack at Ranch House in August of 2007, by CJTF-82, but I too was anxious to move our forces closer to the Pech River, where we had the road and did not have to rely 100 percent on helicopter resupply. Wanat was a district center, and after several *shuras*, we felt we could work with the local leaders and the Afghan police at Wanat to positively improve the security, governance, and development of the town and surrounding area. We estimated we could also work with the population, who had been less than welcoming, thinking they would respond to economic and security incentives (as they had in 2006–2007). Given what we knew, I believe the decision to establish a base at Wanat was sound. It made good sense. For sure, Lieutenant Colonel Ostlund had been pushing for it for many months (he wanted to do it in winter, when the cold and snows would have given us greater advantage). What we did not know made a significant difference to the advantage of the attacking force: the villagers could be and were induced to support the insurgents, including abandoning their homes and stores for use as fighting positions, as well as what I believe to be 100 percent complicity in supporting the attack by the local Afghan police station. There were few locations in RC-East where an entire village or town was completely hostile to ISAF and Afghan Army forces, the Korengal being an exception. Wanat proved to be another. We did not fully understand the human terrain of the Waygal Valley and Wanat, and made assumptions that improved economic development and better access to governance would sway the people away from the insurgents. We were wrong.

Was this unit, Chosen Company from Ostlund's battalion, the right unit to conduct Rock Move? No doubt after almost fifteen months of war in the frontier and mountains of eastern Afghanistan, the unit was battle-weary, fatigued, and ready to go home. That said, they were one of my very finest combat units, deeply experienced in mountain fighting, well led at every level, and proven in combat. Our alternative was to wait for the battle handover to the incoming 1st Battalion, 26th Infantry (TF Blue Spader) from Colonel Spiszer's 3rd Brigade, 1st Infantry Division, and then conduct Rock Move, closing Bella and moving to Combat Outpost Kahler at Wanat. In my analysis, most new incoming units took about ninety days in combat before they were fully able to use all the tools at their disposal, as well as synchronize fully with the upper-echelon intelligence, army aviation, and close air support capabilities that the Brigade and CJTF provided. None of us in command from company to division thought we should delay. I still believe to this day that Chosen Company was the best choice.

JEFFREY SCHLOESSER

Operationally, did we outfit 2nd Platoon of Chosen Company for a successful move, build-out, and occupation of the outpost? The battalion had assembled one of the most capable fighting forces in the 173rd area of operations: it was formed around 2nd Platoon and an Afghan National Army platoon with three U.S. Marine advisors, a platoon medic, a platoon forward observer, a mortar section with 120-mm and 60-mm mortars, a three-soldier TOW team with ITAS, and a six-soldier combat engineer team, plus company commander. They had a total of seventy-three soldiers, with significant crew-served weapons mounted in up-armored Humvees, as well as a Long Range Advanced Scout Surveillance System (LRAS3) thermal sight with a rangefinder. They had support from Low Level Voice Intercept teams. Artillery support from Combat Outpost Blessing was two 155-mm cannons on call, and they enjoyed priority of fires from guns at Asadabad. Although only two howitzers were at Blessing, they were M777 lightweight 155-mm models each capable of firing five ninety-five-pound high-explosive or illumination rounds per minute out to a range of almost twenty miles. An advantage of artillery over close air support is that weather has a far less significant impact on the former's use. In addition, close air support might be busy elsewhere in the region, but the 155-mms could always be counted upon.

These were very significant resources. I think they should have been sufficient and appropriate for the mission. Knowing now what we did not know then, we could have sent up an Apache attack helicopter team for a day and night sortie, working the area between Bella and Wanat—almost an old-time division cavalry mission, executed by army aviators, curious humans with an eye for the out-of-place, and the lethal systems to confront what they discovered. But these were precious resources needed throughout the entire area of operations, and without more indicators, which we did not have then, would not likely have been approved.

There are multiple learning points to consider when looking at the combat outpost, its placement, and the observation post, as well as the tactical routine.

Placement of the combat outpost: the intent, in line with counterinsurgency doctrine as published in *Army Field Manual (FM) 3-24*, recently revised in 2006, was of aligning with and among the local population, to be as close as feasible to the village and people of Wanat, and yet still be defensible. The actual placement of the outpost was below the village itself, so that the roofs of the hotel and some houses overlooked the defenses, and would provide superb firing positions for the enemy. The land for the base had been the subject of multiple *shuras*, haggling by the landowners, and had literally taken months to secure. At first look, it is easy to say we should have done a better job of site selection: the outpost was too close to the village, and the buildings of the village and the surrounding steep hillsides dominated the base. That said, the whole point was to be as close to the people as we could get, and we had had plenty of experience with mountaintop outposts that dominated terrain, and yet were so far from the people as to be ineffective. They were also hugely expensive to maintain logistically, as they were essentially dependent on helicopter resupply or airdrop. Given what we thought we knew and what we wanted to accomplish, I cannot fault the placement of the base. We knew what we had, and had taken measures to ensure we could defend the base such as it was.

Inside the outpost, the very significant firepower, including the single 120-mm mortar and 60-mm mortars, was exposed to enemy fires from positions overlooking the base, and became the first targets for destruction, along with the equally exposed TOW missile system. Placing and building a good mortar position is tough work for an experienced mortar section, and in the end, we could have done better: neither mortar was able to be effectively employed during the attack. And the enemy did a superb job of locating them, and through direct and sustained fires, very much limiting their use.

The two battlefield surveillance systems, the TOW-equipped ITAS and LRAS3, were powerful means to find, fix, and in the case of the TOW, finish a maneuvering insurgent force, especially under the cover of darkness (they could be lethal out to a range of four kilometers, day or night). But they need to be manned, turned on, and used. At Wanat, the LRAS3 was dismounted and used intermittently to conserve battery power. Before the attack, including one sighting the night before, two groups of men were seen in the surrounding rides by the ITAS, but were not targeted. The LRAS3 was not in operation until right before the attack. In either case, it's easy to say the men should have been targeted, but in combat of this nature, it was still important to make positive identification beforehand, which can be a challenge—especially if, as I suspect, the men were hiding their weapons.

The observation post (OP) at Topside was established on nearby high ground one hundred yards from the outpost at the base of a large mulberry tree and incorporated large boulders; on the other side of the OP was a creek at the bottom of a rocky and treed ravine that was not visible from either the Topside OP itself or the combat outpost, but that would allow attackers cover and concealment to approach Topside unseen to within hand grenade range. As General Patton noted in his own memoir, we should avoid establishing positions below large trees since they prove to be both an aiming point for the enemy and can cause wounds themselves to the soldiers below when hit with fires. And dead space, especially that close to any position, must be covered by another position in overwatch, and should also include preplanned and registered indirect fires, claymore mines, trip flares, and the like. At Wanat, the platoon indeed employed wire and claymores in the dead space to some effectiveness; remains of enemy dead were found caught in the wire, "blown out of their sandals."

As the attack progressed, Topside became a fighting position and sucked manpower from the outpost to reinforce and prevent the OP from being totally overrun. Eight of the nine soldiers killed that day were killed at Topside. Instead of a battlefield asset, Topside was the major liability of Combat Outpost Kahler.

In hindsight, it is clear the mountainous, complex terrain limited the unit's options for placement of the OP, and the intent to center with the local population led to the combat outpost's site adjacent to the village. Aggressive patrolling both day and night would have helped both.

We did not send out any real patrols beyond the confines of Kahler, the tactical control point (TCP) on the road, and Topside. The unit felt the construction of the defenses was the priority, and used its manpower in filling HESCO bastions, sandbags, limited digging-in, and the like. The Afghan Army platoon was likewise used to build defenses. A series of sustained, small-unit patrols through the village, and up into the ridgelines, would have been extremely helpful in spotting the enemy maneuver the day and night prior to the attack. As it was, the enemy maneuvered into the high ground surrounding Kahler and Topside, the villagers abandoned the village, and the enemy used rooftops, windows, and the like to seize premier firing positions overlooking the outpost, all undiscovered or at least unrecognized for what they were, until too late.

After almost fifteen months of war, the American soldiers did not fully trust the Afghan soldiers, and so the Afghan platoon was not used to conduct far-ranging patrols, or to overwatch the police station, or to gather human intelligence based on talks with the villagers and locals in the hillsides. In truth, the Afghan troops deployed that day were generally deeply suspicious of the Nuristanis, which may have kept their leadership from pushing outside the base as aggressively as they should have.

On the ground at Kahler, a series of incidents took place to delay the supply of construction materials, assets, and water, as well as the arrival of Captain Myer. There is no doubt that the soldiers worked very hard to build the outpost as quickly as they could given the delays and extreme heat, and they clearly thought through the pros and cons of the placement of OP Topside, ultimately choosing the location they did for ease of reinforcement and a direct line of movement from the main outpost. When Captain Myer arrived on July 12, he inspected Kahler and the observation post at Topside. Seeing the situation, he decided to begin a series of patrols the next day, as well as build a series of small outposts on higher ground to overwatch the base and Topside.

Unfortunately, the enemy attacked in the early morning hours of July 13.

In the end, when history is written about this battle, I believe there will be two things that stand out. First, seventy-three soldiers fought with extraordinary bravery to defend the COP and OP, fighting for their comrades and for life itself, against a skilled, well-positioned, well-equipped, locally supported, and determined foe. This battle will long be remembered for heroism, valor, and selfless sacrifice for one's fellow soldiers.

As it should be.

Second, I believe the strategic decision to withdraw from Wanat within a few days after the attack will long be examined, cross-examined, and critiqued. It was my decision, made with close consultation with company, battalion, and brigade commanders, as well as my staff and deputy commanding generals, but in the end, it was my decision to make and have executed. By choosing to withdraw—and I have explained my rationale earlier—I handed the enemy a strategic victory, which they crowed about for months. They were joined by a U.S. domestic press which I had hoped would provide balance and detailed investigative reporting, which it did in most cases, but a few damned those who fought or who supported the defenders that day.

After what I saw as the corrupt, duplicitous actions of the local elders, villagers, and Afghan police at Wanat, I was unwilling to risk another American soldier's life to help them. We worked closely with elders in every one of our fourteen provinces: some were trustworthy, some not, and our soldiers and their leaders' attitudes reflected their experiences. It took one event, such as an ambush after a *shura*, to make a young officer and his entire platoon jaded. But never had I experienced a wholesale treachery led by the local elder leadership and followed by an entire village and its police force. Given that level of deceit, and its effect on soldiers' lives, I think it would have been impossible for our soldiers and their leaders to regard them—elders, villagers, police—as anything but the enemy.

To those that say this battle was fought for nothing, that these men gave their lives for nothing, after we withdrew, I strongly disagree. We went to Wanat to help the local people secure themselves, connect them to a national and regional government that intended to provide education, medical care, and basic services they lacked, and boost the local economy through focused, rational, and relevant investment. This was noble work. The elders of Wanat and the villagers that followed them proved unworthy, but we at least tried, and our soldiers fought well, with honor.

Sometimes, in war, that is as good as it gets.

PART 2

CHAPTER 11

"We have to understand that the situation is
precarious and urgent in Afghanistan."
Senator Barack Obama

Saturday, July 19, 2008

C ODEL (congressional delegation) Reed was a misnomer. True,
Senator Jack Reed, a Democrat from Rhode Island, was the senior
senator. A graduate of the U.S. Military Academy at West Point, he had
served in the active army in the 1970s and later in the reserves. Now
he was a key member of the Senate Armed Services Committee. His
companion, Republican Senator Chuck Hagel from Nebraska, was no
novice either; he was a Vietnam vet who had fought as a sergeant squad
leader (his younger brother Tom was in his squad) with the 9th Infantry
Division, earning two Purple Hearts. But everything about this CODEL
was focused on junior Senator Barack Obama, a Democrat from Illinois,
from the small legion of Secret Service agents who flew in days earlier to
review our plans and prepare for contingencies, to the deep interest by
Ambassador Wood and General McKiernan in this particular delegation.
It was July in an election year, and Senator Obama was the presumptive
Democratic nominee for president of the United States.

CODEL Reed was coming to RC-East by way of a stop in Kuwait,
where they met with senior military leaders and Iraqi political leadership,

ate chow with soldiers in the dining facility at Camp Arifjan, and played some pickup basketball with troopers that drew wide media attention.

We were ready by Saturday morning, and so the day started normally: some early PT, the stand-up at 8:00 a.m., and the 9:00 a.m. combat update with the intelligence and operations team. Afterwards, I reviewed Senator Obama's speech on Iraq and Afghanistan that he gave before he departed the U.S. I was impressed. For a junior senator short on foreign policy and national security credentials, it was a well-written and focused speech. And I tended to agree with his assessment and his way ahead. I found the part on an Afghanistan way ahead most interesting. He said he would send two additional brigade combat teams to the Afghanistan theater, add more Predators and helicopters, and increase U.S. support to Afghan non-military assistance by $1 billion per year. He wanted to win, and was willing to put in the resources to do so.

I could have written that part of the speech myself. His comments on Iraq seemed to focus on disentangling the U.S. from a war that should not have happened. I had always thought our invasion of Iraq would negatively impact our counterterrorism fight against al-Qaida worldwide, including in Afghanistan. When I led the war on terrorism planning team on the Joint Staff from 2001 to 2003, I had a very serious one-on-one discussion with the then chairman of the Joint Chiefs of Staff (CJCS), General Richard Myers, about this very point in late 2002, when the planning for a possible Iraq invasion was dominating Pentagon routine. It was morning and I had seized on a blank spot on my calendar to go down to the Pentagon gym for a quick workout. No sooner had I changed into PT gear than my executive officer paged me, and told me the CJCS needed to see me right away. I headed to General Myers' office immediately, without changing. Sometimes he had no-notice meetings with the secretary of defense, or a White House meeting that popped up. I ran up the several flights of stairs to his office, still in my army gray T-shirt, PT shorts, and running shoes.

The conversation was classified, but I will never forget the closing. I told the chairman, one time too many apparently, that I was sure the Iraq invasion would wreak havoc on our counterterrorism fight in Afghanistan and globally. I still naively thought I might be able to change his mind and maybe the course of a war. I was mistaken.

General Myers reminded me I was a professional military officer and a key member of his staff. Did I have a moral objection to removing Saddam Hussein from power? After living on two borders of Iraq, Jordan and Kuwait, I hated Saddam with a passion.

No.

If not, it was my duty to get on board, to support whatever the president ultimately decided, to stop being a naysayer, and to proactively help in thinking how to mitigate the negative and accent the positive impacts from a potential Iraq invasion.

Chastened, but with a bit more wisdom exiting the office than what I had when I entered, I said I understood, and headed back to the gym to change.

Less than a year later, I would deploy to Mosul, Iraq, as the assistant division commander of the 101st Airborne Division.

At 12:15 p.m., CODEL Reed touched down at Bagram Airfield. We did the standard meet and greet for congressional delegations and senior leaders—"Welcome to Bagram, site of Alexander the Great's military camp in 329 BC, and things haven't changed much since"—and headed to my headquarters. Located in a former Soviet hangar, the multi-level inner building centered on a tiered joint operations center where more than a hundred staff officers, non-commissioned officers, and civilians coordinated and tracked the counterinsurgency operations throughout all forty-eight thousand square miles of our area of operations. The narrow metal passageways felt right at home for the sailors assigned to the CJTF; I often felt like I was back on the aircraft carrier USS *America* as we supported special operations forces in Haiti in 1994.

As we entered the building and made our way up the stairs to the big conference room, with me leading the three senators, Obama next to me, the staff who were not in the operations center popped out from open office doors, at corridor corners, from the latrine, cameras and cell phones in hand, all trying to meet and get a picture with Senator Obama. Stern conservatives who I knew to be firm Republicans, liberal left-leaning Democrats, others who likely would be classified libertarians, some who said they proudly refused to vote as long as they were professional soldiers: it didn't matter, as everyone seemingly wanted to meet and get a picture with the senator from Illinois.

We made it to the conference room finally, and I gave the CODEL our CJTF-101 campaign brief. Their questions were on point, and I answered frankly. I had gone on record that we were underresourcing the Afghanistan theater, and that my command needed more troops, surveillance and reconnaissance assets, and resources to be successful in any kind of timeframe that I thought the American people would grant us. All three senators agreed.

It was a zoo making our way out of the headquarters, with seemingly everyone in the building lurking in the corridors to get a picture or a handshake. We made it outside, paused for a quick photo op in front of Old Abe, our 101st Airborne Division War Eagle statue, back-dropped by the Stars and Stripes and the flags of the NATO countries and allied coalition fighting in Afghanistan, then jumped into armored SUVs, headed to see the special operations task force co-located at Bagram.

The next stop was Jalalabad, and in the midafternoon heat we boarded a C-130. Senator Obama and I sat up in the cockpit area, directly behind the pilots, so he could get a good look at the terrain. As we flew, we talked about the land we were flying over, the people dwelling on it, and the insurgency that plagued them. He was an apt listener, asked cogent and detailed questions, and seemed to be sincerely interested in learning about this country and our war, rather than just confirming his own thoughts and opinions.

At Jalalabad, Colonel Chip Preysler and his team briefed the senators, followed by the provincial reconstruction team. Finally, we had a small group meeting with Governor Sherzai. Outspoken, sometimes caustic, but with Afghan tribal and warlord bona fides a mile long, Sherzai spoke about what was needed in Nangarhar as well as all of Afghanistan. I thought he made an impression on the CODEL, but was it positive or negative? I could not tell.

It was late in the day as we boarded my Black Hawk and headed west, towards Kabul. The sun was still above the mountain ridges as we flew over our operating base at Mehtar Lam, the capital of Laghman Province, and then outposts at Kutschbach and Morales Frazier in the Tagab Valley of Kapisa Province. It was my favorite time of the summer day in Afghanistan, the heat lessening, the golden light deepening the dramatic hues of the multicolored cliffs, the fields of green crops, some of them poppy, and the dark evergreens that dotted the mountain slopes too steep to harvest. Riding in the far-right aft seat next to the big window in the sliding door of the helicopter, Senator Obama, the fading sunlight reflecting off his dark sunglasses, soaked it all in.

We dropped the CODEL in Kabul, where they were to meet with General McKiernan and the ambassador, as well as see President Karzai the following day, Sunday.

In my journal that night, I wrote that Senator Obama had asked the right questions, and that I had observed a magnetism and charisma that really surprised me; he had always struck me as somewhat aloof on television.

I wrote Patty and our daughter Kelly an email that night. I told them McCain didn't have a chance, and I was sure I had just spent the day with our next president.

It was late evening that same day and I was exhausted. The day prior, Friday, had been one of those Afghan days that training or education just did not, maybe could not, prepare you for. I had heard on Thursday about a Pakistani woman arrested in Ghazni by the Afghan police on suspicion of plotting an attack against the provincial governor. Apparently, she was just outside his compound, dressed in the standard Afghan blue burqa, a head-to-foot dressing with a knitted eye covering that made women in the country who wore it appear essentially alike, almost ghostly inconspicuous. Allegedly, she was drawing a map, and had poisons and other chemicals in her bag, and had many documents and papers, some handwritten, that were of great interest. She had been transferred to the Afghan National Directorate of Security (NDS), and we would send a U.S. Army and FBI team to meet with her in the morning.

On Friday morning, the staff told me that the Pakistani woman had been shot and would be en route to our Bagram Airfield Hospital. I was told she apparently was shot before our attempted interrogation, likely by one of the U.S. Army soldiers.

The day ended at midnight with an update on our Pakistani lady guest at the hospital. She arrived in critical condition, but our surgeons were experts on trauma and gunshots, and I was confident in her care. And mystified about who she really was.

The next day was devoted to CODEL Reed. It was late Saturday before I could turn my attention back to her. By then the intel team and FBI liaison were confident: our Pakistani guest, who was recovering from successful surgery for a gunshot wound to the abdomen, was a Pakistani-born, Massachusetts Institute of Technology and Brandeis-educated neuroscientist. She was also allegedly married to al-Qaida 9/11 planner Khalid Sheikh Mohammed's nephew, and she had been on the FBI's Most Wanted Terrorist List since 2004. Her name: Aafia Siddiqui.

I made sure we had adequate military police protection with Siddiqui, both to protect our docs and nurses as well as Siddiqui herself. We were not really prepared to host an injured alleged terrorist for a long period in the Bagram hospital, but she needed to recover before we either moved her to our detainment facility, or out of Bagram. Frankly, I was anxious to have her out of our care, and out of our hair. I was all too ready to transfer her to the FBI.

I sent the email to Patty and Kelly about the day with CODEL Reed and Senator Obama, not mentioning Aafia Siddiqui, and got up from my desk to leave for my room. It was around 10:00 p.m., it had been a challenging day, and I was ready for a couple of hours of rest. The phone rang. The operations chief needed to brief me on a time-sensitive target. Now.

I got the brief—it was for a classified target—and the risk analysis. I approved using Hellfire missiles from a drone and 105-mm cannon from an AC-130 special operations gunship, and waited.

At midnight came the results: four enemies killed.

I went to my room and tried to sleep. Aafia Siddiqui and CODEL Reed did not keep me awake. What kept me awake, like most every commander in combat, were the life-or-death decisions I made.

I could only hope that the four dead were the right four.

CHAPTER 12

"The strength of a wall is never greater nor less than the courage of the men who defend it."
Genghis Khan

Sunday, July 27, 2008

By late July, it was apparent we would receive some sort of troop increase, but exactly how much and when, no one could tell. Wednesday evening, July 23, the Joint Chiefs of Staff J-3, Lieutenant General Carter Ham, called me. An old friend, we had worked together in Iraq, when his much smaller Task Force Olympia, formed around the army's first Stryker brigade, took control of northern Iraq from the 101st Airborne Division, where I was the assistant division commander. He faced a looming insurgency with fewer forces than we had in Mosul and the surrounding countryside, and I ruefully remember wishing him good luck as we sat on metal folding chairs in my office, which doubled as my bunk room at the Mosul Airport terminal. He smiled, said they would do their best, and I knew he would be asking for more troops right away. I had hoped his requests would not fall on deaf ears.

Now it was my time to ask for more troops and resources, and Carter was in a position to help as the operations officer for the JCS, the Joint Staff in the Pentagon.

"Admiral Mullen met today with the president." If anyone was prepared to brief on our situation in Afghanistan, and particularly along the volatile eastern border with Pakistan, it was the chairman. I trusted him to take our case to the commander in chief.

"You may get a BCT." A brigade combat team would address my request from the past month, plus give me additional troops for what was emerging as a significant fight along Highway 1 and for Kabul itself.

"Plan on it."

I was excited about the possibility of receiving another brigade combat team, but the next call I received was from the CENTCOM deputy J-3, Air Force Brigadier General Gregory A. Biscone. *Not so fast.* Yes, we could get a BCT, but CENTCOM wanted to take the brigade headquarters and some of its troops and move them elsewhere, likely to the south, where the Taliban were having success against the British and Canadians.

I had my work cut out for me to convince CENTCOM that we, CJTF-101 and Regional Command-East, needed this brigade. The entire brigade combat team.

Since the Taliban's announced spring offensive, they had been successful in pressuring my forces throughout RC-East. By late July, the insurgents had created havoc on Highway 1 between Kabul and Kandahar. With IEDs planted into culverts, dug into the asphalt, or stuck inside a dead dog or goat, followed by a complex ambush with RPGs and small arms, the Afghans could no longer safely travel the highway in either direction. The logistical supply convoys, most contracted from civilian firms, were being specifically targeted. It wouldn't be long before they would refuse to drive the highway if we couldn't make improvements, and soon. The highway attacks, plus attacks in the capitol itself like the Indian embassy bombing, had led to a growing public perception echoed by the media that the Taliban and a broader group of insurgents were at the "gates of Kabul."

While Kabul was not my responsibility to safeguard, its approaches from the north, east, south, and west were. We had to secure the gates of Kabul.

CHAPTER 13

"If men will not act for themselves, what will they do
when the benefit of their effort is for all?"
Elbert Hubbard, "A Message to Garcia"

Monday, August 4, 2008

Weather in Afghanistan is unpredictable. With the deserts of Iran to the west, the Chinese Taklamakan and Gobi deserts to the northeast, the Himalayas—the highest mountains in the world—to the east in Tibet and Nepal, the vast Kazakh steppes to the north, and with the tropical humidity of the Persian Gulf to the south, almost anything is possible. At Bagram, the Hindu Kush mountains act as a shield, sometimes blocking or at least ameliorating heavy winter snows or devastating windstorms that begin to the north or west. But sometimes the weather had its way, and it severely impacted our operations.

Ambassador Wood was supposed to visit, but the weather was atrocious: early morning gusty winds turned to thirty knots, then to forty knots as the morning wore on. Soon the sun was obliterated by the wind-driven dust and dirt. The ambassador's helicopter was on hold at Kabul.

Back in my office, I looked at the latest set of metrics that we had. Since our transfer of authority in early April, we had lost seventy-three troopers. Of that number, sixty-two had been killed in action. The rest had died of accidents, medical issues, and suicides. The civilian casualties were much too high as well: in spite of our precision, we inadvertently killed Afghans during our operations. When compared to the deliberate targeting of civilians by the insurgents, our numbers were low, but I knew we had to radically reduce the civilian toll.

We did not try to specifically count or announce to the media exact metrics on the number of insurgents we killed, but the round numbers were high. How long could they take casualties like that?

I pondered the metrics. If our fight were a war of attrition, with enemy and friendly duking it out to produce the most casualties on the other side, we—ISAF, and our Operation Enduring Freedom U.S. forces—would clearly be winning. But this was a counterinsurgency, and most of us commanders believed that we could not kill our way to winning. The insurgents had proven remarkably resilient to attrition. Soon after an enemy battlefield commander was killed, they were replaced, sometimes with someone even more brutal, or skilled, or both. With the Pashtun code of honor that demanded revenge for those we killed, a virtual safe haven in the Pakistan frontier for recruiting and training, and deep-rooted corruption embedded in Afghan politics, business, and culture, I was convinced attrition warfare was a sure way to guarantee we would not win this before the American public, or their elected officials, threw in the towel. The last thing we needed was a replay of the Vietnam War.

In hindsight, maybe winning wasn't even possible. Or at least not winning in the conventional sense, with one side giving up, suing for peace, or evaporating from the battlefield, the other side claiming victory.

"Hey sir, the ambassador is going to try to fly in soon," my aide Andy said. It looked like the weather had eased up some. We headed out to the flight line, and I shelved my nagging thoughts for the moment.

The runway at Bagram heads north to south. The sky was still a sickening, dusty yellow-green color, with a lightless sun just evident as it began a slow descent in the late summer afternoon.

We drove down to the VIP ramp adjacent to the taxiway and parallel the main runway; it was about midway down the runway itself. The winds were picking up again, and we had to squint to keep the dust from blinding us. I was pretty certain that if the ambassador had been able to depart Kabul, he would not be able to land here. Not in this dust storm.

"Call the operations center and find out if they took off. Tell them they won't be able to land here."

Then I heard engines from afar. The sound was south and the winds were out of the northwest, and so strong that they drowned out most sounds. I heard the engines again. It was an aircraft.

Incoming to Bagram.

Our own 101st Airborne Black Hawk pilots flew the ambassador's helicopter. Surely they were not going to try to land!

Andy came back. "The ambassador scrubbed, sir. The Black Hawk crews may have to remain overnight down there at Kabul."

The engines were louder. Something was approaching the airfield, and fast. I could tell it was not a helicopter by the sounds then: it was a turboprop.

Suddenly a C-130, low but not low enough, fast, way too fast, came down the runway. With the wind-driven dust, the plane just suddenly appeared out of the sand and dirt.

He was halfway down the runway and had not touched down, and he was moving much too fast.

"He will do a go-around," I said to Andy. Or crash, I thought.

The pilot slammed the plane onto the runway almost directly in front of us. It careened down the runway, tail sliding to the right, left wing lowered, as the winds had their way.

The plane skidded off the concrete runway into dirt. The four engines were still at max power, and the dirt and sand that were kicked up enveloped the plane.

We jumped back in the SUV and sped down the taxiway to the plane, calling the operations center en route. The pilot had killed the engines when we got there, the back ramp was down, and troopers were piling off the plane. With the wheel gear collapsed, the C-130 rested in the dirt on its belly. I could see the flag painted on the tail: it was a United Arab Emirates C-130.

The aircraft was quickly evacuated. Fire trucks arrived, then an ambulance from the hospital, then other emergency vehicles. The Emirati air crew and their SOF passengers gathered on the tarmac away from the aircraft and emergency teams. Some smoked; others gathered in small groups, talking in subdued tones, hard to make out in the winds. No one seemed to be seriously hurt. Lucky.

I once spoke good Arabic, and could still get around fine, but the pilot's command of English was impeccable.

"So why didn't you go around?"

"We were low on fuel. With the winds so bad, we could not have made another pattern and approach."

We closed the airfield for five hours. We had to divert five Bagram-based jets returning home.

We were lucky.

The next day our female Pakistani guest in the Bagram military hospital was extradited to the United States, to face charges. I was very happy to see her go. Later I would find out she was charged and eventually convicted of two charges of attempted murder, plus other related charges, and was sentenced to eighty-six years in federal prison.

Late that afternoon, we had our weekly secure video teleconference with the secretary of defense. In my battlefield update, I briefed Secretary Gates on highway security throughout Afghanistan, and told him how we were concentrating on ensuring bridges and key culverts were not destroyed. General McKiernan told the secretary that I needed the entire brigade combat team in RC-East, if and when the brigade was deployed. I was grateful for that comment. At the end, Secretary Gates gave us an update from the White House and Pentagon on progress to have General McKiernan appointed as commanding general, U.S. Forces Afghanistan. I would be appointed his deputy.

"One to two weeks more."

I was ready to get that done. I had moved from a reluctant believer in the necessity of such a move to a true supporter, especially if

McKiernan's mandate would be operational rather than my more limited "support to all U.S. troops in Afghanistan" charge that came under that National Support Element-U.S. Forces Afghanistan hat. It was clear to my team and myself that ISAF was not organized to help plan, synchronize, or control the various efforts of the separate regional commands, which resulted in essentially five different campaigns in Afghanistan: north, south, west, and ours in the east, plus the capital region of Kabul. McKiernan's weekly commanders' update video conferences and monthly commanders' conferences in Kabul were helpful, but mainly kept us aware of what the other regions were doing. We all had varied enemy and friendly situations, distinct terrain, and different national caveats to adhere to. Our resulting counterinsurgency operations could not have been more dissimilar.

It had been six years since the U.S. had invaded Afghanistan and the Taliban government had fallen. Seeking refuge in the frontier of Pakistan, the Taliban and al-Qaida were able to reconstitute and then sustain a fairly low-level insurgency in the south and east, and any chance of quickly defeating them and the Haqqanis was lost when the U.S. invaded Iraq in early 2003. Afghanistan became an economy of force area, a euphemism meaning it wasn't a priority for troops, equipment, money, or resources. The lack of an integrated and capable ISAF war-fighting organization at the operational level was one symptom of this overall deficiency—in this case, a dearth of resources and creativity.

At 3:00 a.m. the next day we held a ramp ceremony in a dusty, windy darkness. With full military honors we farewelled a U.S. Marine Corps captain who died of wounds received in combat. In a smaller ceremony immediately following, we paid respects to a soldier who had committed suicide. I knew this policy (my own to make) could be controversial, especially back home, and there were arguments to be made either way. In the end, I could not in good faith to our profession of arms allow the same military honors for someone who took their own life in war, as the person who was killed in combat, or who died of wounds, or of injuries or illness sustained in combat.

Dawn brought worsening winds, and we had to postpone a flight to Kabul to meet Ambassador Wood and brief CODEL Reid: Majority Leader Senator Harry Reid and fellow legislators.

Meanwhile, Governor Sherzai from Nangarhar continued to press Colonel Spiszer at Jalalabad, myself at Bagram, and General McKiernan in Kabul to release a certain Mullah Rabbani from our Bagram detention facility. The mullah, also known as Mullah Mohammad Shinwar, was clearly closely linked to the governor, but had found himself in the wrong place at the wrong time, and had been swept up in one of our operations. Sherzai was livid, threatening President Karzai with resigning if I didn't immediately release the mullah. Frankly, my staff hadn't convinced me the mullah was Taliban or a terrorist, but that kind of information came from interrogations and good intelligence staff work that took time—even days—after a detainee arrived at the Bagram facility. I did not have that much time in this case. Ambassador Wood wanted to talk to me privately on this one.

The weather improved by afternoon, and Mark Milley and I flew to Kabul Airport, where our security team drove us to the U.S. embassy. At the ambassador's residence we met Ambassador Wood, Senator Harry Reid and his national security advisor, and Senators Nelson, Menendez, Isakson, and Bingaman. I hugged Reid's national security advisor: Jessica Lewis Schloesser was married to my brother Chris. We sat down and I gave a brief but very blunt campaign update. I knew the CODEL was exhausted and on the wrong end of their biological clock, but the senators asked smart, probing questions.

What was truly happening in Afghanistan? What was the role of Pakistan? Would additional U.S. and foreign troops make a true difference?

During a break, Ambassador Wood, Milley, and I huddled about our mullah detainee. It was clear this was a major issue with Sherzai, and President Karzai had asked the ambassador for his direct support.

Mark and I agreed that the political fallout was not worth the gain. If it turned out the mullah really was bad, we would hunt him down. And the next meeting may not go as well for him.

I told the ambassador I understood.

I immediately ordered Mullah Rabbani of Shinwar released from our Bagram Theater Internment Facility, and transported that day back to Nangarhar and Governor Sherzai. The mullah was back with Governor Sherzai by 7:30 p.m. I wrote that night in my journal that neither Mark nor I was convinced of his role in the insurgency, not at all sure we had the right guy.

But Sherzai now owed me one.

I flew back in the early evening to Bagram to a briefing from the staff on options to close various outposts. We had to withdraw from those like Wanat, but also like Keating, which was still occupied, that were too far away from our supporting larger bases, too hard to support, and did not have either a significant and direct positive impact on local populations or a negative impact on large numbers of insurgents. We could not continue the status quo.

I received a quick status check on the second 15-6 investigation of the Wanat battle that I had ordered continued. The first one had been completed essentially in-house with the 173rd Brigade Combat Team's deputy commander as the investigating officer; while I did not disagree with his findings, I wanted a further look at the battle from an investigating officer not so close to the unit. This particular investigation would be wider and seek more of the context in which the decisions were made, and it seemed on track.

On Friday, I got in my normal run around the airfield. Overnight I had received a report that a special operation may have inadvertently killed four Afghan noncombatants, all civilian women. We would of course investigate, try to make financial amends if at fault, and continue forward. As I ran, I wondered at it all: how to continue to press our special operations, which were so effective at capturing or killing Taliban and other insurgents, with the very clear need to end or at least reduce civilian casualties. We could not kill them faster than our own operations served to recruit them. And an inadvertent death of a civilian was a family and tribal calamity that required revenge. Money could sometimes help, but blood revenge was the most honorable thing in Pashtun culture, under their code of *Pashtunwali*. We created future enemies every time we killed a civilian noncombatant.

Back in the office that morning, I turned to a breaking story from the Office of the Secretary of Defense. A soldier at Zerok Combat Outpost, located only twelve miles from the Pakistani border, had used social media and a public forum to complain about his chain of command, the living conditions, and the readiness of the outpost. I had not been to Zerok recently, and I was concerned. I would go see for myself—today.

I headed first to Ghazni, where we met with an incoming Polish brigade team from Task Force White Eagle on a predeployment site survey and Brigadier General Grzegorz Buszka, the senior Polish officer in the country. I needed the Poles to take over Ghazni Province, which would free a U.S. battalion to position elsewhere. I was a big believer in the Poles because they had a strong martial disposition, were well equipped, and were proud to be given responsibility for an entire province in RC-East. We needed to set the conditions for their success—the naysayers included the current provincial governor—and so we helped set up camps and build a small runway for their MI-17 and Hind helicopters (their versions of assault and attack helicopters). In the heat and altitude, the heavy Hinds needed a running start when loaded with ammo and gas.

I understood the issue. It had not been that long ago, a decade or so, when I needed a runway and a running takeoff to get my heavily loaded MH-47E special ops Chinook airborne. That the Poles were bringing their own helicopters was extraordinarily helpful, and well worth the cost of a short runway.

After an aerial recon, we dropped the Poles at Ghazni, and Command Sergeant Major Vince Camacho and I headed to Zerok outpost.

We landed at the outpost and met the company commander and first sergeant. Camacho went one way and I the other, but both of us inspected the base defensive plan and measures, preparations for combat, and the overall living conditions. I had junior non-commissioned officers take me through the living areas: metal storage shelters embedded in dirt and rock, bug-infested and wet, humid, and fetid.

After quietly comparing notes with Camacho, I decided the soldier who complained in public to the Office of the Secretary of Defense was right. We had failed our troopers.

I radioed my operations center and Currahee 6, Colonel Pete Johnson. I was relieving the Zerok Combat Outpost chain of command, and the sergeant major and I would stay at the base until a new command team arrived.

I told the company commander, first sergeant, and platoon sergeant I was relieving them then and there. The outpost's defenses were weak, the unit unready for a sustained attack, undisciplined, the soldiers' morale poor. And the living conditions were embarrassing.

Relief in a war zone was in my mind an extraordinary measure taken because of extraordinary circumstances. I felt this was one of those circumstances. We, and I, placed huge responsibility onto the shoulders of young commanders and their non-commissioned officers in RC-East, and delegated significant authorities to them to execute the extremely difficult missions we assigned them. Each outpost was a world unto itself: isolated, exposed to severe weather and usually amazingly difficult terrain, alien to the locals, and targeted by a seasoned and resourceful enemy, who knew the weather, land, and people better than we did. I expected our leaders to uphold the standards learned in military schools and practiced in training and combat. I felt this particular command team had not done so, and that the soldiers deserved better.

I was fully aware that relief in combat, especially for a company commander and senior non-commissioned officer, could be a career killer. Camacho and I flew back to Bagram that evening after the battalion commander flew to Zerok and replaced the command team. On the Black Hawk flying over the stark, barren land, I felt crappy. I was responsible for the outpost and the soldiers stationed there, and I had poorly served the latter. But I was equally responsible for the leaders, and I felt I needed to serve them better too.

Over the course of my command in Afghanistan, I fired several officers and non-commissioned officers. A handful were clear-cut: criminal actions or violations of the Uniform Code of Military Justice. Most were judgment calls, what we commonly call "lost confidence in the ability to command" or to lead, and in these I wrestled with each case. These leaders were not purposefully negligent, nor deliberately incompetent, but along the way of their development, training, or preparation for this war, they missed something, and that absence was magnified in combat. A few of these leaders I knew well; in a very few cases, I had personally selected them for their positions. In most situations, I had met them on the battlefield or the joint operations center or they were just part of my far-flung command, coming from units throughout our army and added to my command once they arrived in Afghanistan. I had always thought of myself as a natural leader, delighted in command, and found command in combat self-fulfilling, but I hated to relieve soldiers. It was a necessary responsibility, but one in which I took no satisfaction.

A few days later, Lieutenant Colonel Pierre Gervais, our CJTF chief intelligence officer, and I flew to Kabul. We spent an hour with the Afghan Armed Forces operations officer, Lieutenant General Karimi, poring over maps, exchanging views of where the insurgents were currently operating, their lines of communications, and where they sought safe haven. The three of us went to Minister Wardak's office, where we spent the next hour and half talking about the friendly and enemy forces dispositions. We talked about our current campaign and its Afghan offshoot, Radu Barq IV, the gates of Kabul, and what we were mutually doing together to guard those "gates." I talked of a winter campaign, one oriented on seeking out the enemy in his safe havens, and of continuous kinetic pressure in spite of the winter cold and snows.

Wardak looked me in the eyes.

"We are short of Afghan soldiers, and you are short of troops. We need to see if we can put together protective groups, under the supervision of the village elders and synchronized with the district and provincial government. Armed, they could help secure the people."

This sounded close to the Afghan tribal watch of old, the *Arbakai* (a traditional, armed, tribal-based community security force). But it was also close to what General Petraeus (now CENTCOM commander) had recommended the day before during a meeting. Was this Wardak's or Petraeus' idea?

I knew arming loosely trained young men with automatic weapons could have obvious downsides, but agreed it was worth having our staff explore it with ISAF.

And so began the Afghan "Guardians," the Afghan Public Protection Program, also known by the acronym AP3.

CHAPTER 14

"I am considering two promises. One is the promise of God, the other is that of Bush. The promise of God is that my land is vast. If you start a journey on God's path, you can reside anywhere on this earth and will be protected.... The promise of Bush is that there is no place on earth that I cannot find you. We will see which one of these two promises is fulfilled."
Mullah Omar

Monday, August 18, 2008

Flanks and boundaries are always areas of grave concern to combat commanders. Our boundary that demarcated eastern Afghanistan and RC-East from FATA and the North and South Waziristan provinces of Pakistan was an example of one of our most challenging flanks. Directly to our east in Pakistan, the enemy could find safe haven and a line of communication and refit that I could not impact, with very extraordinary exceptions in the heat of battle in directly observed pursuit of an attacking enemy force. But friendly unit boundaries could also be challenging.

In the middle of RC-East was the city of Kabul, surrounded by Kabul Province. We did not control or secure Kabul Province. Regional Command-Capital did. By late summer, security for the city itself was primarily Afghan Army and police, and the outside districts had recently transitioned from Italian to French oversight.

At the far eastern edge of Kabul Province was Sarobi District, located about midway between Kabul city and Nangarhar, and south of RC-East's Kapisa Province. A rugged, mountainous, and bleak area, its saving feature was the Sarobi Dam and Lake. Built on the Kabul River, the dam provided limited hydroelectric power and was the source of irrigation for the farmers nearby. The Kabul-Nangarhar highway bordered the lake, went through a tunnel near the dam, and squeaked through the narrow mountain cliffs on the way to Jalalabad. In the spring and early summer, the lake water was an inviting bluish green, and flying over it periodically in my Black Hawk it reminded me of high alpine lakes back home. It helped make the village of Sarobi ruggedly appealing, at least from the air. It was like a small island of cool water, green fields, and trees, surrounded by wasteland.

Under the Italians, little that drew my attention seemed to occur in the district. I didn't think they did any significant patrolling in Sarobi outside of the area immediately around Forward Operating Base Tora, just south of the lake. There were rumors of an Italian truce with the Taliban, but I wasn't certain anyone could have a real truce with Gulbuddin's HiG, which is who we thought operated in Sarobi. And regardless, we had our hands full to the immediate north, in our own sector, Kapisa, and Tagab especially.

By late summer, the French had begun reinforcing their forces in Afghanistan as part of President Sarkozy's commitment to the war. A very capable French task force organized around the 8th Marine Infantry Parachute Regiment was coming to RC-East and Kapisa Province, which would be a vast improvement on the small French OMLT and limited U.S. SOF and regular forces we currently had there. As part of this buildup, we were in discussions to "chop" part of Sarobi District, including the Uzbin Valley, to RC-East in the coming months, even as the French reinforced the RC-Capital security forces as well.

By August 15, the transition from Italian to French forces in RC-Capital was complete, and the French had set out to aggressively patrol the Sarobi District. A patrol that day from FOB Tora up the Uzbin Valley to the remote village of Sper Kunday had been warned about Taliban in the area, and the French reportedly told the villagers they would be back in the coming days.

It was late afternoon on August 18th at my headquarters, and the joint operations center and I were fully engaged with a series of serious attacks at Salerno. While Pete Johnson had plenty of forces to deal with what had so far occurred, we were very concerned that this was just one part of a larger series of synchronized enemy operations that would attack NATO and Afghan forces as well as local populations, timed specifically for Afghan Independence Day. About 4:15 p.m., we were alerted that a French patrol operating from RC-Capital's Operating Base Tora had troops in contact, and that an accompanying U.S. SOF element had requested close air support. We immediately cycled two F-15Es their way to Sarobi District's Uzbin Valley.

Running essentially north by northeast from Sarobi village to the hamlet of Sper Kunday, the Uzbin Valley was a stark yet populated mountain valley with a number of narrow passes, some of which were less gravel or dirt roads and more mountain trails. At almost seven thousand feet in altitude, with mountain peaks well above, it was a literally breathtaking area to patrol for most NATO troops.

As we tried to understand what was happening to the French forces in the firefight, we pulled our liaison officer for French forces into the JOC, as well as contacted RC-Capital. Communications were extraordinarily poor with the troops on the ground, and the F-15Es reported being unable to engage, yet stayed on station. We dispatched two A-10 Thunderbolt close air support aircraft to the site of the battle, hoping that they could get better situational awareness of the tactical situation, as well as engage the attackers.

We learned that a reinforced French patrol made up of two French platoons, including one from the 8th Marine Infantry Parachute Regiment, and another from the Régiment de marche du Tchad (Ad Hoc Regiment of Chad), along with a platoon of Afghan National Army and a platoon from the Afghan National Police, plus a handful of U.S. Special Forces, departed FOB Tora earlier in the day for a multi-day operation into the Uzbin Valley and back to the village of Sper Kunday. It was a motorized patrol, and the marines were reportedly outfitted with the French wheeled armored personnel carrier, the Véhicule de l'Avant Blindé (VAB). Lightly armored and relatively lightweight, it was a reasonably good counterinsurgency vehicle for the mountains of Afghanistan, providing mobility and some protection from small arms for up to ten troopers. But the VAB was not an armored fighting vehicle, any more than the U.S. Humvee was. An exposed crew gunner sat or stood in a low turret of the VAB, normally manning a light 7.62 or heavier 12.7-mm machine gun. We didn't know exactly what the Afghans were driving, but thought most likely they were in the standard light Hilux pickup trucks, leaders in the cabs, and soldiers or police seated in the back, exposed, and only sometimes mounting a light machine gun. The U.S. Special Forces were almost certainly operating from up-armored Humvees.

Our best situational awareness in the joint operations center came from the pilots of the A-10s and F-15Es: The enemy had ambushed a lead element of the French patrol after they had dismounted, leaving some number of VABs lower in the valley. The enemy had closed with the lead friendly element and the friendly close air support had almost no communications with the French. A quick reaction force from Tora had arrived about an hour after the attack started, but they seemed to be pinned down already somewhere south of the village. The situation was grim.

We pushed out Kiowa Warriors, thinking they might be able to use their very low-level "eyes on" to help mark friendlies, so we could engage the enemy with their rockets and guns as well as the heavier GAU cannon on the A-10s. We also moved medevac helicopters so they could pull out the wounded, if they could land. By 6:00 p.m., the situation on the ground was critical; some French elements were out of ammunition, some almost surrounded. The Kiowas and A-10s engaged, danger close. We knew this was dicey, but holding our fire would have almost certainly resulted in at least one French platoon's total destruction.

The French used two of their Kabul-based Caracal helicopters to push out ammo and some reinforcements, and haul back wounded. Their initial reports, filtered through RC-Capital and ISAF headquarters, told of desperate close-in fighting, almost no radio communications with the forces in contact, except the quick reaction force, and most units low on or out of ammunition.

There were several dead, several wounded, and some troopers were missing.

We were balancing the Salerno attack with other smaller firefights in RC-East as well as an IED targeting Afghan police in Nangarhar. Working with the special operations task force, we re-prioritized airborne surveillance and reconnaissance assets as well as their AC-130. We soon had both a Predator over the Uzbin Valley as well as an AC-130, which was able to provide highly accurate heavy cannon fires.

Around midnight, the situation at Sarobi stabilized somewhat, just as fresh attacks in Salerno heated up.

ISAF special ops forces inserted into the Uzbin Pass after midnight found more dead and the missing. We heard reports, later verified, that some of the French troops had been stripped, and at least one mutilated, not unlike our U.S. troops at Tangi Valley.

By morning, we knew the toll: nine French soldiers had been killed in action, another trooper had died in a VAB when a road gave way, and some eighteen French and four Afghan soldiers were wounded. Estimates of insurgent casualties were fifteen killed and some eighteen wounded, but since the enemy usually did a superb job of retrieving their dead and wounded, it was a guess.

We moved an Afghan Commando outfit with U.S. SOF advisors into the Uzbin Valley to track the insurgents, and later targeted several groups of Taliban or HiG as they sought to disperse into small villages in nearby Laghman Province, which was in RC-East and under my command.

Within twenty-four hours, surviving French soldiers told senior commanders of a lack of intelligence, lack of sufficient ammo, and few radios in the initial patrol. They also claimed that our close air support or Kiowas had inadvertently fired on them, during the close-up fight. *A Blue on Blue.* I spent most of August 20 trying to ascertain the allegations, working with my RC-Capital counterpart, French Brigadier General Michel Stollsteiner. Both General McKiernan and General Dempsey needed the truth, soonest. I had almost no way to quickly investigate the report, and relied on Stollsteiner and his team. By late evening, they had ascertained there were in fact no blue-on-blue fires, and the chief of French forces said as much publicly.

Looking backwards later that night, I was relieved that we had not inadvertently killed friendly forces; in fact, I was somewhat surprised. The decision to engage when troops were in very close contact, almost hand-to-hand as it was, was fraught with the potential to kill the very people we were attempting to save. And yet it was the right decision. In my opinion, the French losses would have been much higher that night without the intervening A-10 and Kiowa support. The enemy had seemingly done a superb job of massing forces, reported by the French to be some 140 fighters, with heavy weapons including mortars and multiple RPGs, and using classic military maneuver to separate, isolate, and ambush—and to almost, but not quite, rule the day. Clearly the French troops fought heroically, and the Caracal, A-10, F-15E, Kiowa, and AC-130 crews were to be commended as well. The fact that the Afghan Army contingent suffered no deaths or seriously wounded was amazing—and troubling if it was determined they had shunned close combat.

But I was deeply upset by the friendly operational situation this fight exposed. My staff and I had little if any awareness of the planning or start of the Uzbin Valley patrol, even as it was just a handful of miles south of our restive Tagab District. Clearly there was some prior awareness in the U.S. special operations task force, with a few special operators joining the patrol. My CJTF had liaison with the SOF task force, and the RC-East portion of my staff had liaison with RC-Capital, but we had zero advanced situational awareness, much less synchronized and supporting planning or operations. I could not blame the ISAF staff as they were a strategic staff, high-ranking and experienced in NATO procedures, but not operationally oriented. Nor did they have a mandate to be such.

It was becoming readily apparent that we needed an operational ISAF command: something below the current strategic-level ISAF headquarters, and manned by leaders and staff with significant war-fighting experience. The primary purpose would be to conduct campaign planning that would synchronize and coordinate the efforts of the various regional commands, and supervise the execution of the campaigns.

We could not allow another fight like Sarobi.

Meanwhile, the war continued throughout RC-East. Down in Ghazni, our Polish Task Force was hit by a large IED on Route Florida, a major roadway, killing three soldiers. This was the largest loss of life for the Poles since they had entered Afghanistan, and it hit hard. It would be national news in Poland in hours. Earlier, Colonel John Spiszer had called with an unusual fatality. One of his TF Duke soldiers in the Korengal had collapsed from heat stroke, and died.

I walked out of my office, down the stairs, and across the hangar to my room around midnight. We had another ramp ceremony to honor two of our fallen at 2:00 a.m., and I needed to get a little sleep beforehand. I was exhausted, my body tired but my mind more so.

Or maybe it was my spirit that was worn out.

And this was only the four-month point. We had another eleven months to go.

Friday, two days later, at 3:30 a.m., I met Brigadier General Buszka and Polish Ambassador Jacek Najder on the ramp at the airfield. I led the CJTF staff and the Polish command and staff in a formal memorial ceremony to honor the three fallen Polish soldiers. It was a dark, humid night, the kind of night that could suck the energy out of you. The Polish Roman Catholic chaplain offered prayers and a reflection in Polish. The faces of the Polish soldiers in formation were strained, hardened by war, stoic, and determined, but deeply hurt by this stinging loss. We were comrades in arms, and I was their operational commander; I felt their pain as deeply as if it had been my own 101st Airborne troopers who were killed.

After the ceremony, Ambassador Najder, General Buszka, and I talked in low tones by the side of the aircraft that would carry the remains back to Poland. The Polish prime minister had planned to be there that night for the ceremony, but had been delayed. He would still come, and soon, to be with the Polish troops.

It was still dark when I went out for a run. It was Friday, and I did eight miles around the airfield. I was soaked from sweat when I got back to the operations center, but the run had settled my mind. Perhaps it was more a sedative for the spirit, but whatever it was, the long run helped.

August had been a really tough month. But we were learning. I needed us to learn faster, and I had to make the learning less of the school of hard knocks and more standards-based procedures and innovative and agile tactics, along with an aggressive, proactive approach.

But how?

CHAPTER 15

"During World War I, while inspecting a certain area, General John J. Pershing found a project that was not going well, even though the second lieutenant in charge seemed to have a pretty good plan. General Pershing asked the lieutenant how much pay he received. On hearing the lieutenant's reply of '$141.67 per month Sir,' General Pershing said: 'Just remember that you get $1.67 per month for making your plan and issuing the order, and $140.00 for seeing that it is carried out.'"
General Omar Bradley

Wednesday, September 3, 2008

We were in a UC-35, a small army passenger jet, headed east to Islamabad, and to meetings with Major General Pasha, who was still the Pakistan Army director general of military operations, as well as our usual pre-meeting at the U.S. Embassy Islamabad. It was relatively early in the morning. We had departed at 6:50 a.m., a small team led by Brigadier General Mark Milley and myself. We were not halfway when my aide told me that the Pakistanis might cancel the meeting. Did we want to turn around?

Milley and I talked. We were totally unsurprised, based on an operation that had occurred just a few hours before, in the darkness of the Pakistani night.

"No, let's continue. No matter what, we should talk with the ambassador and the admiral. See how much damage has been done."

I had made numerous notes to talk about with Pasha. The Pakistanis had made hay about their ongoing operations in Bajaur, but I wanted them to realize that we were closely tracking the entire border, and it was going from bad to really bad. The statistics were telling: There had been 264 attacks along the border initiated by the enemy from January to August of the previous year, 2007. This year, on our watch, we counted 349 for the same period, a 32 percent increase in violence generated from their side of the Durand Line. In just the last thirty days, we had had eighty-seven attacks: everything from artillery, mortars, attempted ambushes, and harassment to small arms and RPG fires. The Pakistanis needed to do more. We were tired of this.

Last night's operation demonstrated our fatigue and our resolve: a classified mission that demonstrated the U.S. would not stand idle and allow the border region to grow increasingly more disruptive.

The gloves were off.

As soon as we landed at Chaklala, the Pakistani air base outside Rawalpindi, we were notified that General Pasha could not meet with us. No excuse or reason was offered. We already knew.

At the American embassy, Ambassador Anne Patterson spent an hour with us. As usual, she was cordial, welcoming, and refreshingly direct about her insights and thoughts on the Pakistan government, the military, and the impacts to our bilateral relationship from these maddening insurgent cross-border attacks into our area of responsibility. She had thoughts on our own operations as well, especially last night's affair. I left our meeting promising to return soon, both of us believing the continued relationship between our CJTF and the upper echelons of the Pakistani Army, and Frontier Corps as well, was too important to allow to languish.

Downstairs in the embassy, we visited the Office of the Defense Representative to Pakistan, and spent an hour with Navy Rear Admiral Mike LeFever, who had replaced Ron Helmly in the job. Mike gave us a sweeping rundown on the Pakistani military operations in Bajaur: "Baitullah Mehsud is their number-one threat to them in Bajaur." Mehsud was the leader of the Pakistani Taliban in South Waziristan and allegedly had thousands of foot soldiers at his call. Mehsud was also very active in Mohmand Province. The Pakistani Army had committed a brigade to fight Mehsud and the Taliban in both Bajaur and Mohmand. Admiral LeFever also reminded us that the Pakistani military was reeling from a significant decline in public support, an echo of what General Pasha himself had told me the day of our transfer of authority ceremony back in April. When I questioned just how committed the army really was, Mike told us that some eight hundred Pakistanis, soldiers and civilians, had been killed this year by suicide bombers, and another nineteen hundred wounded. These losses could not continue.

"What will be the impact of our cross-border operation?"

Clearly the Pakistanis sent a message today; the visit cancellation would be reported all the way to Foggy Bottom, as well as the Pentagon and Fort Bragg. But none of us knew if it would make a tangible long-lasting negative difference in what had become an increasingly important relationship.

"You need to meet with Major General Tariq Khan, the new inspector general at the Frontier Corps."

In mid-May I had flown to Peshawar to meet Khan's predecessor, Major General Alam Khan Khattak, at the Frontier Corps headquarters for the North-West Frontier Province at Bala Hisar. The fort itself was historically impressive, located on a hilltop with commanding views of Peshawar and the surrounding countryside. Khattak led me on a tour and told me a little of the fort's history. It was said Babur built the fort in 1526 after capturing Peshawar, and Afghan Pashtun King Timur Shah Durrani later used it as a citadel.

The Frontier Corps intrigued me. Created by Lord Curzon, viceroy of British India, to police and provide border security along the frontier with Afghanistan, the Corps was made up of local recruits. They came from the villages and frontier they patrolled, spoke the dialects, and knew the elders. Some of the most famous units, like the Khyber Rifles and Chitral Scouts, had strong combat records, and were well equipped and trained. I thought the Frontier Corps held potential for my plans to strengthen our military relationship and cooperation along the fragile border. As a counterinsurgency force, they were exactly what we needed working among the tribes, and fighting off the Pakistani Taliban.

We flew back to Bagram, where I promptly told my staff to get me back on Pasha's schedule.

"Oh, and I want to go back to the Frontier Corps. I need to meet Major General Tariq Khan."

That afternoon I hosted retired Lieutenant Colonel James "Maggie" Megellas, a true war hero from his service in World War II with the 82nd Airborne's 504th Parachute Infantry Regiment. Maggie had earned a Distinguished Service Cross and many more awards for heroism during combat in Italy, the Netherlands, and Germany. Now ninety-one years old, Maggie was still a ball of fire, and was going out to some of our smaller forward operating bases to spend time with our troopers. He was a true inspiration to listen to, and just to be around him and his electric personality was empowering.

If only more of our near constant VIP meetings and visits were so enjoyable. I left the session upbeat, my spirit renewed.

The next day was our quarterly commander's assessment brief that we held at the Bagram Jirga Center. As a senior commander, I was always wary of large and lengthy commanders' meetings or canned briefings: it was usually a waste of subordinate commanders' time, their staff's time, and my time. I very much preferred to fly to their turf, and receive periodic updates while seeing for my own eyes the conditions on the ground. I usually had Command Sergeant Major Camacho with me, and he went his own way with the senior non-commissioned officers as soon as we touched down. Generals Mark Milley or Jim McConville would sometimes come along, but they had their own specific responsibilities as deputy commanding generals and had their own designated Black

Hawks to get them where they needed to go. I often tried to bring a staff officer or two from the CJTF staff. They were always grateful to get out and see Afghanistan beyond the wire of Bagram, and I found their fresh insights remarkably helpful.

As a leader of any size of organization, I found that seeing with my own eyes and hearing with my own ears were remarkably helpful in achieving an understanding of what was really happening on the ground, and bringing along a staffer for similar insights was enabling for them as well.

But periodically it was important to take the time to get all the senior commanders and their sergeants major together to compare notes, and hopefully learn from each other's initiatives, lessons, and mistakes.

The commanders of the three brigade task forces in our AOR, Pete Johnson, Currahee 6; John Spiszer, Duke 6; and Scott Spellmon, Warrior 6, joined my senior staff and our deputy commanders, Mark Milley and Jim McConville, along with the Combined Security Transition Command-Afghanistan (CSTC-A) commanding general, Major General Bob Cone. Bob started us off with an assessment of the Afghan Army, as well as his work to equip, man, and train the Afghan forces.

Bob was a good friend and a superb army trainer who had previously commanded the National Training Center for almost three years, pushing the center to incorporate counterinsurgency tactics and techniques into its training. I trusted his judgment. As commanding general of CSTC-A, he had direct and sometimes daily contact with Minister of Defense Wardak, Lieutenant General Karimi, and the chief of the Afghan Army, General Bismillah Khan. At least once a month when I was in Kabul, I would visit Bob at his headquarters. A larger, stronger, and more capable Afghan Army and Afghan Border Police (ABP) was a key enabler of our overall strategy and operational campaign plan, and the border police played an outsized role in our winter campaign. We wanted and needed capable partners.

After Bob was finished, each brigade commander briefed, informally, most with no PowerPoint charts at all, on how the three components of our campaign were going in their areas: security first, then governance, then development. In my mind, they flowed in that manner. Without a secure local population, or at least what reasonably passed for security in 2008 in Afghanistan, neither good governance nor substantial development could be expected to be possible, and certainly not for long.

In our area of responsibility, some 80 percent of all violence took place in 25 percent of our 174 districts. In those districts lived a little less than 30 percent of the total population of RC-East. They could be tough places; in these districts we averaged nine insurgent attacks per day, whereas the other 75 percent of the districts had one attack every sixteen days.

Five districts accounted for the majority of violence: Pech in Duke's AOR, which included the Korengal; Bermel and Sabari districts in Currahee's Khost Province; Tagab in Warrior's Kapisa Province; and Sayad Abad in Currahee's Wardak Province.

In July, the CIA estimated that there were some sixteen to twenty-two thousand insurgents in Afghanistan, with half, seven to eleven thousand, in our sector. And the majority of those were in or close to our "top five" districts.

We knew why the insurgents massed in RC-East; after all, many of the rat lines from their safe havens in the FATA of Pakistan ran through our sector, the mountainous terrain provided cover and concealment, and Kabul—the insurgent's crown jewels—lay in the center of our AOR.

As each commander talked about their operations, be they kinetic security ops, support to good governance, or working hand in hand with the provincial reconstruction teams on development and governance projects in their areas, I tried to wring out positive and negative lessons that we all could share. The daily patrols in the small villages and larger towns combined with precisely planned "knock and grabs" for those insurgents we located each day and night were meant to provide increased security for the locals: I wanted no Afghan to wake up to find a Taliban or other insurgent night letter, or worse, a headless corpse outside their compound walls.

It was hard for me to get precise statistics on just how much of the violence we tallied was as a result of our own operations into areas that had provided previous safe haven. As we added more French and Polish troops, we were increasingly expanding our operations in their sectors as well as in areas where we moved U.S. troops they had replaced. What was abundantly clear was that overall violence in RC-East in 2008 would be the highest since NATO arrived in 2001. It was already 30 percent higher year over year from 2007.

I worried that too many of our troops spent too much of their time chasing the insurgents in a relative handful of districts, protecting a minority of the overall population. We were making some progress taking the fight to the enemy, but we had to begrudgingly acknowledge the enemy was doing the same to us.

We spent a long time reviewing every provincial governor in RC-East. I tried to meet with a different governor each week, usually on their turf at their provincial center, and had my own thoughts on many of them: in my view, the best, like Governor Sayed Fazlullah Wahidi of Kunar, were caring, competent public servants who were doing an effective job with the limited resources provided by the Afghan central government, plus our own relatively extensive initiatives, to bolster the provincial and district leadership. The majority were not polished leaders, had differing ideas of public accountability, and desperately needed the advice they received from the provincial reconstruction team's commander and their State Department or USAID deputy. One or two of the governors were ineffective, politically connected appointees who were no better than thugs.

We worked with what we had, but I did my best to get the Independent Directorate of Local Governance (IDLG) director general, Mr. Jilani Popal, out into our provinces and districts to meet the leaders the central government appointed.

The development projects were generally a good news story. We had nearly doubled our own Commander's Emergency Response Program (CERP) funds provided to the CJTF and dispersed to the brigade commanders to support their own and the reconstruction team's priorities in their area. They included major road-building and paving projects in Kunar, down to small micro-hydroelectric turbines in high mountain streams in Panjshir, providing power to isolated villages. And then we had the major USAID and non-governmental organization (NGO)-funded projects, such as the USAID Khost-Gardez Pass Road. In several of these latter projects, our role was to explain the importance to the local population while preventing the insurgents from destroying the project during or after construction

Brigadier General James McConville led our development efforts, and had taken a small agricultural development program and figured out how to radically expand it. Reports from reconstruction teams indicated that agricultural knowledge, which had been passed down orally in a culture with a 10 to 15 percent literacy rate, had vanished as tens of thousands of farmers perished or stopped working the fields after twenty-plus years of conflict. As a result, U.S. civilian and military leaders sent American soldiers with agricultural expertise to Afghanistan to reintroduce that lost expertise among far-flung rural communities. Although the new program represented a marked change in how the coalition interacted with rural Afghans, it built upon a concept used successfully by U.S. citizen-soldiers during two decades of Central American deployments. The soldiers were organized into ADTs (agricultural development teams). There was a small team from the Missouri Army National Guard in Nangarhar and one from Texas in Ghazni already, but McConville wholeheartedly supported the program, planning for a significant expansion of the original effort during our fifteen months in Afghanistan.

The governors wanted more.

The ADTs were essentially professional farmers, agricultural scientists with advanced degrees, soils engineers, ranchers, beekeepers, veterinarians, you name it. For Army National Guardsmen, their combat tours in Afghanistan would be spent advising local farmers on everything from crop substitution, irrigation, animal husbandry, and harvest storage and processing to marketing the fruits of the farmer's labor. They were invaluable, a combat multiplier that I could not put a price on, and I too wanted more of them.

I was convinced that a small ADT, often just the size of a four-soldier fire team plus a leader, had a hugely disproportionate positive impact. Of course, they were vulnerable, and required security overwatch to ensure they were not ambushed or kidnapped. But it was worth it in my mind. I knew it would be years, maybe decades, before these efficient farming and husbandry methods would take hold in this tribal land, the people there so suspicious and distrusting of outsiders and foreign ways. But it was one of the best ways we could find to eventually wean the farmers off of poppy production, and the circle of opium production that seemed to enrich the Taliban more than the poppy farmer.

We concluded after all had briefed and we had had plenty of discussion that we were making progress, but much too slow, and somewhat uneven. We could clear, but then not hold. We could transform the local environment in many locations, but not in our most insurgent-infested areas. We could help connect the people to their provincial and central government, but could only marginally make those leaders better leaders. We were not losing, but none of us thought we could win this thing on the timeline we were on. We needed more resources. Not dollars, we had enough. We needed boots on the ground. Predators in the air. Farmers teaching farmers.

It was September. I had made my request for more soldiers and aerial intelligence, surveillance, and reconnaissance assets in June.

The support within the Pentagon and CENTCOM was significant. But I still had no clear commitment for our CJTF or RC-East.

It was time to speak more clearly.

The next evening my aide and public affairs officer, Lieutenant Colonel Rumi Nielson-Green, and I drove over to a small nondescript concrete and plywood building. Behind a simple backdrop, the public affairs team connected me to the Pentagon Press Room via a form of video teleconference. My second Pentagon press briefing began.

I hated to read from a script, thinking it often made leaders look unsure of their topic and, at worst, insincere. Years ago at Fort Campbell, when I was a battalion commander, our division commander was then Major General Jack Keane, a master at what appeared to be ad-libbed public speaking, but who inevitably was on message, inspirational to private, colonel, or civilian, and remarkably interesting. I studied him and his speaking method then, and I still tried to follow what seemed to be his basic and simple precepts: know your topic; know your audience; connect your audience to your topic in an interesting way; and speak simply but forcefully, with heartfelt passion.

The routine for these briefings was for me to make a statement about our current status in RC-East, followed by an open question-and-answer period with those journalists who had decided to attend that morning's brief back at the Pentagon. I had a fuzzy screen that allowed me to see the audience and moderator, and they me, likely no more clearly. The audio connection was solid. If they could not make out every detail of my "fuzzy" body language, they could hear my voice, my tone, my passion.

I started off with the bad news: *Insurgent attacks in Afghanistan had increased twenty to thirty percent since 2007.*

It wasn't hopeless, however. I said, "We are making steady progress," but defeating the seven to eleven thousand insurgents in RC-East "will take longer the way we are doing it now, as far as the resources we have."

"I'd like to speed that up," I announced, and made the argument for more U.S. troops, saying the numbers we needed were "in the thousands."

Then I laid out our winter campaign.

"This campaign has got two components. One of them is a strong military offensive and the other is a developmental surge."

I clearly told them that we were taking the fight to root out the insurgent where he hid in the winter: "We will pursue them wherever they run. We will attempt to intercept them, and we are going to destroy their resources. My intent is to eliminate the support areas within our sector to diminish the enemy's ability to operate next year."

I said that using some $480 million in 2008 CERP funds, we would "match the power we have here, both the hard power…as far as the [military] operations that we're going to do on the ground with our troops, as well as soft power, and that's the CERP, then, the development funds…"

I told them we would be seeking to provide jobs for the people most vulnerable to insurgent recruiting pitches: "They'll be doing things such as clearing ice and snow from roads, doing construction training workshops, road maintenance, distribution of essentials to villages that are basically isolated, such as food and clothes."

I said all that was needed, and we would also be providing roads, wells, schools, clinics, micro-hydroelectric plants, and more.

There were a few questions, and the broadcast was soon over.

I'm sure I was not as articulate as Jack Keane, but I was pretty certain they could hear and feel my passion. I was convinced this winter campaign would work because I felt the enemy was getting cocky and would seek to keep the pressure on us and the Afghans over winter, rather than retreating fully into the tribal areas of Pakistan. We would seek out those who stayed, employ those fence-sitters who just wanted to feed their families, and what I could not say publicly was that we would work with the Pakistani Army and Frontier Corps to make the Pakistani tribal areas equally inhospitable, should the insurgents cross the Durand Line. And our special operations teams would also help hunt them down, and show no mercy.

The questions were fair, educated, and showed a willingness to listen to what I had to say. I was honest—*no, I did not believe we were losing in Afghanistan, just not winning on a timeline the American people could support over the long term.* A few wanted me to wander into classified areas, such as the recent border operation, but I could not and would not go there.

At the end of the brief, Rumi and I reviewed how we thought the conference had gone. We thought I got our message out. We would have to continue to echo my points with our weekly engagements with visiting journalists and think tank experts. I knew that in strategic communications, one must constantly communicate, communicate, communicate. Like many senior leaders, speaking to journalists was not in my comfort zone, but I also knew it was a critical responsibility that I had to embrace, and improve upon.

CHAPTER 16

*"It is foolish and wrong to mourn the men who died.
Rather we should thank God that such men lived."*
General George S. Patton Jr.

Wednesday, September 10, 2008

ost soldiers just called it "Wilderness." Technically renamed Forward Operating Base Tellier after Sergeant Zachary Tellier, a fallen paratrooper from the 82nd Airborne Division, the base was carved into the mountainside along the KG Pass Road. In spite of the sporadic traffic that used the sometimes dirt, sometimes gravel, sometimes paved road that was under construction, the area was remote, generally hostile to our presence, and felt like you were a very long way from fellow American or NATO troops. This description fit many of our remote operating bases, but this one more than most. So "Wilderness" it remained.

We flew late in the morning from Bagram. As the Black Hawk banked and slowed for landing into the landing zone, I got a good look at Wilderness. I was no stranger to the base, and I could see Kilbride and Heater waiting along the edge, trying to avoid the downwash of chalky dirt and small rocks that served as our initial greeting every time we landed to see our troops.

Captain Tom Kilbride and First Sergeant Eddie Heater, of Troop C, 1st Squadron, 61st Cavalry, were one of those command teams that seemed textbook-made for their roles as commander and senior non-commissioned officer of a remote American base plopped down in bad-guy country. Tom was just under thirty and looked like a Hollywood soldier, but had years of combat experience leading progressively larger units in Iraq and now Afghanistan. Heater was the proverbial senior "non-com," head shaved, articulate in the blunt way I found so refreshing in American non-commissioned officers, and serious as a heart attack when he needed to be. I trusted these guys with a real challenge: keep the Khost-Gardez Pass Road open, and keep the Haqqani network from stopping the road's continued improvement and construction.

But I was deeply concerned that they did not have enough resources to be successful. There was more and more intelligence indicating massing of insurgents right across the border, and the Salerno attacks also indicated foreign fighters were increasingly involved in attack planning and execution. Kilbride and his troops had just had a significant operation in which they killed twelve insurgents in a shoulder-high field of corn while having one man wounded by small arms fire. After the battle, the soldiers found a camera among the dead. The playback was chilling, showing large numbers of enemy fighters traversing mountain tracks, well armed, and with what looked to be quasi-military bearing and training. The video showed American soldiers, in one instance standing around in the open, completely vulnerable to enemy attack. Luckily, the insurgents had been content with filming their opponents for later study, not in attacking them then.

Kilbride and Heater gave me a good rundown of the operation, and their concerns. Jalal Haqqani had recently said in the Taliban media that he "banned" the construction of the KG Pass Road, and his fighters routinely placed night letters in the villages that sat adjacent to the road, warning against any collaboration with the construction crews, Afghan forces, or Americans. He clearly could not push us off Wilderness, but he could make the road work even more dangerous to the civilian construction crews, and to those of Kilbride's cavalry troop who patrolled the road and surrounding countryside.

We walked the firebase, which was improved in defenses and amenities since my last visit. They even had a brick-and-mortar dining facility, where we stopped to grab water and meet the CBS journalist and cameraman embedded with the outfit.

Lara Logan and her cameraman had been at Wilderness for days, had witnessed and recorded several of the operations, and were well versed in the situation. We sat down in the mess hall and talked about the situation in Pakistan as well as in this part of eastern Afghanistan. Rumi Nielson-Green, my public affairs officer, had told me Logan was no pushover. She was an attractive and fit blonde born in South Africa, with a friendly smile, and I was certain our soldiers initially found her presence this far forward in the fight disorienting, but welcome. Impressively, she knew more about the Haqqanis, and the Waziris across the border, and in general, more about this particular AOR and the war here, than any of the previous journalists I had talked with.

I felt it was my responsibility to keep our American public informed, so Rumi ensured we had a steady stream of seasoned journalists in RC-East, many of whom I allowed to embed with units, and others with limited time that I had fly with my deputy commanders or me for a day as we circulated the battlefield. It was a calculated but mitigated risk: we had to ensure their safety, as much as we could, and we never knew exactly what they would write or say. I had to trust that the majority really wanted to know what was factually going on, and that as long as we—Rumi, and both Mark Milley and Jim McConville, our deputy commanding generals who also briefed journalists—were straight shooters, and did not try to spin our mistakes or challenges, I felt we had a reasonable chance of getting our message out.

CBS' *60 Minutes* was doing a piece on Afghanistan, specifically Forward Operating Base Wilderness itself, and Lara was their foreign correspondent. Rumi and I agreed that I would be interviewed on camera during the time Logan was embedded at Wilderness.

It was a bright and warm afternoon when we met out near the landing zone for the simple interview. Two metal chairs facing each other and the cameraman with a sound mike were the set. Lara asked questions, probing questions, and I did my best to honestly answer them.

"In 2005 I was told the same thing as 2006 and in 2007, 'Oh it's not the enemy's stronger, it's that we're more successful,'" she said. A statement, not a question.

"Well, you know I'm not telling you that," I said. "I'm telling you that the enemy did increase from twenty to thirty percent this last year and you haven't asked yet but I'll tell you they are doing more complex activities, which concerns me greatly. So I'm not here to blow smoke up anybody's dress. I'm not."

She asked about foreign fighters, the Pakistani safe haven for the enemy, and the porous border: "That seems like an impossible task."

"I think it makes it extraordinarily difficult," I responded. "There's no doubt in my mind. Americans should know that we defend ourselves and we fire right back inside Pakistan because it's a threat."

We talked after the interview as I walked back to the Black Hawk. She said she was pregnant, and that she wanted to travel for a story on the other side of the border, the FATA, later that month. I was surprised about the former and doubtful about the wisdom of the latter, but kept my opinions to myself.

I never did see the *60 Minutes* piece, "Fighting in a 'Hornet's Nest,'" while I was in Afghanistan, but both Patty and Kelly saw it back in the States. They gave me grief for the "not here to blow smoke up anybody's dress" comment.

"What were you thinking?"

Two years later, at an army course for soon-to-be three-star generals, they showed us the interview. The army's top public affairs officer, a brigadier general and a colleague, focused on my comments. He said I was clearly at ease with the press, knew my message and the background information, and knew how to subtly answer the questions asked and get my word out.

I think he gave me an A for honesty and the overall interview, but a D for my word choice! Years later, I still reflect on the interview: preciseness is important to leaders, whether in directing a complex operation or communicating to a public audience.

A week after the interview, a Humvee patrolling outside Forward Operating Base Wilderness hit an IED, killing four soldiers and an interpreter.

On Friday morning, September 12, at 8:45 a.m., Sergeant Major Camacho and I were back on the airfield ramp, the sun already hot, the troopers in formation sweating, as we paid honors to two troopers: Chief Warrant Officer Four Mike Slebodnik and Private First Class Michael E. Murdock. I did not know young Murdock, who had been killed in action at COP Lybert near the Pakistani border the day prior, but that didn't matter. He was one of my troopers, and every death was personal to me.

I did know Mr. Slebodnik. Years before, Mike and I had served together. A family man with small children, Mike was thinking of getting out of the army. He had enlisted right out of high school, served as an aero-scout observer in Operation Desert Storm, and had clearly paid his dues. We talked a long while, and I could see Mike didn't dislike the army or army aviation. He just needed a new challenge. A way to actualize all that he knew was in himself.

Why not try out for the Night Stalkers? Mike knew of my background with the 160th Special Operations Aviation Regiment. He was intrigued.

I don't know if it was our talk that kept Mike in the army. He went on to serve as a senior chief warrant officer. At the time of his death, he was one of the most experienced armed reconnaissance pilots in the 101st, and was flying and leading in the 2nd Squadron, 17th Cavalry.

On Thursday, September 11, Mike had been piloting his Kiowa Warrior near Combat Outpost Najil, in Laghman Province. An insurgent fired at the aircraft and a single round hit Mike in the leg, severing his femoral artery. His co-pilot took over and got Mike to the base where he was treated first by medics, then medevacked out. He bled out before making it to the hospital at Bagram.

So here I was at Mike's ramp ceremony. This was not the first time I felt I had helped keep a soldier in the army, only to then have them killed in combat.

Kneeling at Mike's coffin, I remembered Steve Reich. Captain Steve Reich had served as a staff officer and company commander in the 12th Aviation Brigade when I commanded it from 1998 to 2000. A former star pitcher for the West Point baseball team who actually played in the minor leagues before being called back to the army, Steve was an incredible athlete and a very quick study. He had a perpetual boyish grin and Disney-movie all-American good looks that belied his age-defying competence. I made him a liaison officer to then Brigadier General Craddock's staff when we moved into Kosovo for the first time. He was brilliant working with a senior staff in the precursor to what became Camp Bondsteel: at the time, little more than hastily erected tents with some concertina wire surrounding them, on a windswept hill.

When we returned to garrison at Wiesbaden, Germany, from Kosovo, Steve and I frequently talked about the army, about combat aviation, and his future. He had a German girlfriend, a doctor, and was thinking about marriage, getting out, and maybe living in Germany. But I could see he was not tired of being an army aviator. We kept going back to our time in Kosovo, and how important the work was.

"Steve, what about trying out the 160th? You are still young enough to be an operator."

And so it went. Steve was an exceptional special operations aviator, and a superb leader. He played an early and important role immediately after 9/11 in Afghanistan, and special operators from the tiered units loved Steve: his youthful exuberance, and yet profound competence.

Steve Reich was killed during his fourth Afghanistan tour. A special operations aviation major with the 160th Special Operations Aviation Regiment, he was air mission commander of a Night Stalker MH-47E sent to rescue a four-man SEAL team that was part of Operation Red Wings, an action to capture or kill Ahmad Shah and his team of insurgents located near Sawtalo Sar Mountain in the Pech District of Kunar, a story told later in the movie *Lone Survivor*. His aircraft was hit by an RPG fired by one of Shah's men, and crashed, killing Steve, seven other Night Stalkers, and eight SEALs, including the SEAL Team 10 ground commander, Lieutenant Commander Erik S. Kristensen. Steve was just thirty-four years old.

As I knelt next to Mike's casket, I was conflicted as I thought of Mike's and Steve's deaths. I thought I should feel remorse, and guilt. Instead, I felt saddened by the loss of a comrade, but strangely proud of being a very small part of their service to their units, to the army, and to our nation. As volunteer soldiers, we didn't get to choose our wars; our nation did that for us. But it was up to us to serve honorably, to "have the back" of our fellow soldiers in our squads, platoons, and companies, and sometimes, thank God only sometimes, to die in doing so.

I got off my knee, said a simple prayer, and gently but firmly placed my two-star commander's coin on top of the U.S. flag draped over Mike's casket. I did the same with Murdock's casket. And I walked away.

At 10:30 p.m. that night, we had a smaller ramp ceremony for two Navy SEALs killed early on the 12th in a firefight in Kapisa. The SEALs had killed twelve insurgents, but lost two men: Senior Chief John W. Marcum and Chief Richard Freiwald. The special operators did many things in their own unique way, and the ceremony out at the airfield ramp was private, with just a handful of us senior leaders from the CJTF attending. The grief was intense among the bearded special operators and the clean-shaven senior special operations commanders as they talked about the two men. These men were not in my command, but they were Americans, fellow warriors, and I shared the grief of their comrades. When it was my turn, I placed my commander's coin on top of the flag-draped coffins, which were already covered by gold SEAL tridents, and stepped off the aircraft into the pitch-black night.

CHAPTER 17

*"The power of decisive leadership develops only from practice.
There is nothing mystical about it. It comes from a clear-eyed
willingness to accept life's risks, recognizing that only the enfeebled
are comforted by thoughts of an existence devoid of struggle."*
Brigadier General S. L. A. Marshall

Saturday, September 13, 2008

Combat Outpost Najil, where Mike Slebodnik was shot, was built on a steep hillside in the Alishang Valley of Laghman Province. Laghman sat astride insurgent lines of communications—mountain trails to be exact—between Kunar to the east and Kabul to the west. The base was close to Alishang village, which acted as the district center for Mehtar Lam District.

Flying north from our operating base and reconstruction team headquarters for this province at Mehtar Lam town, we flew over several remote settlements built above the Najil River, where the dirt road that connects the outpost and district center to Mehtar Lam, Jalalabad, and Kabul parallels the river. Babur, a direct descendent of both Genghis Khan and Timur (Tamerlane), camped and hunted in the valley around 1520. He later conquered Kabul, and later yet founded the Mughal Empire. From the air, it did not look like much had changed since: the rock and sunbaked homes looked timeless, and there were no vehicles in sight along the road.

There wasn't much to indicate that the area had seen significant action during the Soviet incursion. I had read that a mujahedeen commander, Sher Pashah, had commanded a small unit in the vicinity. Surrounded in Alishang village by Democratic Republic of Afghanistan soldiers and their Soviet advisors, Pashah lost fourteen fighters in minutes, with another fifty wounded, and many of the village civilians dead or wounded. Using mortars, RPGs, and heavy machine guns, they were able to break out, and eventually prevail.

There was no sign now of that battle. But I knew in the Badrow Hills north of the valley and the Hindu Kush even further to the north lurked waypoints for transiting insurgents, and Combat Outpost Najil, established in late 2006, was proving to be a real irritant to the insurgents' freedom of movement. And hence it was a target.

A young lieutenant and his platoon sergeant met Camacho and me at the helipad. We hoped to see improvements since our first visit to Najil. Manned by a platoon of National Guardsman from 1st Battalion, 178th Infantry Regiment, of the 33rd Brigade Combat Team from Illinois, they had not been part of our train-up, nor had we been part of theirs. Camacho had gone ballistic as he saw the misplaced fighting positions, the sad mortar pit, and the overall crappy living conditions. Since they did not know our standards, we made no reliefs, but we did make immediate changes, plus got them more resources, which clearly they needed, everything from sandbags to a functioning field kitchen.

It was midday and still hot in mid-September. We walked up to the top of the outpost along the dusty, steep road that traversed the camp from top to bottom, sweating in the dry yet intense heat. The fine chalky dust covered most things in camp, and soon we looked as dirty as the rest of the soldiers who called Najil home. Clean running water was scarce, showers rudimentary to say the least, but the soldiers were in good humor, positive, and proud of the work they had done.

"Best mortar pit in Afghanistan, sir!" said the mortar section sergeant, and I had to agree with him. He and his team, most from Chicago or the immediate area, had rebuilt the entire pit, and it was now perfectly positioned, postured for immediate action, and yet protected from incoming. I had seen a fair number of mortar pits in the mountains and hills of Afghanistan, and this was really good.

"I believe you are right, Sergeant. You all have really done a great job here. I am impressed."

I did not say that often.

Vince Camacho was impressed too, but would never say so. Instead he pulled aside some of the non-commissioned officers and had a good talk, checked on the chow with the younger troopers, which was improving, and found a .50-caliber machine gun that he didn't think was in proper position. He helped them move it to expand its useful field of fire.

We flew back to Bagram in the late afternoon for the combat update brief.

Overnight, Combat Outpost Najil was attacked. It was a complex attack by more than a handful of fighters, using mortars, rockets, and RPGs to try to overrun the outpost. It turned out Camacho had been right. The .50-caliber machine gun in its new position was devastating, and the mortar team earned their pay too. The defending platoon from Captain Luke Gosnell's Company C killed a good number of insurgents, captured a few, which was rare, and overall did a superb job of not only defending Najil, but really putting the hurt on the insurgents in the valley.

I have been asked in the years since our deployment about our National Guard units in CJTF-101. I don't have much patience for those who denigrate the guardsmen, their leadership, or their willingness and ability to fight or work the rest of counterinsurgency operations. I often wished that we had been able to train with the National Guard units prior to our deployment, and ensure they had our standards and tactics and technical procedures from the start. I wished the same for every non-101st active unit that came into the CJTF; in some limited cases, we were able to send observer-mentors to the brigade-level train-ups, and in others we were able to send out intelligence and operations guidance, but it was not the same as being in the same chain of command for months or years prior to deployment. I couldn't fault the units, active or guard; it was the way the army decided to address the multiple deployments of brigade and smaller-level units. While I understood the intent—the flexibility to deploy brigade combat teams independently of the division headquarters they were associated with and had trained under—it was a challenge to build cohesive formations with similar cultures when the first time you worked together was on the battlefield. But the overall performance of the many National Guard units and their soldiers in our deployment, be it an infantry battalion, an engineer brigade, the numerous army aviators, or the small agricultural development teams working with Afghan farmers, was really good.

Later in the week, TF Duke's Commander Colonel John Spiszer and I flew to Kabul, landing in the field within the Armed Forces Headquarters Complex. We picked up General Bismillah Khan (General BK), the chief of Afghanistan's army, as well as Lieutenant General Mohammad Ghulab Mangal, the deputy minister of the interior, responsible for the ANP and border police, and the 201st Corps commander, Major General Rahim Wardak. Months earlier, General BK and I had resolved to spend time together visiting our troops, rather than just meeting every few weeks in his headquarters or at one of the ISAF briefings called by General McKiernan. The Kunar and Nuristan area was a major effort for both of us and our respective troops; in several camps, we were now partnered with the Afghan Army and border police, training together, patrolling together, and fighting side by side when needed. That is where we headed.

General BK and I got along very well. He was a big man, burly, with a cropped beard that was more gray than black. A Tajik from Panjshir, Bismillah Khan had been a soldier since attending Kabul Military University. During the war with the Soviet Union, he fought with Ahmad Shah Massoud. When the Taliban took over in 1996, he became a senior commander in the Northern Alliance fighting them. He had been army chief of staff since 2002. Unlike some in the Afghan leadership, General BK was a real fighter. As we flew together, he would point out obscure fighting positions in the hills and mountain slopes, and tell of the battles that had taken place there.

General BK's English was not strong, although I suspected he understood far more than he let on. My Dari and Pashtu were almost nonexistent, so we spoke using General Wardak's assistance, as he spoke good English.

We had some contentious issues to deal with, and we discussed them as we flew along the Kabul River, past the Sarobi Dam with its almost surreal emerald water and over the green fields of Nangarhar. Since I arrived, BK and Minister of Defense Wardak had asked me for further assistance in a village far to the north in Nuristan, along the border of Chitral, deep in the towering mountains of the Hindu Kush. They insisted that insurgents were using Barg-e Matal as a rendezvous and kickoff point into Nuristan after crossing high mountain passes from the Pak North-West Frontier. They had army troops and police there, but could barely keep them resupplied. My staff and I had been over their requests multiple times, and my intent was to consolidate our far northern outposts, not expand them. They were all generally remote, the roads and trails nonexistent or so vulnerable to accidents and attacks as to be unusable, and therefore air-centric for resupply and combat support. I had no intention of giving in to placing U.S. or ISAF troops at Barg-e Matal, but did agree to help from time to time with aerial resupply.

In turn, I wanted General BK's approval, or at least grudging concurrence, for my plan to close Combat Outpost Lybert, an isolated outpost in northern Kunar east of Gawardesh that had outlived its usefulness. The outpost was named for Staff Sergeant Patrick Lee Lybert, who along with Staff Sergeant Jared Monti was killed in action on Hill 2610 in June 2006 during a 3rd Squadron, 71st Cavalry operation. Hill 2610, a mountain at least eight thousand feet tall, was just west of the ridgeline that became Combat Outpost Lybert, established in late summer 2006. In September 2009, Sergeant Monti would be awarded the Medal of Honor, posthumously.

It seemed most of the outposts and operating bases in Kunar and Nuristan were named after fallen troopers: Lybert, Monti, Fritsche,

Keating, Bostick, Lowell, Restrepo, Honaker-Miracle, Fenty. I knew it was an effort to honor our fallen, to give their death some meaning in a war with sometimes opaque and often temporary tactical objectives. But when it came time to close these outposts, it was gut-wrenching for the soldiers that occupied the sites, as well as those who had fought alongside their namesake, perhaps even seeing their deaths. And back home, the families found it heartrending, confounding, almost as if, by closing the outpost named for their loved one, we were culpable in a second death. We were killing their memory.

We landed first at Forward Operating Base Joyce, near Serkani. Captain Mark Davis, commander of Company D, 1st Battalion, 26th Infantry, met us. General BK, Mangal, and Wardak headed to see their Afghan troops and police, while Davis gave me a walking tour of the operating base and we discussed plans for its expansion. Joyce was named after a fallen trooper too: Lance Corporal Kevin Joyce, from E Company, 2nd Battalion, 3rd Marines, killed in action in Kunar in June 2005.

Next we flew north to Naray, landing at Forward Operating Base Bostick. Again the Afghans went to be with their troops, and Lieutenant Colonel Jim Markert, Task Force Raider commander, and his operations officer Major Tom Nelson and I discussed their plans for future operations in TF Raider's area of operations.

We headed back south to Asadabad, where we visited Afghan and U.S. troops together, then went into town to meet Kunar Governor Sayed Wahidi. Asadabad Provincial Reconstruction Team Commander Dan Dwight came along. It was clear he and Wahidi had forged a close working relationship, and quite possibly an actual friendship. We talked about the big day we would have tomorrow, with the visit of a high-ranking dignitary.

In the late afternoon we flew back to Kabul, where we dropped the Afghan generals at Bismillah Khan's headquarters. It had been a long day in the late summer humidity and heat, but I was satisfied. This was far better than endless meetings in stuffy offices, bent over maps, describing to each other the terrain and the troops we had on the ground. Here we saw it, could talk with the troops themselves and their leaders, and make decisions.

Before we parted, General BK agreed with me: *We should close COP Lybert.* I gave the order as soon as I returned to Bagram.

Wednesday, September 17, was yet another hot summer day at Bagram. I started the day with terrible news: an IED outside Wilderness had killed five. I wanted to fly out to the outpost myself, but knew that the last thing Kilbride and his soldiers needed right now was the division commander in their midst. And I had other duties to attend to that day.

The midmorning sun was a blinding white on the Bagram Airfield tarmac as the C-17 taxied in. General Dempsey (still the acting commander of U.S. Central Command) had already arrived, and we greeted Secretary of Defense Robert Gates as he bound down the aircraft steps, looking fresh and well rested in a pressed dark suit and tie.

The secretary had met earlier with President Karzai and Minister of Defense Wardak in Kabul and visited the U.S. embassy.

I first met Gates on a cold, overcast day in February 2008 at Fort Campbell, Kentucky. He had flown in to preside at Mark Milley's promotion ceremony to brigadier general. I greeted him as he got off his Gulfstream executive jet at Campbell Army Airfield, and we rode together over to the promotion ceremony, and then again later in the day as he met with spouses of units deployed to Iraq, and to a short visit to our Wounded Warrior Transition Unit. Mark had been the secretary's junior military assistant, and they got along fabulously. During that visit, I found Gates to be open, friendly, inquiring, and a very quick study. I hoped this time to build on that early rapport. We got in my Suburban, and headed to the special operations task force camp inside Bagram. Secretary Gates' senior military assistant, Lieutenant General David "Rod" Rodriguez, rode with us.

Vice Admiral Bill McRaven, an old friend and the special ops commander, met us at the SOF headquarters, a plywood-on-plywood building that looked like it had been built by combat engineers and Seabees in a week, and yet oozed with technology.

The special operations task force brief centered on the cross-border operations that had been executed and others in planning. I could tell from Gates' questions that he was measuring the risk and payoff from what had already occurred and its blowback, especially in Pakistan, and the potential gain. Maybe we had already made our point to the insurgents and the Pakistani government, such as it was inside the FATA and Waziristan. We could not tolerate an insurgent safe haven on the border.

The next stop was lunch for the secretary with troopers at the dining facility. It was a good mix, and Gates shooed us generals away. Rod and I had lunch together, and I gave him my assessment of the situation in RC-East.

The next stop was back across the airfield to the 455th Air Expeditionary Wing. Brigadier General Mike "Mobile" Holmes was the commander and met us outside the operations center. Mike was a balding, crusty-looking F-15 fighter pilot with an easy smile and a relaxed style that put airmen at ease and yet got results. He was hugely competent at coordinating and providing air power and close air support for all of Afghanistan. We worked together to apply combat power when and where needed to achieve the counterinsurgency effects our commanders needed on a variety of very diverse fronts.

Mobile and his team briefed the secretary on how they did precision targeting and close air support, and the measures they used to avoid collateral damage and civilian casualties. The secretary was deeply interested and I could see he was taking mental notes. Next, we walked outside to a parked A-10, and Gates got a walk-around brief from young officers and NCOs while the press watched and filmed. The A-10 "Warthog" is not a sleek fighter jet or a massive high-technology bomber. It is a weapon of war, the infantryman's and tanker's ground war, a chubby but menacing airframe built around a high-speed, absolutely devastating GAU-8A Avenger 30-mm cannon which fires 3,900 rounds a minute, each shell almost a foot long and weighing a pound and a half.

Close air support (CAS) in Afghanistan was critical to our troops, ISAF, and the Afghan security forces. By late summer 2008, the U.S. and ISAF had been beaten up in the press and by President Karzai for what seemed to be a growing number of civilian casualties, many resulting from aircraft supporting ground units during a troops-in-contact (TIC) response. In some cases, the insurgents attacked from *qalats* or buildings where women and children were present, unbeknownst to us. The pressure was intense to reduce the casualties, and General McKiernan had recently put out orders placing limitations on the use of close air support. Part of Secretary Gates' visit to the 455th was to determine how we targeted and how we attempted to reduce collateral damage.

On the battlefield, I thought the A-10 was the best fixed-wing close air support platform. It operated low and slow enough for the pilot to actually see the target with his own eyes, and discern the friendlies that may be nearby. And the GAU 30-mm was a highly accurate but devastating weapon system which could be used with friendly troopers fairly close. I knew that the fast movers, usually F-15Es or F-16s but sometimes the B-1B bomber, had advanced sensors that gave their pilots situational awareness, day and night, but their weapons loads were usually 250- or 500-pound bombs, which made engagements near troops in contact very difficult and dangerous, even with modern precision targeting and guidance. But no matter the platform, when the fight was on and the enemy rounds incoming, it was hugely reassuring, and often a game changer tactically, when close air support came on station, be it an A-10, F-15E, or B-1B. The air force close air support, and navy and marine when we received it, saved many an American, NATO, and Afghan trooper's life during our fifteen months in Afghanistan. Years later, I still thank those I meet who flew or supported those missions.

We crossed back to the other side of the airfield and boarded a waiting C-130. The secretary and I climbed up the short ladder into the back end of the cockpit. Sitting side by side, we watched the aircrew go through startup and taxi. Gates was quiet, as if thinking through what he had just seen. Aloft, we flew towards Jalalabad, the crew pointing out key terrain and camps along the way. Sitting down on the backbench, it was hard to see, and Gates didn't say much, nor did I. I figured he was probably feeling the time zone shift and the heat, and could stand a short break.

At the Jalalabad airfield, TF Duke Commander John Spiszer met us as we piled off the ramp of the C-130, and we walked over the fist-sized gravel to Spiszer's headquarters, another plywood building, but considerably less impressive in its kit than the special operations headquarters. Kunar Governor Wahidi and the Asadabad Provincial Reconstruction Team leaders, including Dan Dwight, were already in the conference room, a fairly large, plywood room with a long U-shaped plywood desk. Spiszer, the governor, and Dwight gave the secretary a detailed rundown of the enemy and friendly situation in the area, with a particular emphasis on Kunar, which of course was one of our most violent areas in all of Regional Command-East. We discussed the role of the Afghan security forces, and focused on the Afghan National Police and border police, and all we were trying to do to professionalize their forces, outfit them with proper equipment and connectivity, and partner with them in operations.

The secretary, Rod, and I went back out to the airfield and boarded my Black Hawk. We returned via Mehtar Lam, where I pointed out our base, and then went to Sarobi, flying almost directly over where the French had been ambushed, and then Tagab. We flew about two thousand feet above the ground, and the scenery was spectacular. Gates sat in the outermost seat, facing out the rear door window, with a great view, as I pointed out key terrain, roads, rivers, fields, and camps, as well as scenes of some of our fights. He was talkative and more animated than he had been on the C-130, and I think he truly enjoyed the flight.

He reboarded his C-17 at Bagram in the late afternoon, and headed to London.

As I wrote in my journal that night, I thought about what the secretary had gained from the visit. He met Governor Wahidi, a standing governor, who was likely the best of the fourteen governors in RC-East. He experienced the professionalism of our air force wing and the special operations task force. Finally, he saw up close the raw, magnificent, but sometimes truly treacherous terrain of eastern Afghanistan, which impacted almost everything we did. I hoped this was enough to make the trip worthwhile.

Later that night, a soldier at Forward Operating Base Monti was killed in action. Five killed that morning at Wilderness plus this soldier. Twenty-four hours later, at midnight, commanders, staff, and I met once again on the dark airfield ramp in front of six metal coffins, and bid the dead a final farewell.

A military ceremony with ancient roots, our ramp farewell was a cathartic rendering of honors to one who served and died serving their fellow comrades, their unit, and their nation. To observe a single ramp ceremony from the sidelines as I did before I assumed command was an emotionally powerful event. You could not help but feel, secretly, fortunate to be alive. But to be a part of a multitude of ceremonies, almost nightly, and to feel the loss as a commander in combat who one way or another ordered these troopers to execute what turned out to be their last operation, was different: deeply disturbing, a rending of my spirit, a cause to examine my previous actions and future plans. And yet, I had to hide that from my soldiers, and my leaders.

CHAPTER 18

"My own soul is my most faithful friend. My
own heart, my truest confidant."
Babur

Saturday, September 20, 2008

That evening we held our normal joint operations center Saturday evening ceremony, where we honored the casualties from the month with moments of silence, as we gazed at their pictures displayed on the main screen. Normally a bustling, high-tempo place with a constant buzz, it was perhaps easy to forget that beyond the Predator feeds of ongoing kinetic ops, blue force tracker maps, and so much more information, all displayed on multiple large screens, there was in fact a real world where troops talked to Afghan farmers, shared tea with local tribal leaders, and at times, did all they could to find and kill a reclusive but stubborn enemy. I reminded myself that night that it was the simple events like this and the ramp ceremonies that served to remind those at headquarters in Bagram what was truly at stake outside the wire.

I was barely back in my office when the operations center called me back. There had been a massive bombing in Islamabad, at the Marriott Hotel. On the large screen was a TV feed, showing major destruction to the front of the hotel, which was still burning, sending a black tornado-like cloud of smoke into the dark sky. There were casualties.

"Have we heard from Colonel Dapore and the liaison team?"

"We are trying to contact them now, sir."

The Marriott served as a home away from home for U.S. and other diplomats, international businessmen, and closet spies, as well as the handful of military liaison teams working with our Pakistani counterparts. It was Saturday night and mid-evening in Islamabad, a perfect time to hang out at the Marriott. It was also Ramadan, and time for iftar, the evening breaking of the daylong fast, and the Marriott likely had one of the finest iftar banquets in Islamabad.

A perfect time for a bombing.

We knew the chairman, Admiral Mullen, had visited Islamabad earlier in the week, and had likely stayed with his security and communications team at the Marriott. The hotel was close to the diplomatic quarter and the U.S. embassy, and was considered to have stringent security. It was common for the U.S. embassy to book rooms for visiting American delegations at the Marriott. Military and other government agency personnel working temporarily at the embassy were housed there as well.

We also knew that Pakistani President Asif Ali Zardari had given his first public address earlier in the day, and had lashed out against homegrown terrorism, declaring his government would stop terrorists from using Pakistan as a safe haven to attack other countries. Zadari's wife, former Pakistani Prime Minister Benazir Bhutto, had been assassinated as she departed a campaign rally in December 2007. The daughter of former Prime Minister Zulfikar Ali Bhutto, she was a groundbreaking female politician: she became the first democratically elected woman head of an Islamic state. Educated at Harvard and Oxford, she worked to deregulate Pakistan's economy, build capitalism, and cut the influence of trade unions. Twice dismissed by Pakistan's president, she eventually left Pakistan for Dubai, where she spent some nine years. She returned to Pakistan in 2007, and was the leading candidate to win the general election for president, scheduled in early 2008. She had made many enemies over the years, but had been a survivor—until December 27, 2007, when after attending a party rally in Rawalpindi, she stood up through the sunroof of her vehicle to wave at supporters. Several shots rang out, followed by an explosion. She died at the hospital.

Her party went on to win the general election, and her husband, Asif Ali Zardari, took her place as president of Pakistan, vowing to wage war against terrorism.

It would take weeks to understand exactly what happened at the Marriott that night. Within twenty-four hours, the Pakistanis said a large dump truck loaded with an estimated thirteen hundred pounds of explosives had detonated as the driver tried to drive through the Marriott's security barriers. The next day, Sunday, the government released a security camera video showing a truck driving up to the barricade, then a small explosion with fire in the truck cab, and the local security guards rushing to put it out with fire extinguishers. The camera freezes. What is not seen is the actual primary explosion, which created a crater twenty-four feet deep and almost sixty feet wide, according to Pakistani Interior Minister Rehman Malik. The blast caused a natural gas leak that set the Marriott on fire, blew down the trees surrounding the parking lot, and left dozens of cars burned-out hulks. Malik said they believed fifty-seven people were killed, and another 256 injured. Among the dead was the Czech ambassador to Pakistan.

That night, we were concerned about our own. It seemed like forever, but was only minutes before Colonel Dapore reported in. He and his team had been eating dinner at the Marriott when the bomb went off. We didn't have any details, but Dapore and his team were OK.

They had been lucky. A National Guardsman from Ohio, unflappable, with an urge to serve where others would not or could not, Colonel Jim Dapore was a perfect choice to lead a liaison team working with difficult partners in an exotic but dangerous place. Dapore and his team were all seasoned soldiers; that's why they were there, after all. Seasoned enough to know that they had cheated death, this time.

We found out later that two U.S. servicemen were killed in the Marriott blast: navy cryptologist Matthew O'Bryant and Air Force Major Rodolfo

Ivan Rodriguez. Several marines had been in the hotel and had been injured. Two days later, at 2:00 a.m. on Tuesday, September 23, we held a ramp ceremony at Bagram for Chief O'Bryant with full honors, as if he had died in our formations in Afghanistan, and sent him home.

On Sunday, the army chief of chaplains, Major General Doug Carver, came in for an office call. He was out checking on soldiers and the ministry teams we had at division, brigade, and battalion levels throughout Afghanistan. Doug was a friend: we had served together in Iraq in 2003 when he was the V Corps and CJTF 7 command chaplain. Doug had come into the army as a field artillery officer in the seventies, left to pursue his chaplaincy studies as a Southern Baptist, and came back to the army. He understood soldiers and soldiering, and I always found him particularly attuned to the demands of leadership in tough circumstances.

I gave him a rundown on how I saw our challenges, especially at the small-unit level; squads and platoons at isolated posts, so remote they saw their battalion chaplain only infrequently. We tried to fly chaplains to many of our outposts, and they would hold small Christian services, not specific to any one denomination. At times, a Jewish Rabbi would come into the theater, and we would do our best to fly him around as well. We had even less coverage for our Muslim soldiers.

I was a huge believer in the need for chaplains in military service. I myself was not particularly religious. Born a Roman Catholic into an army family that moved frequently, I attended Catholic schools in Minnesota, Kentucky, and Hawaii, but felt much more at home in the public schools that made up the majority of my education. As a child, my parents and I routinely went to Sunday mass, usually followed by brunch at the officers' club. I still remember 1964 to '65 at Schofield Barracks, Hawaii, my father resplendent in his army white uniform, my mother in a fashionable brightly colored dress and matching hat, as we socialized with friends and my father's fellow company grade officers as we waited to file into church. The kids hoped the chaplain's sermon would be short, so we could head to the officers' club and the awesome brunch they served, followed by horsing around on the O club grounds as our parents enjoyed a quiet Sunday with friends.

And then the 25th Infantry Division deployed to Vietnam, and the fathers were gone. We still went to church, and sometimes brunch, but it was never the same again. Some of my friends' fathers never came home, at least not alive. It served as a sober awakening for an eleven-year-old, and I saw religion differently from then on. As an adult, and later as a parent, I was a poor example, usually avoiding church. But Patty and I still ensured our kids grew up Catholic, with all the sacraments. I think my children and certainly Patty knew that I had my doubts about Catholicism in particular and organized religion in general. I seldom went to church, and usually as a family we were the "bad" Catholics who attended church on Christmas and Easter, but not in between.

But in war, or just when deployed, I gravitated back to church. Maybe it was the simple services in a field environment that appealed to me. I will never forget the Sunday service our chaplain held in the cramped and heaving forecastle of the USS *America* as we steamed through rough seas to invade Haiti in 1994. I was a battalion commander in the 160th Special Operations Aviation Regiment, the Night Stalkers. The plan was bold and complicated, involved joint operations at night from the aircraft carrier and our sixty-plus helicopters, including my twenty-five-ton heavy Chinook helicopters, and there were many unknowns. I wasn't alone in the forecastle praying that evening.

Later, in deployments to Albania, Kosovo, Iraq, and now in Afghanistan, I regularly attended services, such as they were. It did not matter if they were Catholic to me or to most of our troopers; the service was a place to think about things other than combat, to seek clarity in the middle of conflicting thoughts that fighting and killing always bring to mind, and to seek solace, even if only temporarily.

"And how are you holding up?" Chaplain Carver had an easy smile, and yet one knew he was actually concerned when he asked. He was one of the most sincere people I had ever met.

I don't recall now exactly what I said to Doug, but I did confide in him. This wasn't my first war, or my first time leading troops in war, or the first time losing soldiers as a result of my decisions. But I was six months into a fifteen-month command tour in combat, and our losses—each one more than a name and face on a card, but a husband or wife, father or mother, son or daughter to someone—burned in my soul.

"Let's pray together," Doug said. And we knelt together there on the floor of my office, hands joined, and he gave the humblest supplication to God I had ever heard.

That night at midnight, I went to the hospital to pin Purple Hearts onto some of our wounded before they would be flown to Landstuhl, Germany, and then on to Walter Reed or Bethesda. At midnight we held yet another ramp ceremony in the darkness. I don't recall if Chaplain Carver attended the ceremony or if he had already departed Bagram. I do know I never thanked him for his counsel. Or for that simple prayer he led with me. It made all the difference.

CHAPTER 19

"I want to let you know that the United States is committed to the people of Afghanistan. We will stand by your side, and do the hard work necessary to achieve our objective. And our objective is for you to become a thriving democracy, and to deny al Qaeda and other extremists a safe haven or a base from which to launch their murderous attacks."
President George W. Bush

Friday, September 26, 2008

I flew from Bagram to Kabul in the early evening. As we flew down the valley, the mountain peaks to the west were still visible in the dimming light, jagged edges already white with early snows.

What would I say to the president tonight?

The security team picked us up at the military ramp of Kabul Airport, and we drove through the city streets slowly. It was Friday night, the weekend, evening prayers were over, and the city scene was lively, the souks packed, women in top-to-bottom blue burqas haggling with street vendors to get the best price, single glaring light bulbs over the fruit, veggie, and nut stands, men pushing wheelbarrows and carts with furniture, used TVs, and satellite dishes, and kids everywhere. We had to watch carefully as they darted out on the roads, chasing beat-up soccer balls.

What could I tell the president that he didn't already know?

The U.S. embassy guards waved us into the first of several gates as we entered the grounds. After security checks of our vehicles and our badges, we drove onto the compound and parked. We walked from the parking area to the main building in silence, the cool air refreshing, the silent, dark grounds a brief respite between the teeming and almost garish city scene and what was to be a high-pressure political event, played out in Kabul and Washington, D.C., with plenty of media attention.

Mister President, thanks for the promises of more troops. So where are they?

Nope, that probably wouldn't be a smart opener.

The embassy admin staff ushered us into the large conference room, one wall a large video screen, already showing the Roosevelt Room in the White House. We could see the long table at which President George Bush and President Karzai would sit, side by side, with their national security teams.

On our side, Chargé Chris Dell was chatting with Governor Sherzai from Nangarhar and Governor Wahidi from Kunar. From my team, we had the provincial reconstruction team commanders and civilian deputies from both Nangarhar and Kunar, as well as the team leads from the applicable agricultural development teams.

Mister President, you can't kill your way to victory in a counterinsurgency war, so we are here to talk about local governance and farming.

True. But maybe a bit too blunt.

On the screen, we could see both presidents' teams as they took their seats on the two sides of the long wooden table. I saw Secretary of Defense Gates and Chairman Mullen, as well as Afghan Minister of Defense Wardak. Off on the side, I could see Lieutenant Colonel Frank Sturek, an old friend and wartime colleague, now a presidential aide.

In walked President Bush and President Karzai, the former in a dark suit with a red tie, a U.S. flag pin clearly visible on his lapel. Karzai was dressed in his trademark dark green and purple robe over a dark suit with a gray shirt buttoned at the neck, every bit an Afghan president.

After a warm welcome from the president and cursory introductions, the secure video teleconference (SVTS), without media, began.

Chris Dell started from our side, and then I spoke, then the governors, the reconstruction team leads, and the agricultural team leads. We each had about two minutes to highlight what we were collectively doing in RC-East to get beyond the "kinetic," the hunting down, capturing, or killing of enemy insurgents and terrorists. We talked about farming, city management, village water and roads and power projects, schools, and more schools. The governors were animated, and Dell had to help them bring their presentations to a close as they took more than their share of time. The reconstruction commanders and deputies were passionate as well, and I did the same to keep us on track.

We talked about the two lines of operation in our campaign that received the least attention in Washington, where National Security Council (NSC) and Pentagon staffers were deeply engaged in our third line, and the kinetic aspects of "separating the enemy from the populace." That night, it was all about linking the local population to their elected and appointed governments at the district and provincial level, and transforming the environment—and the people's lives—through economic development, medical care, and education.

President Bush and Karzai were engaged, friendly, and clearly comfortable with each other, the topics, and the forum. I couldn't recall whose idea this had been, perhaps someone from the NSC team like Lieutenant General Doug Lute, but I could never recall from the past such a high-level meeting on such earthy but fundamental topics. Frank Sturek spoke as well, relating his experiences as a battalion commander in Afghanistan.

The president thanked us all. As the camera focused on him, I could see his face clearly. After eight years in the job, almost all at war, his gray hair and lines beneath the eyes were a given, but his expression was one of focused concern, of true interest in this "other" side of war, and he looked at ease.

The media were ushered into the Roosevelt Room, and both presidents spoke. President Bush said that, in listening to us, he heard progress, and felt there was promise and hope. President Karzai recited some of the statistics on education, roads, and medical care, and then thanked President Bush and the American people for what he called fifty to sixty years of progress accomplished in the preceding five to six years.

It was truly a media moment, a political moment somewhat staged, with those of us in the U.S. Embassy Kabul as backdrop, shown on screens in the Roosevelt Room. But President Karzai was genuine, articulate, and very clearly thankful: "You can't imagine here in Washington, especially at the White House, how much difference you have made to the lives of the Afghan people," he said.

After listening for six months to Karzai condemning U.S. and ISAF forces for civilian casualties, night raids, and our inability to close the border to insurgents, his words were welcome.

I flew back to Bagram well after midnight. The cabin of the Black Hawk was blacked out, and as we flew back up the valley, there were few lights below, the farmland and small family compounds barely visible in the ambient starlight.

Was this worth the presidents' time?

If governance and development truly were as important as our counterinsurgency plans said they were, then yes, it had been time well spent. I thought the president had heard about initiatives that he wasn't previously aware of, especially the agriculture development teams. His overall support and emphasis to the National Security Council staff as well as the Pentagon could be critical to the continued money we received to fund these initiatives. And talking about this "soft" side of the war was important for the American and NATO public to hear. We could capture or kill insurgents and terrorists all day and night, and still not win this war, unless we convinced the Afghan people to throw their lot in with their government. For that to happen security was absolutely critical; but so were good local governance and more development, medical care, and education.

What we had not spoken of that night was the proverbial elephant in the room: corruption. Corruption so raw, so entrenched, and pervasive in this society that it eroded many of the gains we made in security and development.

And only the Afghans themselves could rid themselves of corruption.

But would they?

President Karzai, Afghan National Day Parade, Kabul, 27 April
2008. Seconds later, the Taliban attacked with mortars and
automatic weapons fire. Photo courtesy of LTC Andy Beyer.

Battle Buddies: Division Command Sergeant Major Vince
Camacho and I in my Black Hawk helicopter heading out to
a combat outpost. Photo courtesy LTC Andy Beyer.

CH-47 crashed in the Kunar mountains at 9,000 feet during a special mission. After inspecting the crash, I ordered the aircraft destroyed with thermite grenades. Photo courtesy LTC Andy Beyer.

U.S. Navy Commander, Shoshana Chatfield and I during my
visit to the Farah Provincial Reconstruction Team, which
she commanded. Photo courtesy of LTC Andy Beyer.

The traditional New Zealand Maori welcoming "Haka," at the
New Zealand Provincial Reconstruction Team's camp in Bamyan
during my first visit. Photo courtesy of LTC Andy Beyer.

First Lady Laura Bush during a visit to Afghanistan, welcomed by
my command team and I. Photo courtesy of LTC Andy Beyer.

Then Senator Obama visiting Regional Command East, including Bagram and Jalalabad. U.S. Army photo, public record.

Brigadier General Jim McConville and to his left, Nangarhar's Provincial Governor Gul Agha Sherzai. Photo courtesy of General McConville.

President Bush during his last visit to Afghanistan in December, 2008. He thanked our troops, visited President Karzai, and took the time to pose for pictures with many of our soldiers, sailors, Marines, and airmen before departing Bagram. Photo courtesy of the White House.

The Chairman of the Joint Chiefs of Staff, Admiral Mike Mullen, and I visit COP Deysie, during one of his many visits to Regional Command East and Afghanistan. Photo courtesy of U.S. Army, public release.

Secretary Robert Gates and I aboard a C-130 aircraft en route from Bagram to Jalalabad. Photo courtesy U.S. Army, public release.

Solider from 4th Brigade (Airborne), 25th Infantry Division, CJTF 101, shares with Afghan children during a village patrol. Photo courtesy U.S. Army, public release.

PART 3

CHAPTER 20

"The inhabitants of these wild but wealthy valleys are of many tribes...
except at the times of sowing and of harvest, a continual state of feud
and strife prevails throughout the land. Tribes war with tribes....
Every man's hand is against the other, and all against the stranger."
Winston S. Churchill, The Story of the Malakand Field Force

Wednesday, October 1, 2008

inally October! I wrote early that day in my small green daily journal.
I woke in the morning with the winter campaign on my mind, practically bubbling with enthusiasm and optimism.

In hindsight, perhaps unreasonable optimism.

After morning briefings, I grabbed a sandwich in the operations center chow hall and headed out to the helicopter. Soon we were climbing over the mountains just east of Bagram, en route to pick up Commander George Perez, commander of the Nuristan Provincial Reconstruction Team.

I really enjoyed working and talking with Perez, but he sure wasn't who you would expect commanding a reconstruction team in the hinterlands of northeastern Afghanistan. A former navy-enlisted man from Corpus Christi, Texas, George had an electrical engineering degree from the University of Texas and had served multiple tours on a variety of nuclear submarines. In command of the provincial reconstruction team since the previous December, he had worked hard to move beyond his temporary base at Qala Gush, building a rough road to Parun that would allow us to establish the Nuristan reconstruction team in the provincial capital. I wasn't convinced the team could thrive in such a remote location. Was there even enough populace in the vicinity to work with? What about security? And was there anything we could really do to improve the lot of such people, the Nuristanis?

It was a brilliant fall day, and it seemed like we could see forever. It was easy to forget the slog of the war as we sought out high mountain passes to cross the Hindu Kush.

Nuristan, land of the enlightened. A province of extremes. Its location in our northeast sector was framed by roaring rivers, stunningly beautiful narrow valleys, and the mountains: still heavily forested by evergreens and deciduous trees, the mountains majestically steep, barriers to human movement, but not to human civilization. They were the ancestral home of the Nuristani people.

Speaking a Dardic tongue with at least five Nuristani-based languages and several dialects, Nuristanis are historically fiercely independent of outside military, political, and religious influences. To this day, they are regarded with deep suspicion by many Afghans, as if Nuristan is a separate land, and Nuristanis an alien people. Reputedly occupied by Alexander the Great's forces in 330 BC, it wasn't until the late nineteenth century that Nuristanis were forcibly converted from ancient Hinduism, Buddhism, and some animist devotions to Islam by the "Iron Emir," Abdul Rahman Khan. Known for centuries as the land of infidels (Kafirs), Nuristan had been deemed "Kafiristan" by the few travelers and authors to visit the remote region. Among the most notable was Rudyard Kipling, who based his book *The Man Who Would Be King* in Nuristan.

The Soviets fought the warlords, mujahedeen, and Nuristanis to no success, ultimately leaving little evidence of their presence behind. Our own U.S. forces had spent considerable blood and treasure in trying to build security—Wanat was just the latest example—but had so far had little success in moving beyond kinetic operations. We needed to assist the Afghan national and provincial government in establishing a lasting presence in Nuristan, and clearly demonstrate to the people that medical care, development, and schools would follow, if that was actually what the Nuristani people wanted. After Wanat, I wasn't so sure.

We picked up George and his team at his headquarters and headed over a high pass even deeper into the Hindu Kush. George too was in a good mood, enthusiastically briefing me about all he would be able to do once he could establish his team's headquarters in the heart of Nuristan, at the provincial capital of Parun.

"Sir, we are one minute out," said Dave, my command pilot.

Outside the Black Hawk window was a bucolic setting: a tightly constricted valley with a rushing narrow river, vibrantly green grass bordering the rock-defined waters, tall dark green firs and pines dominating among shorter deciduous trees (they looked like cottonwoods), their leaves turning yellow, the blue sky almost an indigo in the high altitude.

I was expecting a small town, or at least a medium-sized village. I could see nothing but mountains, trees, grass, and the rushing waters.

We landed on a flat landing zone pointed out by George, and got out of the aircraft. Following George and his team, we crossed the river on a simple one-log bridge, no handrails or ropes to balance oneself, and waded through a green sea of tall thigh-high grass to a dirt and rock road. We were met by a few local Afghan Army soldiers, who walked with us, pulling a very loose form of security. My own security detachment was forward and behind George and me as we walked along the road. We learned from the Afghans there were no trucks to be had that day.

I was just fine with that. It felt good to walk, to stop and talk to villagers, herders, and the curious who stopped along the road, astounded by the sight of American soldiers in Parun.

I too was curious. The people were markedly different from their fellow Afghans to the south and west. Women walked boldly without burqas, their brown, brunette, red, and even blonde hair in scarves. The kids rushed around, trying to touch our uniforms, being kids, their eyes strikingly green or blue or light brown. The men seemed taller than usual, confident as they reassured us that Parun was quite secure, that even Qari

Zai Rahman, Nuristan's al-Qaida and Taliban shadow governor, had been unable to penetrate this mountain redoubt.

Shadow governors: the Taliban did their best to place "governors" loyal to the Taliban in each of our provinces. In isolated cases, they upheld the former Taliban political and judicial system, such as it was. In most cases, the shadow governors spent the majority of their time outside the province and usually even outside of RC-East, since we tried our best to identify and target them for capture or killing. In the fall of 2008, we were having some limited success in doing so.

Normally, I would have met with Provincial Governor Jamaluddin Badr. He was recently appointed after his immediate predecessor, Hazrat Din Noor, had been tragically killed in a car crash. Noor himself had just taken over as governor a few months prior, after long-term Governor Tamim Nuristani had been fired by President Karzai in the political fallout arising from comments he made condemning U.S. forces in the July 4 Apache engagement of pickup trucks at COP Bella. No stranger to Americans, Governor Nuristani, whose father had been the mayor of Kabul until the Afghan communists took over, had lived in the States, working as a cab driver and eventually opening up restaurants in Brooklyn and Sacramento. He had a reputation for speaking his mind and of seeking to keep space between himself and the national government in Kabul, and his comments this time had gone too far. A shame, because he was the closest thing Nuristan had to a technocrat. The Parun Provincial Reconstruction Team had been his brainchild.

Governor Badr was traveling out of the province, so this trip was all about allowing me to do an assessment of the terrain and the infrastructure, such as it was, and get eyes on the town.

We walked through the main street, the town's only real street, a narrow dirt and rock lane with no evidence of recent motor vehicles other than ruts. The mountains pressed close on one side, and then again on the other side of the river, which was a few hundred meters away. Homes made of stone, with enormous timber beams forming the roofs, stacked their way up the sides of the mountains. Roofs of many homes formed the entranceway and porch of the next home, and so on, up the mountain.

I was told there was a hotel and a store, but was never certain I actually saw either during the tour.

It was a beautiful day, and I was enchanted by the almost impenetrable but striking terrain, the ruggedly handsome and confident people, and the fine autumn weather. We seemed to be a long way away from our war further south.

We re-boarded the Black Hawk and flew along the road back out of the valley. My predecessors had spent millions on expanding what had been no more than a rough mountain trail into a minimally passable single-lane road, unpaved, that connected Parun to the rest of the province. Commander Perez wanted to locate the U.S. reconstruction team with the provincial government and especially its governor, and to provide development assistance in what was Nuristan's largest economic center and only major town.

I had my doubts. But as we dropped George off at his headquarters, we agreed I should meet with the new governor when he returned to Nuristan, and meanwhile planning for the team's relocation could continue.

I wrote that night in my journal about the trip to Parun, noting how beautiful the mountains, the valley, and the river had been, and how intriguing I found the remarkable townspeople. But I was also concerned. The lessons of Wanat haunted me: Was this mountain valley and the team's site defendable? Would the people support the reconstruction team and actually help keep it secure? Would the effort actually make a difference in our counterinsurgency campaign? I would need to return to Nuristan to seek answers to these and many other questions that nagged me that evening.

After some years of reflection, what I should have done was review each and every combat outpost in RC-East, some one hundred, for a comprehensive reappraisal of its ultimate purpose weighed against the security risks, the means to mitigate those risks, and the troops and resources at hand. I had taken my 101st Airborne inspector general, Lieutenant

Colonel Craig Jones, and tasked him with an ongoing, near constant, on-the-ground status check of our major operating bases and outposts that covered security, troop welfare, and the like. I did not ask him to conduct a total review of the purpose versus reality of each location, and given the immensity of the task, I doubt that would have been possible. We were fighting a war, after all, and the tactical operations trumped the strategic analysis almost every day.

That night I stayed in my office working late on what was to be a published instruction to all of our U.S. and NATO troops in the CJTF and RC-East. The idea for a "tactical guidance" began the evening of September 23, as several of us senior leaders in the CJTF sat in my office talking about what we had, and especially, had not, accomplished so far in our campaign. We were focused on the various tactics, techniques, and procedures of our combat formations; we had sat or stood through many small and larger unit post combat after-action reviews, and we were not satisfied with the results. The night turned into a bitch session, with all of us voicing frustration. Finally, I called it to an end, with orders to have the staff develop a letter of tactical guidance to our commanders.

In the evenings since, I had pulled together my own ideas and jotted them down. As my thoughts coalesced, I decided that the audience could not be just commanders; this instruction needed to be addressed to every soldier. And it needed to clearly and concisely explain the "why" of our upcoming operations, how I wanted commanders and especially non-commissioned officers to think of what had heretofore been considered a winter lull in fighting, and most especially, convey my intent: our goals, objectives, and how we would carry ourselves as we accomplished what would be a very challenging set of operations to seize the initiative from the insurgency and not give it back—our winter campaign.

I made some progress on the tactical guidance that night, and ensured the team knew I was personally taking pen to paper, but also wanted their ideas and feedback. This was far too important in my mind to allow my ego, or "wisdom" as some might say, to get in the way of a clear communication of commander's intent to each and every member of our CJTF and Regional Command.

On Saturday, three days later, I headed back to Nuristan. Combat Outpost Lybert was on the far eastern rim of RC-East and Nuristan Province, perched on a mountain ridge a few miles from the Pakistani border. Near the village of Gawardesh, the camp ostensibly overlooked a rough road that became a mountain trail over a narrow pass and led into Pakistan's North-West Frontier Province. Lybert was established to observe and block insurgent movement along the road. Imperfectly situated, observation even with the Long Range Advanced Scout Surveillance System from Lybert was difficult, although it seemed useful in causing the insurgents to not often use the route.

Perched high on the mountain ridge, Lybert was not an ideal location to mingle with the local villagers as it was quite a trek up and down the mountain. That said, the outpost's aide station had done a healthy amount of business serving the local villagers since our own CJTF had arrived in 2008, and that was helpful in keeping their allegiance for the time being.

As we made our approach for landing on Lybert's ridgeline landing zone, I was reminded of the huge role that trees, timber and forestry, played in Nuristan and Kunar. Once heavily forested, competing factions from both sides of the Durand Line had over-logged the mountains, denuding many of the slopes. Other slopes looked to have been burned a few years ago. Rumor had it the fires had been purposeful, a result of murderous competition. In hindsight, we were slow over the years in fully understanding the lumber trade in eastern Afghanistan, and so made many bad decisions that led to violent confrontations with local villagers, most notably in the Korengal, where we established our main outpost on the site of a sawmill, and got drawn into a confrontation that fixed us in place on the wrong side of ever winning over the lumber-smuggling Korengalis. Armed with set-piece counterinsurgency doctrine drilled into us at the Joint Readiness Training Center and a typically American exuberance to "roll up our sleeves and get things done," we often found ourselves naively confounded when the locals really did not desire all the good things we offered them, such as a closer working relationship with their district, provincial, and national government through paved roads. Turns out the government was trying to restrict and regulate the lumber trade, and the locals wanted none of that.

We were learning. Slowly.

Task Force Raider's Major Matt McCollum, who was leading an advanced command element from the 6th Squadron, 4th Cavalry, met me at the landing zone. If I decided to close Lybert, Matt would lead the effort. Matt introduced me to First Lieutenant Ian Lipsitz, who led the 2nd platoon of Battery A, 1st Battalion, 6th Field Artillery Battalion, and Second Lieutenant Chad Lorenz, 1st platoon leader of Troop C, 6th Squadron, 4th Cavalry. Ian's platoon had taken over in July. On September 11, Lybert had been attacked, with the enemy bringing forces from three sides in spite of the ridgeline defenses, and this is where Private First Class Michael Murdock had been killed (we conducted a ramp ceremony for Murdock and Mr. Slebodnik on September 12).

We talked about the firefight and Murdock's death. Ian had far more details than I had previously known, since he was Murdock's platoon leader. Murdock was shot while in a hut, donning his body armor. That didn't change anything in my mind—his death very much disturbed me—but I didn't say that to the soldiers in front of me.

Chad Lorenz's platoon had been part of the quick reaction force after the battle, and had never left.

We walked the entire base, and ventured out of the wire to see how the enemy had approached on three sides during the September 11 fight. We talked about the limitations: it was hard to get up and down the mountain to work with the villagers, hard to resupply except by helicopter, and it was a long way from Jalalabad. It was also difficult to actually observe the pass and mountain road that was its purpose. I peered through the big scope (LRAS3) at the pass not so far away, and saw how the ridgeline blocked a full view of both the pass and the trail that came down on the Afghan side.

"Close it," I said to Matt, as we walked back to the Black Hawk.

But I was thinking of young Michael Murdock as we left.

★ ★ ★

That night the chief, Colonel Tom Vail, came in with my division lawyer (JAG). We had a "Congressional" to respond to, and not much time, in spite of being at war.

It was on Wanat.

First Lieutenant Jonathan Brostrom was the platoon leader killed at Wanat along with eight other soldiers. I had initiated two internal Army Regulation 15-6 investigations right after the battle, the first of which was conducted internally by a senior officer, the deputy commander in Chip Preysler's brigade. The second I had ordered to ensure we were looking beyond the brigade-level of operations and support. I reviewed both of the findings and agreed with them, and sent them upward to my commander and the Pentagon.

Brostrom's father, retired Army Colonel Dave Brostrom, had flown from Hawaii to Washington, D.C., where he met with Virginia Senator James Webb to request a further investigation. There were twenty-six questions to be answered. Less questions and more accusations, they were a stinging critique of the chain of command, from company and battalion to CJTF. I don't believe the 173rd was included in the questions at the time, but that too would change.

I knew Dave Brostrom as a fellow soldier, army aviator, and a colleague. I did not know him well, but respected him for what I did know. We both had had sons in the army, and at war. My son, Ryan, now a captain, was at Fort Bragg after a year in Iraq as a combat engineer platoon leader finding and removing IEDs. His son, Jonathan, had died leading his platoon at Wanat, under my command. Like the chief, I was initially angry at the direct accusations that went to the very core of our professional conduct of the war, and appeared to allege we commanders were directly negligent, and responsible for the deaths of nine soldiers, as well as the horrible wounds of those who survived.

I did believe in command responsibility, and I accepted the ultimate responsibility for the battle of Wanat. I rejected the concept that we—my staff, or the company, battalion, or brigade commanders or their staffs—had been *negligent*. We had prepared a sound plan to build a vehicle patrol base and ultimately a combat outpost, and had resourced it as well as we could. The enemy had surprised us, massed, and fought well. The reinforced U.S. platoon fought better, and held at Wanat. We in command were responsible, yes, but not negligent.

I wrote in my journal that night that I had to place myself in Dave Brostrom's position. He had lost his son; I had not. He had not served in Afghanistan, and for those of us who had, it remained a very foreign war to describe to others. It was our war, and he saw us as responsible for his son's death, as well as those who had died along with Jonathan that day.

I made a recommendation to General McKiernan that he request another investigation of the battle, and that a senior officer outside of my CJTF lead the investigation. In the meantime, I directed the chief to ensure we answered the Congressional as best we knew.

Two days later we flew from Bagram to Khost to meet with the provincial governor, Asala Jamal. I routinely and often met with the fourteen provincial governors in Regional Command-East, and this trip was like most others, entailing a lot of staff and personal preparation followed by significant work on the ground between our U.S. or NATO forces and my security team, to ensure we would have a relatively safe place to actually talk for a lengthy period of time. In the provinces, especially the more remote ones, we would usually land my Black Hawk close to the meeting site and walk over to the meeting. In others, like Khost, held in or near towns or cities, we would land and drive over, usually in up-armored military vehicles. Either way, it was hardly a modest, or inconspicuous, entrance. We of course knew we were being observed and reported on by insurgent supporters, and always planned to depart within a few hours. We were almost always successful in departing before insurgents could rally and mount some sort of quick operation.

We landed at the Khost provincial capital center (PCC) on the outskirts of the city, and with Task Force Glory Commander Lieutenant Colonel Dave Ell leading, took a couple of MRAPs down the hill to Governor Jamal's home. He met us at the door and enthusiastically led us into his outdoor gardens. It was early October, but the weather in Khost tended to be warmer and more humid than the rest of eastern Afghanistan, and the garden was still beautiful, bright exotic flowers mixing with roses and green bushes. We sat under a shaded area beneath a large tree, and sipped cool water and boiling hot sweet tea.

Governor Jamal was an interesting character. Pashtun, born in neighboring Paktika in 1966, he had received a degree in economics outside the country, and worked in banking and later within the non-governmental organization community outside of Afghanistan during the Taliban years. Reportedly close to President Karzai, he returned to Afghanistan after the fall of the Taliban and worked with the Afghan Stability Program in rural development. Karzai appointed him governor of Khost in August 2006.

The governor was not a tall man, slightly balding, with a close-cropped graying beard and fashionable glasses: he looked more like a university economics professor than a governor of one of the most difficult and violent provinces in Afghanistan. But his appearance belied a strong, aggressive personality, deep intelligence, and a Western-oriented technological bent. He wanted to change Khost Province, knew what needed to be done, and that made him a Taliban target. He had survived repeated attempts on his life, usually when in a security convoy. That's why we were coming to him this time.

Jamal was a survivor, and knew well how to reap maximum benefits for his people while cooperating with U.S., NATO, and Afghan forces. CERP funding, allocated at the CJTF level and distributed on a program basis to the local U.S. commanders to support their initiatives for development and governance, was always a focus of all of our governors, for it was a direct, timely, and relatively un-bureaucratic investment into their province. Jamal was a master at working with the provincial reconstruction team and task force to garner these funds. When he took over as governor, his province was receiving $6 million in CERP; in 2007, $25 million. For 2008, we had allocated $55 million and he was asking for an additional $13 million before the year's end; we were predicting $80 million the next year. In a poor country like Afghanistan and within one province, that was real money, and could make a substantial difference, if wisely spent.

After pleasantries about the weather, his children in Canada and mine in the U.S., and the beautiful garden, we began our meeting. I thanked him for his leadership, saying he was fearless, culturally sensitive to the multitude of tribal issues in Khost and in neighboring Pakistan's North Waziristan, and was, nevertheless, forward-looking. I congratulated him on working with the reconstruction team and Lieutenant Colonel David J. Ell's 4th Battalion, 320th Field Artillery's Task Force Glory to build a number of important projects, including work on the KG Pass Road, the Khost Airport, and a commerce center. The previous year, the CERP had paid for some fifty schools, three hundred wells, thirty dams, and over fifty kilometers of road. If the schools had teachers, the wells and dams water, and the roads helped connect the people to their governance at the district and provincial level, then it was money well spent.

That was not always the case in RC-East, and Brigadier General McConville and his team were systematically reviewing every new CERP request to ensure it made common sense, and that we built no schools without students and teachers, no waterless dams, and no roads to nowhere.

The governor thanked us all. We talked about tribal politics, voter registration, and the impact of our special operations on the security of the province, as well as the negative impact some of the activities had on his legitimacy. Civilian casualties were a big issue, and we had to do better.

"How is security?"

Jamal told me the districts were safe. I must have had a wry expression, as he immediately qualified the statement, noting in Sabari District, the "people were supporting the enemy."

I spoke to a few other districts I was concerned about.

"Why not consider an Arbakai? You must give them weapons," Jamal asked me.

The idea of an armed, tribal-based community security force was not new. In Pashtun areas of Afghanistan, the Arbakai was a traditional, honorable method of enforcing peace, and if not peace, relative law and order. Derived from the Pashtu word for "messenger," Arbakai were not an armed, paid militia (or Lashkar), which was often seen as outside of cultural norms, and often not honorable. Tribally appointed, each member of an Arbakai was honor-bound to enforce the resolutions of the local jirga as well as ensure a corruption-free enforcement of laws. A centuries-old solution to community security in eastern Afghanistan and the frontier that was now part of Pakistan, this type of local policing had pretty much been done away with by U.S. and NATO forces plus the Afghan Army and police. I had heard of some localized attempts to reinstitute Arbakai in Paktika, but we had been less than supportive, so far. President Karzai had called the Arbakai illegal, and the U.S. administration wasn't supportive either: Just how would the Arbakai interface with the national police and the central government? But General Petraeus and Minister Wardak had both suggested a protective force that sounded like an Arbakai to me.

I couldn't promise our support, but said we would look at it and I would discuss it with my boss, General McKiernan.

The governor walked us out to the MRAPs. His compound seemed secure, and the modest but well-kept home with extensive gardens was a sanctuary, at least for the time being. I wished him well, and to stay safe, and we boarded the MRAPs for the ride back.

It was clear to me that Governor Jamal was the real thing: an educated, forward-looking Afghan leader who was working hard to improve his province and the lives of its residents. We needed to keep him alive. I wished we had more governors of his ilk.

CHAPTER 21

"By the North Gate, the wind blows full of sand,
Lonely from the beginnings of time until now!
Trees fall, the grass goes yellow with autumn.
I climb the towers and towers
to watch out the barbarous land:
Desolate castle, the sky, the wide desert."
Rihaku (Li Po), translated by Ezra Pound,
"Lament of the Frontier Guard"

Wednesday, October 8, 2008

I went for a run early in the morning. Before sunrise, the mountain air crisp, cleansed by a solid half hour of rainfall the previous day, it was one of those rare runs in a war zone that invigorates both body and soul. The tall mountains just to the west of Bagram were snowcapped, and as I ended my run back at the headquarters the dawn turned the very tips of the jagged peaks a golden orange. I lingered outside by the pull-up bars for just a few minutes, as the colors turned brighter, the snow on the peaks whiter by the second.

In late morning, we boarded my Black Hawk and flew south. Way south. It was a seventy-five-minute flight to Forward Operating Base Kushamond, located near the seam between RC-East and RC-South and close to the Paktika-Waziristan border.

Never in Regional Command-East had I seen a more desolate site for a base camp. Established by U.S. Army combat engineers in late 2001 and early 2002, Kushamond was first occupied by Polish troops and meant to secure the primitive road network in the area. It had not seen significant enemy action, and was realigned under U.S. forces as we prepared for a larger, more capable Polish brigade to assume command and control of all of Ghazni Province. Captain Jeff Farmer's Company C, 1st Battalion, 506th Infantry was in charge, with troops from Company A, 62nd Engineers helping to build out the camp. In addition to his three rifle platoons and headquarters platoon, Farmer received a 105-mm artillery platoon, a military police platoon, a maintenance section, and the battalion physician's assistant plus some headquarters medics because his unit was so far from other American elements in RC-East. They had their work cut out for them. Kushamond was enormous by company base camp standards, and had direct access to an adjacent Afghan Army camp, which our troopers were partnering with.

As the Black Hawk slowed on short final, I could see the entire camp in context. Everything looked to be dust-colored and dust-covered: a dirty light brown was the predominant hue, the plywood "B-huts" (simple plywood living quarters, usually housing a handful of troopers) and desert-painted Humvees providing scant contrast in their only slightly darker or lighter hues.

There wasn't a tree in sight for miles.

A few dirt roads, more like trails, started on the western and northern horizon and cut straight pathways to the camp's perimeter. If there was a village to be had, I couldn't see it. And it seemed like I could see for miles as we descended.

We set down on a helipad, and got out. Dave would have both Black Hawks refueled here at Kushamond and then shut down in a corner, to await our return flight. This was unusual: the aircraft usually dropped us and immediately departed, getting fuel at a larger base and awaiting a call to return. That kept the enemy from targeting the outpost I was visiting, in hopes of destroying the helicopters.

But there was no place to go for fuel this far south other than Kushamond itself. Best of all, it had almost no enemy fires.

Except for last week. As we walked through the ankle-deep "moon" dust of the base, camp Commander Captain Farmer told me they had received some small arms fire last week, with no damage or casualties. They had been at Kushamond for months and had never been mortared or rocketed.

We walked through the camp's spartan sleeping areas and chow hall. The headquarters building was a work in progress, as were the perimeter towers. The camp was too big for its purpose, too big for the company manning it to guard it 24/7, train with the Afghan Army partner unit, and do much significant patrolling via Humvees out to the villages, which I was reassured did exist, beyond eyesight.

Just why would we maintain an outpost here? I thought to myself as we walked around to the artillery position. I was glad to see the two well-maintained 105-mm howitzers. If the enemy ever did try to approach Kushamond in any meaningful way, our soldiers would need their own firepower for some time before we could get attack helicopters or close air support overhead.

What was the base's task and purpose? Were the road networks still so important in this remote area of RC-East to justify the base? They certainly were important to resupplying the outpost, that I was sure. It seemed that now the base was most important for the role it played in training and working with the Afghan National Army. Without our presence, support, and daily example, I doubted the ANA unit stationed at Kushamond would be effective.

There was no doubt the U.S. soldiers were doing their best, given the austere location and equally austere provisions. They deserved better support if we were going to keep this base open. I knew any move on my part to close Kushamond, given its location and closures I was already directing in Kunar and Nuristan, would be strongly opposed by the Afghans.

As we departed in the late afternoon, I again got a bird's-eye view of the camp and its environs. This was the end of the earth. This kind of place must have been in Bob Dylan's mind when he wrote "All along the Watchtower." As we flew north, with Jimi Hendrix's version of the song in my head, I pondered the future of Forward Operating Base Kushamond: Should I try to close it and free these troops to serve elsewhere in RC-East?

★　★　★

The next day, General Dempsey told me in a video conference that he had read my tactical guidance, approved it, and complimented us on the concept and the content.

General McKiernan soon approved it as well, and we went to press.

The staff produced a five-by-seven-inch card: on the upper-left corner was our CJTF-101 emblem, complete with a small image of Afghanistan in the center. In larger font was the title: Eagle 6 Tactical Guidance. Then below in short paragraphs I laid out what I wanted us to do regarding our enemy. In simple language I laid out the "why" first: *My intent for the Winter Campaign and operations in Spring 2009 is to tactically, operationally, and publicly seize the initiative from the enemies of the Afghan people, causing Afghan "fence sitters" to choose their government over the insurgents.*

Then I laid out our objectives:

> We must secure the population and separate them from the enemy. To do that we must execute an aggressive winter offensive that drives the enemy to the point where he is off-balance, unable to influence the people, and is incapable of prosecuting actions on his own terms.
>
> We must force the enemy to react to us by avoiding predictability and executing sustained and unexpected offensive actions. When contact is made (by them or us) attempt to fix the enemy then complete his destruction with violent action. Use non-kinetic means (quick wins) to immediately support and protect the people, then cement gains with sustained efforts to keep the enemy isolated and unable to influence the population.

When the enemy breaks contact, exploit. When it makes sense, employ a force that can be quickly inserted into an area to pursue or block a fleeing enemy element. Maximize the use of fires to fix and destroy him. We have tactical and operational flexibility with our lift and mobility. Maximize this potential.

Employ sniper teams and small unit ambushes in areas of known enemy activity. The value of a successful sniper or small unit engagement cannot be overstated – it drives the enemy off balance and disrupts his freedom of movement, exposing more vulnerabilities we will exploit.

We are tough, well equipped, and well led – as are many of our ANSF partners. We can and must conduct sustained combat operations in the enemy's previous safe havens and sanctuaries in Afghanistan, sometimes mounted, often dismounted, sometimes away from our fire support, most often in close support by CCA and CAS. We own the night, and we must maximize this incredible advantage.

I believe significant numbers of enemy will remain in Afghanistan this winter to rest, recock, resupply, and prepare for operations in 2009. Find them. Present them four options: capture, death, reconciliation, or flight out of this country. Use air assaults followed by complementary search & attack operations to identify and clear enemy winter support areas. In addition to inevitable success hitting these sanctuaries, these efforts "flush" the enemy and trigger activity and movement which we will exploit with increased HVI raids. (HVI: high value individual)

In all you determine to do to implement this guidance, understand that I fully realize decentralized operations to force the enemy off balance, create opportunities, and maintain operational and tactical initiative will require tough decisions and some amount of reasonable, calibrated, and calculated risk. I trust you, your commanders, and our troops. We will win. Let's get after it.

Air Assault!

MG Jeffrey J. Schloesser

Eagle 6

As we went to press and then distributed the guidance cards to each and every trooper, I hoped to invigorate our kinetic operations during a time heretofore regarded as a winter battlefield lull. I knew ancient armies fighting in the Afghan Hindu Kush had often gone to camp for the coldest, snowiest months, not unlike other more modern armies when faced with extreme, dangerous temperatures, hazardous or impossible supply lines, and low or non-existent visibility. But I also knew Alexander had forced an early spring crossing over the nearby 12,625-foot Khawak Pass in deep snows and ice that surprised his foe and led to battlefield success. And that was in 329 BC.

In the tactical guidance, I was seeking a balanced approach to mission command orders. I wanted to communicate clearly that we had to do more to be successful, and it started with the first leg of our counter-insurgency triad of focus on the enemy, focus on the people, and focus on development. We couldn't get to the people or the development without better success against the enemy, and I was convinced the winter gave us an opportunity. Our intelligence indicated many of the insurgents would "winter-over" in Afghan sanctuaries, seeking to exploit their placement among certain local tribes and their relative battlefield positions. I was sure they would try to fight when the weather and the conditions gave them a temporary advantage.

I wanted us ready for those fights. I wanted us to aggressively seek out the enemy, and cause them to fight, flee, or reconcile.

I saw in a previous war what happened when we miscalculated enemy intentions. By late summer in 2003 in Mosul, Iraq, we had defeated and disbanded the Iraqi Army. But then we learned what a newly organized group of former Iraqi soldiers could do to disciplined, well-trained conventional troops, when the insurgents determined the time and place of their attacks. Swallowing hubris, we learned daily in the tough school of the urban battlefield. Few of us knew that the war had just begun.

By now I had seen that the enemy we were fighting in Afghanistan was every bit as difficult to predict, in both intentions and capabilities.

My enemy, our enemy, was diverse, distributed among the populace, impassioned with his cause, and viewed our conflict with ancient eyes. We Westerners were in a hurry; the insurgents were ready for multi-generational battles. I was truly impressed by the skills, range, and commitment of our foes. In cheap rubber sandals, they could outclimb us on snowy trails. With AK-47s and SKS carbines from the Soviet War they would snipe us from hundreds of yards, sometimes with a shot that killed one of us. With cheap Chinese and Indian rice cookers, and rusty nails and broken, oily bolts, they would fashion depressingly effective and destructive IEDs.

If we were ever going to get to the focus on the local people and their development, we had to do better than the insurgents. We had to *be* better at counterinsurgency than the insurgents were at insurgency.

The tactical guidance was my way of communicating at all levels, from colonel to private, that we had to do more to win this.

On Monday, I did an hour-and-a-half interview with Jacques Follorou of *Le Monde*. It was important to get the word out to all of our audiences about what we were doing, what the insurgents were attempting to do, and the criticality of increasing our capabilities, be it more troops, increased surveillance and reconnaissance, or MRAPs. The French had their nose bloodied in Sarobi, and were committed to increasing their troop strength in both RC-Capital as well as under my command in Kapisa. I needed the French public to know how important their role— their troops as well as public support—was to our overall success.

I believed in an open press, but was aware that our enemy was media-savvy and very sophisticated, and therefore supposed they read or listened to our interviews for information and intelligence. I also knew the journalists were always in search of a "story" that provided insights, revelations of something not previously known, or of deep human interest. It was my job to ensure we talked to our various audiences in ways that strategically communicated information they needed: what my own troops needed was different than the American public, which was different than the detailed views we provided to our elected officials, and in turn that was different than the broader narrative that interested our NATO partners. Because we actually exist as a military in the United States to support and defend the Constitution, which provides for freedom of the press, I felt what we said had to be without "spin," and had to be as fulsome and frank as possible without providing critical information to the enemy, who was always listening. All of this was no easy task.

From the start of our deployment we planned an aggressive media approach that supported our campaign, and public affairs officer Lieutenant Colonel Rumi Nielson-Green was a master at working with the media outlets and journalists, many well-known, as well as our command group team. Like everything at this level of war, from CODELs, and high-ranking military visitors to think tank intellectuals, there had to be an empowered gatekeeper, otherwise the sheer numbers would overwhelm us. Tom Vail, my chief, was the gatekeeper for all visitors and delegations other than media. Rumi was our gatekeeper for journalists. I thought she did it very well, but more than once she had to convince me to take on yet another reporter, TV crew, or author during our jammed daily schedule.

But convince me she often did. In the past two weeks, I had flown Fox News' Dana Lewis with me to Kapisa, the Uzbin Valley, the KG Pass Road, and Forward Operating Base Shank, a total of four hours on camera and tape. A few days later, I did a National Public Radio interview with Tom Bowman. And yesterday, I had had a one-hour interview on film with *Army Times'* Michelle Tan. Looking back after the *Le Monde* session, I was satisfied with these outreach efforts, at least from their diverse scope: from Fox to NPR to *Army Times* to *Le Monde*, I hoped our message was getting out.

South of Kabul were two provinces that were a working demonstration of our relative weakness in the summer and fall of 2008. To the east was Logar Province, with the Kabul to Gardez highway leading to the eastern approach of Kabul. Our small camp at Altimur did not have enough troops or mobility to broadly influence the province, nor did our Czech provincial reconstruction team operating out of Forward Operating Base Shank, and the insurgents had more influence at this stage with the locals than we did. Wardak Province guarded the southern gate to Kabul, as Highway 1 ran from Kabul southward towards Kandahar. It was a real highway by Afghan standards, built with foreign funds over the last few decades and repaired and paved since 2002 by the U.S., to the tune of $270 million. It was the key line of communication between the two largest cities in Afghanistan, and the transportation conduit for bus and car service for the local population. It was also the focus of aggressive and largely successfully insurgent efforts to at least appear to threaten Kabul, as the Taliban had done in 1996, blockading the city first, and eventually overrunning it.

The enemy was masterful at planting simple but effective and destructive IEDs in the many culverts along this stretch of Highway 1, and often added a complex ambush to the attack after the IED stopped one or more vehicles. They were heartless, targeting civilian buses as well as our contract and military resupply convoys. An attack against a contracted convoy earlier in the summer destroyed almost fifty trucks carrying supplies and fuel. The insurgents rounded up drivers who hadn't fled and beheaded several of them. These drivers were not U.S. or NATO soldiers or even Western contract drivers. These were fellow Afghans and Pakistanis out to make a buck by driving for the local Afghan trucking company we hired to move routine supplies.

The Tangi Valley attack against our CSTC-A soldiers occurred two days after the convoy attack. Our resulting brigade-level air assaults to find and capture or kill the perpetrators had been limited in scope and duration: most of the troops had been moved from other locations in other provinces for the punitive operation, and were needed back in those areas too. After achieving our limited goals, we moved those troops back to their AORs.

Our outposts in Wardak were as limited as Logar. Just south along the mountain chain edging Kabul's southern exposure to Highway 1 we had a company-level camp, Forward Operating Base Airborne. And along a feeder valley that started in the mountains southwest of Kabul and linked eastward to the highway lay Jalrez Valley, where in spring of 2008 we had constructed a small outpost called Kote Ashrow. We knew the enemy was in the mountains rimming the valley, and used it as a safe haven to plant IEDs and conduct ambushes along Highway 1. In an "economy of force" move, we were trying to stop or at least limit the enemy success emanating from Jalrez until we received the additional troops I had requested back in June. We had decided to place the majority of that new incoming unit, recently announced to be the 3rd Brigade Combat Team, 10th Mountain Division, in Logar and Wardak.

I was convinced the brigade would be powerful enough to fight the various insurgents in this area, a mix of Taliban, HiG, and foreign fighters. With better control over the insurgents, the unit could make much more progress than we had had so far in governance and development. The Czech PRT would be more effective with better security.

The 3rd Brigade wouldn't deploy until January, so we did what we could with the forces we had.

That meant limited operations from Forward Operating Base Airborne and our Kote Ashrow outpost, supported periodically by air assaults of a platoon or two into the valley or the villages and towns nearby, seeking to find and fight the enemy and reassure the local villagers.

I first saw Kote Ashrow on July 17, when it was a platoon outpost established literally on the rooftop of a stone house on high ground overlooking the road. The senior non-commissioned officer was Staff Sergeant Moriarty, who along with twelve of his soldiers was doing his level best to partner with a small platoon of about twenty Afghan Army soldiers, and a handful of Afghan police. As he led me along, it didn't take long to see all they had: no concrete Texas barriers for force protection, just some wire atop poorly made concrete blocks, an ITAS, and a 60-mm mortar.

And the Afghans' two D-30 howitzers, which they assured me they could operate effectively, as long as they were in direct fire mode. I was struck by the situations in which we put our troops and leaders. And being just a few days after Wanat, I knew not to underestimate the enemy. I flew back to Bagram with a host of changes to make, and immediately, at Kote Ashrow. The outpost was better now, with more troops, more weapons, better force protection, and better living conditions, but it still was sparse. We had to keep the enemy off-stride.

The operation that day air assaulted troopers near the town of Nerkh. We were sure Nerkh was an enemy safe haven. We were not sure if the locals were complicit with the insurgents or had been persuaded by force of arms, but we were taking no chances. We had learned tough lessons elsewhere.

When I got back to the operations center, the mission was still ongoing, but we had succeeded in getting the Taliban's attention. They quickly massed and attacked our troopers as they made their way through the orchards and fields that bordered Nerkh, and we had a real fight on our hands.

We moved close air support to the vicinity, and the combined and coordinated fires really took a toll on the insurgents. We hunted from the ground and air that night and throughout the next day, a relentless pursuit. They fought back with small arms and RPGs, and we had several troopers wounded. But the enemy had made a fatal mistake in exposing a fairly large force in terrain that provided us ample opportunity to track, locate, and destroy them, and we did. We killed almost fifty insurgents over the two-day operation, and knew many more had been wounded, as Afghan reports came in from the more remote villages further in the mountains of tens of injured Taliban who were seeking medical treatment.

Operations like this one in Jalrez and Nerkh would have to suffice until the 3rd Brigade Combat Team, 10th Mountain Division, arrived in three months. Looking back later the next day, I was certain we could keep the insurgents off their game, and prevent an actual takeover of a district or provincial center. I was almost equally convinced we could not keep the enemy from all-too-frequent small battlefield successes—IEDs, ambushes, kidnappings, beheadings—that would continue to influence perceptions. Most importantly, we had to address the perception of the locals, of the Kabul elite, of the media, and the world, of an endangered capital: the enemy at the gates of Kabul.

Over the fifteen months in combat, we conducted multiple offensive operations like the one at Nerkh, big and small, on a daily basis throughout RC-East. When combined with the counterterrorism operations conducted by the special ops task forces, they were critical to keeping the insurgents off-balance, at least as much as we could.

There was not much time to sleep that night, but not because of the Nerkh operation. Pete Johnson's brigade combat team and staff along with my CJTF team in support had that fight well under control, and my Deputy Commanding General for Operations Mark Milley and CJTF Operations Officer Colonel Brian Winski reveled in the action. As the division commander I watched them wage the battle, and seeing no need to intervene, did not.

Brian Winski had not been part of the 101st Airborne Division staff when we deployed to Afghanistan as CJTF-101. He was actually in school, completing a war college-equivalent fellowship. When I decided to replace our senior joint operations officer, Milley and many others told me Winski was our man, and I remembered his competence and leadership as the 101st's chief of current operations in Mosul, Iraq, back in 2004. We called, he volunteered to deploy, and in what seemed like a handful of days he joined us in Bagram, in charge of our entire joint and combined operations staff, and a key interlocutor to all of our ISAF allies as well as the Afghan and Pakistani military staff. As modest as they come, with a character that exuded the "Follow Me" precepts of the infantry branch, and supremely competent, Brian was the perfect officer for this complicated position.

I found over my career that finding the right person for the toughest jobs is really hard. I discovered the importance of personal chemistry: some people are instant and accurate judges of that chemistry; I, on the other hand, developed relationships more slowly, and in some cases, realized I had made an error in entrusting a key job to someone who I ultimately could not trust with that responsibility, often because the required level of competence exceeded their experience or training, or because of some issue in character, theirs or mine.

I trusted Winski and Milley with my life as well as those in my command, and so headed off to bed. At 2:00 a.m., after grabbing some ninety minutes or so of sleep, I returned to the operations center to sign legal documents concerning three detainees, then held a ramp ceremony for two soldiers killed in action: a soldier killed by the Afghan police, and a soldier from up in the Korengal, killed in action during a dismounted patrol.

The next morning was Saturday, October 18, which turned out to be beautiful at Bagram and Bamyan, and so after an early morning run and less than two hours of sleep, we boarded the Black Hawks and headed southwest, deep into the Hindu Kush.

Our commander for Bamyan and Parwan, Colonel Scott Spellmon, flew with me. Scott commanded the 1st Maneuver Enhancement Brigade (MEB) out of Fort Polk, Louisiana. A West Point graduate with a master's degree in civil engineering, one might not expect a Corp of Engineers officer commanding troops responsible for a counterinsurgency fight in Afghanistan. But Scott and his 1st MEB soldiers were perfect for Bamyan and Parwan. Neither province was a hotbed of insurgent activity due to their remoteness, insularity, and relative local populace homogeneity. But both provinces had low-level insurgent activity and both needed extensive work to assist the local governance and to build infrastructure. In the case of Bamyan, it was worse—to prevent famine.

This wasn't Scott's first war. He had served in Desert Storm and later in Iraq during Operation Iraqi Freedom, and he was a confident, skilled, and personable leader.

This was my fourth trip to Bamyan. All of Bamyan Province was remote, with narrow passes east, west, and north that allowed limited truck and car traffic when the weather was good. The peaks on both sides of the passes were Hindu Kush peaks: towering, jagged, snowcapped, beautiful to behold from a safe distance, and terrifying if you found yourself on a slope or in the air in bad weather. Then they were killers.

In spite of their remoteness, these highlands that lay within the Hindu Kush and the Paghman Range had a long, bloody history that stretched more than two millennia. Not far from the town of Bamyan was "Red City," believed to have been constructed around 300 BC. Built into solid reddish rock about fifteen hundred feet above the valley floor, with multiple tiers for buildings and homes, it must have been something to see in its prime. It was utterly destroyed centuries ago. Not far were the ruins of the citadel, the Shahr-e Gholghola, capital of the Ghorid Empire. Also utterly devastated. The standing Buddhas, one almost 175 feet tall, sculpted out of soft rock into the canyon, dated from about the fifth century AD, and were part of the Buddhist Kushan Empire. Surrounded by a Hindu Buddhist monastery named the "Place of Shining Light," the site had attracted the devout, who carved hundreds of dwellings in the rock face. Facing the Buddhas amid narrow but lush green fields and a rushing river, Bamyan town dated back at least from then, and travelers on the ancient Silk Road mentioned the Buddhas and Bamyan. But history had mistreated the tiny, bucolic village. Waves of invaders conquered the highlands, the Sassanids replaced the Kushan, and then came the Hephthalites, the Saffarids, and the Ghaznavids. Finally, the ultimate destroyer arrived in Bamyan in 1221.

Genghis Khan and his Mongol army of some thirty thousand troops roared into the highlands and the Bamyan Valley in pursuit of Jalal al Din Mingburnu, ruler of the Khwarezmian Empire. Holed up at Bamyan, Mingburnu's troops fiercely held off the Mongol siege. Then Mutukan, grandson of Genghis Khan, was killed in combat, reputedly by an arrow from the Khwarezmian fort. Khan's rage was immense: in spite of extraordinary casualties, his troops captured all of Bamyan, and Khan swore that nothing—no person, no animal—would survive his revenge. Men, women, children, animals, all were slaughtered, and the countryside laid to waste. The Place of Shining Light became known as the City of Sorrows.

As we flew up into the valley, I spotted the gigantic empty holes in the red rock mountainside to the north. The Buddhas were long gone, as if struck by a leprosy that ate away rock as if it were flesh, destroyed by Taliban cannon and explosives in the spring of 2001. Regarded as apostate icons by the Taliban, who had no sense of history other than their narrow interpretation of Islam, the destruction of the Buddhas of Bamyan was just one in a string of unconscionable acts perpetuated against Afghans, their culture, and their rich history during the painful years of Taliban rule.

To my left, I could see the short rock and dirt strip that was the Bamyan airstrip. At just short of ten thousand feet of altitude, hemmed in by mountains, it was a challenge for fixed-wing aircraft to use. For our Black Hawk on such a beautiful morning, it meant keeping our gross weight reasonable: carry no heavy loads, watch our fuel, and ensure we didn't take one passenger too many.

I could see the New Zealand base camp just adjacent to the airstrip. Manned by a diverse lot of New Zealand soldiers and civilians, they were well suited for the mountains and high altitude of Bamyan. They seemed to get along well with the local Hazara population, which was critical.

Just a couple of weeks prior, I had flown up to the reconstruction team for their transfer of authority. The outgoing commander, Colonel David Tracey, was giving up command to Colonel Rich Hall. It was a great show, with Maori martial traditions interlaced with British Commonwealth. It reminded me of my first real experience with the New Zealand defense forces, during one of my first trips to Bamyan and the reconstruction team. I had been forewarned. When confronted by half-clothed, menacing warriors, chanting what could only be a life-or-death warning, give honor due, but don't retreat. And don't ever look at the token they toss your way, even as your role is to retrieve it, while never breaking eye lock on the warriors: eye to eye, warrior to fellow warrior.

In the hot dust of the Afghan spring, surrounded by stark gray and black bare peaks, I stared unblinkingly at what must have been the entire contingent of the New Zealand reconstruction team's soldiers, shirts off, strongly built, with only their fiercest faces showing. The haka was a spectacle and an honor I will never forget.

After I had done my part, retrieving the token without breaking eye contact, without fear, but with respect, I was greeted, and made to feel a part of the New Zealand team.

After that welcome months ago and a few more visits, I was a real fan of the reconstruction team. The province itself was a major challenge: incredibly undeveloped, starkly beautiful, and embarrassingly dirt-poor. When rains did not come on time, and crops failed, people starved.

We drove from the base down the narrow road into town in unit SUVs. We were ushered into a nondescript building, and then into Governor Sarobi's modest office. Behind a simple wood desk sat Afghanistan's first and only woman governor, the country's leading female and Hazara politician. With a genuinely friendly smile, she greeted us, shaking hands, and indicated that we should sit in several somewhat worn but clean stuffed chairs.

Habiba Sarobi was in her mid-fifties, a short compact woman with a round, pleasant face, a hint of brown hair peeking out from the shawl she wrapped around her head, and granny glasses perched on a light brown nose. Educated in Kabul, she had studied medicine on a World Health Organization fellowship in India and was a pharmacist; later, she fled to Pakistan with her children during the Taliban years. She became an educator and eventually led the Afghan Institute of Learning. After the fall of the Taliban, she was appointed by President Karzai to be minister of women's affairs. Four years later he appointed her to be Bamyan's governor.

Sarobi was frank about her governorship. She could be a governor of Bamyan because Bamyan was much different than most of the other thirty-three provinces of Afghanistan. Hazaras, like the governor herself, were in the majority. They were Shia and overall less conservative than the Sunnis of Kandahar, especially about the role of women in society and the economy. The Hazaras were reputedly descended from Mongol invaders, looked different than the majority of Pashtun or Tajik Afghans, and had often been relegated to subservient status in Afghan society. But

Bamyan was their home, and although life was tough, brutally so, they were equal up here.

We chatted about First Lady Laura Bush's visit to Bamyan in June as we sipped fiercely hot sweet tea from tiny glass cups. I complimented her on her selection by *Time* magazine as a "Hero of the Environment." She smiled, and said she would personally show me her work, the Band-e Amir Lakes parklands, if we could fly there together later in the day. I asked about security. Sarobi told us that the security situation was worsening, and she wanted more Afghan police stationed in her province to better patrol the roads and passes. At the time, there were no significant Afghan Army units in Bamyan, and the New Zealand security team was the primary way we in RC-East influenced Bamyan's security. I asked the governor if she wanted me to talk with Minister of Defense Wardak about stationing an Afghan Army unit in Bamyan. She said no, she preferred more police, not soldiers. I hoped she was right.

We spread out maps and reviewed road projects, which New Zealand and the U.S. were funding. But the main topic was food insecurity. It had been a bad harvest, and without extensive World Food Program shipments of basic foodstuffs, her people would starve. I promised as much help as we could provide, and told her about the agriculture development teams we were bringing to several other provinces. She immediately said she wanted a team too.

We drove with Governor Sarobi up to the airstrip and boarded our Black Hawks. Sitting next to her, with Scott and Rich following on maps, we flew further west. I had done an extensive aerial recon of Bamyan in early October, and had seen the huge engineering effort expended to build simple gravel roads. I had also overflown the soon-to-be national park at Band-e Amir Lakes, which, frankly, seemed far-fetched. Miles from Bamyan, the lakes were deep azure, the deep blue sky and that of the pristine snowmelt water complemented by sheer white and gray stone of the surrounding cliffs.

I thought then, *We are in Afghanistan, not Wyoming or Utah!*

This time, with Governor Sarobi's narration, her passion and enthusiasm quite evident through the aircraft intercom, it was easier to at least understand her dream. She saw tourism as Bamyan's key to survival, and future prosperity. She was working with the UN and other NGOs to rebuild the Buddhas at Bamyan, which had been a site of religious tourism since the sixth century. Archeologists could excavate the Red City and citadel and build a small museum to display the artifacts. And at Band-e Amir she saw the gorgeous alpine lakes as places for solitude, for recreation, for tourism just like we had in the western U.S. national parks. One part of my brain told me it was a crazy idea, not feasible in our lifetimes. The other part said maybe this is just what Bamyan needed.

We flew back to the town and dropped the governor and Rich Hall off, then headed back down the long, narrow pass to the Shomali Plain. I really liked Governor Sarobi and deeply respected her. For over two thousand years her land, Bamyan and the highlands, had known only grief from foreign invaders. I thought we—my soldiers, our PRTs, our leaders, myself—were different this time. But we would have to prove it.

CHAPTER 22

"A just man walketh in his integrity; his children are blessed after him."
Proverbs 20:7

Tuesday, October 21, 2008

As a regional commander, I had little to no routine interaction with President Karzai. I first saw him in person at the Afghan Independence Day debacle in late April, and admired his fearless determination as he quickly regrouped and immediately got on Afghan TV to denounce the insurgent attackers and reassure his people. I later met him at General McNeill's change of command ceremony. Later still, I briefed him and President Bush over video teleconference. It was hard to gauge the man. In person, he appeared serious, even intense, well spoken, more articulate in English than most world leaders, and impeccably dressed in the role of Afghan president.

But Karzai seemed to have a split personality when I listened and read his media interviews and all-too-frequent denunciations of U.S. and ISAF troops and our operations. His allegations made it seem like we deliberately targeted Afghan civilians, and the accusations profoundly disturbed many of my leaders and me. Most of our soldiers did not pay close attention to Karzai's press releases, and those who did often characterized Karzai as just another politician, saying one thing to one group, something else to another, with truth an unimportant and bothersome issue best ignored.

But to those of us who led troops into combat and sometimes to their deaths, what Karzai said *was* important, and the more he ranted against NATO and ISAF, the more I came to dislike this man whose country we were trying to defend.

I had seen press reports of Karzai, reportedly surrounded by yes men and sycophants, holed up in his palace and walking the corridors, talking to the paintings on the walls. I had seen intelligence reports that discussed his emotional state and stability, and one had to give the man credit for maintaining his composure and sanity in the sometimes feudal, always tribal politics of Afghanistan, and surrounded by less than cordial neighbors.

By October, I often thought that Karzai was truly wacko. If not unhinged then he was deliberately trying—for reasons unknown—to denigrate those who sought to help his country, while ignoring the atrocities of the insurgents and especially the Taliban. After some of his most egregious statements against NATO, I wished I could tell him what I thought, in person, to his face.

My time came on a cloudy Tuesday in late October.

Late morning, I was in my office when I got a call from General McKiernan. President Karzai was ill, perhaps very ill. He needed to be seen by a doctor, preferably at a hospital. Could I send Black Hawks to the palace to pick him up and bring him to our military hospital at Bagram?

Of course I said yes, and the staff and Jim Richardson's aviation brigade quickly got two Black Hawks en route to Kabul and the presidential palace. We alerted the hospital commander and his staff.

My driver Staff Sergeant Chris Keepes and I drove the short distance to the hospital and waited out by the medevac pad. I didn't know what to expect. McKiernan had few details about what was ailing Karzai, just that it was important to get him to a good doctor right away. I thought the president would have had his own doc, maybe even his own clinic in the palace. But given the still developing medical capabilities in Afghanistan in 2008, from what I had seen, I didn't blame Karzai one bit for seeking out our military hospital.

The Bagram military hospital, officially known as the Craig Joint Theater Hospital, was a level III treatment facility, and provided the best and most comprehensive medical care in the country. Long out of tents and located in a well-built concrete building with a modern surgery and intensive care unit, and manned by the best trauma docs and nurses in the army and air force, the hospital had saved hundreds of lives since we had arrived in March. American lives. Polish lives. French lives. And many, many, others, including Afghan soldiers and civilians.

Whatever was wrong with the president, I was confident we could help.

The Black Hawks were quickly back, and taxied to a side ramp, not wanting to occupy the medevac pad just in case we had an urgent trauma casualty come in. The crew chief got out of the still-running aircraft, opened the side doors, and out came the president, along with the flight surgeon we had sent to care for him in the air. A large traveling party followed Karzai. He came directly for me. We shook hands as I greeted him, and smiled a small smile. He looked in pain, his face sallow, pinched. We walked together a short way. He knew who I was, which I found amazing, and recalled my brief over the video teleconference when he visited the White House.

The docs latched onto the president and whisked him off to be examined. We chatted with Karzai's staff, who did not seem to be worried now that he was with us.

I lost track of time as we waited and talked; his staffers were fluent in English, very much acquainted with our overall situation in RC-East, and curious to learn more about our daily operations. Some of the team went off on a hospital tour.

About an hour later President Karzai and the doc emerged. Karzai looked better already. The doc said he had a case of early pneumonia, and with meds and rest could keep it from worsening. Karzai promised to cut back his hectic schedule, at least for a few days, and he thanked the docs and nurses hovering around him.

The president seemed in no hurry to return to Kabul and his palace, and lingered. We talked about the situation in the east, and he asked probing questions that impressed me. An aide came up and whispered into the president's ear, and then they were off, not out to the aircraft, but deeper into the hospital wards. We followed.

I lagged behind the party, and so was surprised as I turned the corner into a large corridor to find Karzai holding a baby, beaming, cooing into the baby's ear. Out of nowhere appeared a camera, and the president and baby posed for pictures, as if it was election time in Kabul. Or Peoria, for that matter. Politicians love babies.

Baby Zahra was the first baby to be born at our hospital. Her mother had been brought in several weeks prior after suffering major injuries in an explosion at her home. The medical team treated her injuries and decided Mom could continue carrying the baby. Zahra was delivered by C-section the morning of October 4. A number of our air force doctors and nurses actually had obstetrics experience and training. Among them, Air Force Tech Sergeant Roopa Shoop, a medical technician at Bagram who worked as a labor and delivery tech back at Nellis Air Force Base when not deployed, helped with the delivery and did the first assessment of the baby. Zahra was a healthy newborn.

After visiting with several wounded Afghan soldiers also being treated at Bagram, we walked out to the waiting Black Hawks. Karzai thanked all of us sincerely. He got on board the aircraft and was soon en route back to his Kabul palace.

I missed my chance to tell the president how I felt about his denunciations of some NATO and ISAF operations. At the time I did not find the opening, the minute or two when he and I were alone when I could bring it up. I was doubtful the president would care one way or another about my angst; he was speaking to a different audience, a local and tribal audience that didn't care about foreign troop morale, but cared a lot about the inadvertent civilian deaths and injuries that came with this kind of war.

Karzai quickly recovered, and soon was back to his normal schedule. And back to his bitter denouncements of our night operations, inadvertent civilian casualties, and intrusions on Afghan lives.

Early the next morning a U.S. special operations team returning from an operation along the KG Pass Road ran into an Afghan Army checkpoint, and in the confusion and darkness, one side or the other fired shots. A firefight broke out, and the better-trained and equipped special operators killed nine Afghan soldiers and wounded four more. Once I found out, I called the ISAF commander. General McKiernan told me to take the lead for consequence management, as usual. He said we should suggest a joint U.S. and Afghan investigation, as we had in the Gora Paray border incident. I called Vice Admiral Bill McRaven, whose operators had been in the fight, and told him what I planned to do. I then called Afghan Army J-3 Lieutenant General Karimi, personally apologized on behalf of the U.S. government, told him I was sincerely sorry as a fellow soldier and commander, and suggested a joint investigation. He accepted.

That evening, after working the blue-on-green firefight all day, I forced myself to admit maybe Karzai had a point.

Some of our operations created more enemies than what they started with. In any society, the inadvertent killing of relatives or loved ones creates anguish, pain, and resentment. In Afghan society, where Pashtunwali and family honor required revenge and retribution, the brothers and sons and even fathers of those we inadvertently killed on the margins of our operations became our new enemies. For every friendly or fence-sitting Afghan we killed by mistake, we gained several new insurgents, sworn to revenge. And they had multiple avenues to extract revenge, from simple but devastating pressure cooker IEDs to suicide vests and cars to joining any one of myriad insurgent groups.

We had to find ways to increase our precision. Karzai and many others, including some NATO commanders, felt we needed to drastically curtail our night operations or our air attacks or both in order to minimize civilian or blue-on-green casualties (meaning US or NATO forces inadvertently killing an Afghan civilian, policeman, or soldier). Most of our special operations occurred at night, and were often as precise as modern combat allowed. Most of our air attacks, be they close air support, AC-130 gunships, or Apache or Kiowa Warrior helicopters, came from responding to troops in contact, and often saved the day for the troopers on the ground. I wasn't about to put artificial limits on either.

But precision in targeting and engagement had to be improved. We had to have better assessments of the raw intelligence and the targeting indicators, attuned to this society, this terrain, and this culture. We had to differentiate between a bridal party walking en masse in the mountains at 3:00 a.m. and an insurgent platoon moving to contact; we had to understand the hundred-year struggle along the contested Durand Line; we had to ensure a nervous Afghan Army soldier or policeman did not start a major friendly-on-friendly firefight with an erratic shot in the dark.

We had to increase our precision even as others worked at cross-purposes. The insurgents often sought refuge among women and children, and the local insurgents were themselves villagers. The Taliban seemed to regard children as instruments of war, and thought nothing of deliberate targeting of schools and schoolchildren. Otherwise friendly Afghans who supported the Afghan government used false reports to ISAF to settle old scores among local or regional competitors, be they family or tribal scores. And, of course, the porous and contested border between the Afghan east and the Pakistan frontier provided numerous opportunities, from "hit-and-run" type mortar and artillery shelling from the Pakistani side, to causing Frontier Corps-versus-border police fratricide, to the sheltering of fleeing insurgents in the villages of the FATA and North and South Waziristan.

Confusion was the antithesis of precision, at least in this fight, and this war was plenty confusing. It was a war my father would have recognized, with his three tours in Vietnam. At the tactical level, most of our enemies wore no uniform, claimed to live among and represent the people better than the legitimate government, and scrambled across the border when odds were not in their favor. At the operational level, small bands of seemingly poorly equipped insurgents could mass with significant firepower for offensive operations at a time and place of their choosing, especially against the host nation armed forces, with effects well beyond the tactical. At the strategic level, the entire outcome of the fighting depended on uncertain support from the American people and their representatives grown weary of war and its costs. And fighting for what? A seemingly irreversibly corrupt host government? The parallels to my father's war were impossible to ignore.

Three days after the governor's meeting, I hosted Brigadier General "Mick" Nicholson in my office at Bagram. Fresh from a National Military Command Center assignment at the Pentagon, Mick was on his way to be the deputy commander for stability at RC-South. We walked around Afghanistan verbally, and I shared my experiences and thoughts since we had assumed RC-East the previous April. Mick was very much up to speed and had insights of his own. As we shook hands and planned to meet in a few days' time in Kandahar, I mentally noted: *He is one of our best and brightest. He knows more about Afghanistan than most.*

I flew down to Kabul for my routine meetings with Lieutenant General Karimi, the Afghan operations officer, and Minister Wardak. I then headed over for my first meeting with the newly appointed minister of interior, Mohammad Hanif Atmar. I was looking forward to meeting Atmar: he was reputedly a KHAD (former Afghan secret intelligence service) intelligence operative with Soviet KGB (main Soviet security/intelligence service) ties when still quite young, then a fighter against the mujahedeen in the Soviet-Afghan war, where he lost part of a leg during a battle at Jalalabad. He left Afghanistan and earned degrees in the UK, and then worked with NGOs involved in Afghanistan. After the fall of the Taliban, he returned home and was appointed to be the minister of rural rehabilitation and development in the transitional government. In 2004, Atmar was confirmed by the Parliament in the same position as part of newly elected President Karzai's cabinet. From 2006 to 2008, he served as the minister of education, and had just been confirmed by the Parliament to replace Minister Zarar at interior.

The minister welcomed us at his office door, joined by his U.S. advisor, Colonel Steve Lynch. Immaculately groomed with a closely trimmed dark beard and short hair, a small balding spot shiny at the back of his head, and gleaming bleached white *shalwar kameez* covered by a dark natty sport coat, Atmar looked the role of a minister. But it was his mind that most impressed me that day.

He showed me to a comfortable chair, limping only slightly as a subtle reminder of his past. He was soft-spoken, and I had to lean forward with my poor hearing to fully hear him. He spoke superb English, and was articulate, measured, and reassuring. This was a man who knew he had much to do, didn't have much time, and wanted partners who could help him achieve his objectives.

"My time is limited, at most eleven months," he said after the beginning pleasantries and salutations. He clearly didn't plan on staying on after the election, no matter the outcome.

He told us of his top priorities: Kabul security, voter registration, Highway 1 security, border security, and police development and counter-corruption.

This was all good: they were my priorities for the ministry and our partnership as well.

Addressing the last point, I mentioned the friendly fire incidents we had had, with Afghan National Police engaging and sometimes killing ISAF soldiers.

"We are so ashamed that our ANP killed a U.S. soldier," he told me.

I was none too proud of our own blue-on-green firefights where U.S. forces had killed Afghans.

We agreed that we needed to collaborate to help promote good police work, get rid of the corruption as much as we could, and equip the forces for success. He wanted to significantly accelerate the professionalization of the police and border police, and I wanted the same thing.

It was a warm, thoughtful exchange, and I left the meeting headed back to Bagram thinking Karzai had chosen well.

It was late afternoon by the time I got back to my headquarters at Bagram, and arrived to terrible news. Captain Robert Yllescas, commander at

Combat Outpost Keating, had been severely wounded right outside the gate at Keating. He was being flown to Craig, our hospital, for urgent surgery. He might not make it to the hospital.

Rob Yllescas had replaced Captain Joe Hutto as commander at Keating soon after my visit there in July. Yllescas had been raised in Guatemala. His American mother met his father at the University of Nebraska, married, and accompanied him to his native Guatemala, where Rob was born and went to school. After attending the University of Nebraska, he was commissioned in the U.S. Army, married, and had two girls. He had served in our nation's wars, twice in Iraq, and then in Afghanistan.

The facts of what happened took time to assemble and flow into Bagram, but eventually we were told Yllescas was leading a joint U.S. and ANA patrol around COP Keating, and had headed back to camp. A rickety footbridge over the rushing river in front of Keating supported only one person at a time, and when Rob crossed, an emplaced radio-controlled IED detonated, throwing him onto the rocky landing zone in the middle of the river. His legs had been badly damaged, plus he had trauma to his head and hands. In spite of insurgent small arms fire that immediately targeted the patrol, Rob was quickly evacuated to Keating's aid station, where physician's assistant Captain Steve Brewer worked feverishly to keep Yllescas alive. Medevac was called for, but Rob's traumatic injuries required immediate evacuation to a surgical hospital, and a Chinook refueling at Bostick was ordered to Keating to pick him up as soon as it could fly to the outpost.

A few bullets were still being exchanged when the Chinook landed on the landing zone, and Yllescas was carried aboard. Jim Markert had ordered Bostick's doctor, Captain Amanda Cuda, to jump on the Chinook before it departed, and on the flight out of Keating, she picked up treating Rob, as Brewer was needed to stay at Keating and treat others wounded in the day's fight.

Captain Brewer and Captain Cuda saved Rob Yllescas' life that day, allowing him the time to reach Bagram, where his shredded legs were amputated, his hand repaired, and head wounds treated during many hours of surgery through the night.

The next day was rainy and cold, with heavy clouds in the passes, a dispiriting type of weather that perfectly fit my mood when I went to see Yllescas and three others who had been wounded in the previous day's fights in RC-East. They would soon be on an air force jet headed to Landstuhl and then the States, and like normal, I presented Purple Hearts to the wounded. I was a professional soldier, very familiar with the ravages of war on the human body, but seeing Rob so badly mangled was deeply disturbing. And I was most uncertain he would make it through these next several days alive.

I was hosting the first tripartite border conference the next morning, but first my staff had set up an early meeting with the new inspector general of the Pakistan Frontier Corps, Major General Tariq Khan. With the Gora Paray incident early in my tour, my relationship with Khan's predecessor had been perfunctory. That couldn't stand; I needed the Frontier Corps to lock down their side of the Durand Line, and if that was not possible, to at least significantly increase security on their side. A good relationship with the commander of the Frontier Corps, the inspector general, was critical in my mind.

At exactly 8:45 a.m., precisely on time, General Khan appeared at my office door. Attired in the winter uniform of a Frontier Corps general, an impeccable navy wool uniform with a calfskin waist and bullet belt and somewhat incongruous leather sandals with white socks, he looked every bit the frontier khan. His British English was smooth, articulate, and learned. The son of a Pakistani feudal lord who was also a cavalry major, Tariq Khan was the real thing: a born and bred frontier warrior with a worldly view and a strong sense of history.

We talked about the security situation in Bajaur and what might be done to improve our coordination. We already had U.S. Special Forces living at Fort Bala Hisar, his headquarters, with a direct line to my headquarters at Bagram. We also had the border coordination center at Torkham Gate to help coordinate among ISAF, the Pakistanis, and the Afghans. But much more was needed.

He told me that he had a deep admiration for General Douglas MacArthur, and what he had accomplished in Japan after World War II. All in all, it was a fascinating discussion and excellent first meeting with a man I would grow to have deep respect for over the coming months.

General Khan and I drove over to the Jirga Center on Bagram, where the tripartite team had formed. Joining Tariq Khan were the Pakistani Army ops planners Brigadier General Amjad and Brigadier General Amer. Major General Rahim Wardak, commander of the Afghan 201st Corps, and his senior staff represented the Afghans. Lynne Tracy, consul general of the U.S. consulate in Peshawar, was there, as was the ISAF ops officer, Brigadier General Mike Tucker.

We all gave briefs on the situation facing our forces, but Tariq Khan's was the most memorable. He said the enemy, the Tehrik-e-Taliban-i-Pakistan, the Pakistani-focused Taliban called the TTiP, and the Tehreek-e-Nafaz-e-Shariat-e-Mohammadi (TNSM), who were not unified, must be defeated "agency by agency," and that he and the Pakistani Army needed our help. We discussed how we could coordinate operations on both sides in time and space for maximum impact on the insurgency. Out of the corner of my eye, I watched the regular Pakistani generals as they listened to Khan, searching for signs of disapproval; after all, this was the most honest and open assessment of the terrorist and insurgent problem in Pakistan by a Pakistani official I had yet heard. I could detect nothing but support in their faces.

At noon, I reluctantly called the meeting to a close. This was truly the first really productive meeting I had had with the Pakistanis and Afghans together, and I wanted it to be the first of many more. As I lingered, my aide pushed me out of the Jirga Center door to our SUV, and off to my Black Hawk, which was already running. We flew down the Shomali Plain, skirting Kabul on the mountainous east side, satisfied that yesterday's low ceilings, rain, and spits of sleet had cleared. This was to be an important event for RC-East at Ghazni and I was the host.

The Polish Battle Group was the largest allied contingent serving in RC-East, larger than a U.S. battalion and smaller than a U.S. brigade combat team, and well armed and equipped. This was the handover between Battle Group Three and Four, and more importantly, this was the transfer of authority in Ghazni from Tony DeMartino's battalion to the Polish Battle Group. The Poles would take over security for all of Ghazni Province, reporting to RC-East and under my command.

In preparation for this, we had improved the camps in the province, increased the intelligence sharing between my headquarters and the Polish headquarters at Ghazni, and built a helicopter ramp and short airstrip at Ghazni. The Poles had carried out their promise to provide their own rotary wing support, and several MI-24/35 HINDs and gleaming new MI-171 assault helicopters were now at Ghazni and ready for missions.

It was a chilly but sunny fall afternoon. The Polish troops stood at attention on the hard dirt plain. Afghan Minister of Defense Wardak and Polish Minister of Defense Klich chatted with General Bantz Craddock, who was now NATO's supreme allied commander Europe, while Ghazni Governor Osmani tried one last time to talk me out of moving DeMartino's battalion out of Ghazni. He still did not trust the ability of the Poles, and I think feared for his life if the insurgency made inroads. But I was tired of Osmani's continued lack of support for the Poles, and as diplomatically as I could told him this was the way it was, and I was convinced it would work just fine. With their integral air support, mobile gun platforms, and the 148 MRAPs the U.S. was providing to the Poles for improved secure mobility, they were both well equipped and well trained for this type of mission in Ghazni Province.

Speeches could be incessantly long during transfers of authority and changes of command, but the afternoon went quickly and even Governor Osmani seemed to come through at the last minute, giving what had to be a grudging acknowledgement of what ISAF and the Afghan ministry strongly supported. The Poles were in Ghazni in a big way, and he needed to work with them as closely as he had the American battalion under DeMartino.

And we needed DeMartino's battalion elsewhere.

CHAPTER 23

"Conquering the world on horseback is easy; it is
dismounting and governing that is hard."
Genghis Khan

November 4, 2008

I spent Election Day traveling to visit troops in Sharana and in meetings and briefings back at Bagram. That evening the results were not yet clear, but I wrote in my journal that I was so relieved to have the election cycle over. It seemed like it had been years of listening to the politicians and pundits alike, and I was thankful to be far away from the epicenter, Washington, D.C.

I had not voted in this election, like most since I became a professional army officer. I had met and briefed Senator Obama, and had seen up close the magnetism and excitement surrounding him, and thought he would be tough to beat.

Instead of the election, a tragic attack down in RC-South dominated the day and night. A female member of a U.S. Human Terrain Team (HTT) had been attacked by a local national, doused with gasoline, and lit on fire. Saved by a fellow HTT member, she was barely alive, with burns over 60 percent of her body. Her boss, the HTT leader, detained and questioned the local national suspected of the attack. He then shot the Afghan point-blank in the face, killing him instantly. Apprehended by U.S. soldiers, he was being held for homicide.

It was an ugly war.

The next morning, the election results were in and Barack Obama had been declared the winner, with 350 electoral college votes and 52 percent of the popular vote. Democrats controlled both the House and Senate. I wrote in my journal that night that I had renewed faith in the American system of government and our people. It was time for a black American to be president, and I was hopeful. Obama was a noble choice, but could he govern such a diverse nation? And what a mess he was inheriting: two regional wars, a global economic recession and housing collapse, and declining trust in the American presidency. The new president would have to be better than good.

The following morning, we flew in a small jet, a UC-35 usually reserved for longer flights to Kandahar or outside the country, on a short fifteen-minute trip to Kabul Airport, shooting an instrument approach through the smoky haze of a soon-to-be winter early morning. Kabul city was obscured by thousands of small wood and coal fires, used for cooking and heat in the chilly late fall. The smoke and haze were reminiscent of all I had read about nineteenth-century London. It stung the eyes and left a bitter taste on the tongue.

I met up with General Petraeus at a waiting C-130, and we flew along with some twenty of his CENTCOM staff back up to Bagram. We briefed our campaign plan, then drove him over to hear the special ops task force, and then dropped him at the dining facility for lunch with brigade commanders. After lunch, he and I boarded my Black Hawk and we flew over Wardak and Logar, and I pointed out where the first incoming troops of the surge I had requested would be positioned. We then headed further southeast to the Pakistani border and Margah Combat Outpost. Lieutenant Colonel John Allred, 2nd Battalion, 506th Battalion commander, met us, and with two young first lieutenants led the general around the small platoon outpost and talked about their patrols and their defenses. We were five miles from Waziristan, launching pad for many insurgent artillery and mortar attacks, as well as enemy cross-border firefights. I hoped we would be spared during the visit. I wanted Petraeus to see the reality of RC-East, but not that much reality on his first visit as the CENTCOM commander.

We flew north to Salerno where he met with Colonel Pete Johnson and the Currahee battalion commanders, then flew back to Kabul. He said it was a good trip. He realized now why I recommended that division, brigade, and battalion commanders return to Afghanistan once they had successfully served there, instead of alternating between Iraq and Afghanistan with no purpose. It took time and experience to understand the terrain, the diverse population, and the incredibly complex consortium of insurgent groups that made up the enemy in Afghanistan.

As I headed back to Bagram, I was satisfied. I sometimes doubted if these trips by senior leaders were really useful to them, but this one seemed to have been just what General Petraeus needed as he took over CENTCOM. The situation was worsening, and it would take more effort, more troops, and more resources—and General Petraeus' strong support and leadership too.

I knew I was not the only commander highlighting the worsening situation in Afghanistan. A few days before the Petraeus visit, I had flown south to Kandahar for the RC-South TOA and change of command. Canadian Major General Marc Lessard was departing, and Dutch Major General Mart de Kruif was assuming command just as RC-South was rapidly expanding its force structure and reach into the southern provinces. A large number of U.S. Marine Corps units had begun operations in the summer, and the situation was increasingly violent. After six speeches, I talked with Brigadier General Mick Nicholson, now the operations deputy, and he affirmed that RC-South would need even more troops to be effective. In one sense, all of us were competing for limited resources, especially as the impact of the Iraq troop surge continued to adversely impact the "dwell" times for U.S. troops at home between combat deployments.

I knew I had a brigade coming soon, as well as MRAPs and more surveillance and reconnaissance, and I had to make sure we made maximum progress with them, in spite of the looming winter.

That same day, I flew back to Bagram midday for a ramp ceremony for Specialist Dan Wallace, a Kentucky National Guard soldier with our 201st Engineer Battalion. When it was over, I went to my office and wrote a short note about the ceremony to Major General Ed Tonini, the commander of the Kentucky National Guard, and to Clarissa "TC" Freeman, civilian aide to the secretary of the army from Kentucky. I realized neither had ever seen a Bagram ramp ceremony, and so I described it for them in a short email:

> TC and Ed:
> Late this afternoon here on the Shomali Plain, Bagram, Afghanistan, several thousand Soldiers, Sailors, Airmen, Marines, and civilians lined the main street of our airfield, standing silently as the HMMWV with Specialist Dan Wallace's flag-draped coffin drove past. With fall upon us, the sky was cloudy and colored in a way only possible here at the start of the Hindu Kush, but no one paid much attention to the sky. All eyes were on the coffin and Wallace's last trip among us.
>
> With the U.S. Flag and honor guard at least 20 men strong, we moved Dan's coffin into the waiting C17, a giant airplane that swallowed those of us honored enough to bid him a final farewell. Two Chaplains guided our prayers, and two by two the commanders of the 201st Engineer Battalion, Kentucky National Guard, and the rest of us who command troops here in combat, filed by for a final salute. It was dark and gloomy in the aircraft hold, matching everyone's demeanor.

I have done almost 100 of these ramp ceremonies: they never cease to hurt, never cease to astound, and never will break my spirit, or those of us left behind.

I am proud to have served with Dan Wallace, a Soldier.

Jeff Schloesser

I could only hope that I was right, that these ramp ceremonies would not break my spirit.

On that Saturday, I flew by Black Hawk to Forward Operating Base Shank, and picked up CNN Pentagon correspondent Barbara Starr and her cameraman. Fresh from embedding with some of my troops at Shank, she wanted to talk with me about the situation along the Pakistan border, and together we would visit Margah Combat Outpost, the same base General Petraeus and I just visited. My staff had told her Margah was one of a series of remote platoon-sized outposts along the Paktika-Waziristan border designed to limit the infiltration of insurgents from the Pakistan frontier to Afghanistan, and she was deeply interested in seeing it firsthand.

I did not know Barbara personally before this trip, but I respected her work. She was one of the Pentagon and defense correspondents who I felt went the extra "mile" to tell an accurate story.

A few minutes from landing at Margah, my command pilot Dave came on the intercom. The outpost was being mortared. I told him to divert further south, to Combat Outpost Malakshay. Located about three miles from the Pakistani border on a steep hill, it too overlooked insurgent infiltration routes. Of course, no one at Malakshay knew we were coming.

I trusted our soldiers and leaders with representing our army and our division, speaking directly with journalists, and without preparation. They often were the best voice: direct, honest, and frank to the point of discomfort, and refreshingly nuanced about the situation in Afghanistan.

We landed on the small helipad outside the wire and scurried up the steep access road and into the HESCO bastion-walled outpost. If the platoon leader or his squad leaders were surprised, they hid it well, as they led us on a tour of the small camp. From narrow perches along the walls they pointed out the infiltration routes used by the insurgents, almost always at night and during bad weather. The mountains and hills were nothing compared to the Hindu Kush up north, but they did canalize the movement across the border, both legitimate and insurgent.

We climbed a narrow ladder to a sandbagged perch above the camp that overlooked the tight valley that led to Pakistan, just a few miles distant. Wearing a blue protective vest and dark green helmet that perched somewhat skewed on her head, her dark-rimmed glasses framing curious, intelligent eyes and a mature face, Barbara was not your typical war correspondent. But she was intense and experienced, and truly excited about being here at Malakshay, on our frontier. It was a cloudy, gloomy day, cold in the wind, but with the camera running, we talked about the outpost, its purpose, and the insurgent movement across the border that we could see in the distance. I was frank about the situation, and I trusted her to factually report what I said.

After an hour and half at Malakshay, the Black Hawk returned and we bid goodbye to the soldiers, and walked out of the camp and down to the waiting aircraft. As we flew back to Bagram, Barbara continued to ask tough questions, good questions that made me think, as she took in the amazingly difficult and jagged terrain below us. She commented how impressed she was with our soldiers. Like so many of our combat outposts, they lived a spartan life of cold and dirt not unlike their grandfathers and great-grandfathers in America's past wars. And while they bitched among themselves about everything from the chow to the boredom, they were professionals at war, and proud to show off for a visiting journalist and their division commander. And I was proud of them.

On Monday morning, I went for my typical run at 5:00 a.m. In the darkness along the perimeter road at the north end of the airfield I heard rockets, a not-too-distant series of explosions. The attack was over within seconds and the night returned to quiet. I turned around and ran back to the operations center, where the watch officer told me the rockets had exploded harmlessly well beyond the airfield and the populated parts of the immense base. *Lucky again.*

But I knew that luck in war was an uncertain presumption, and vowed to ratchet up our security patrols outside the wire.

By 7:30 a.m., I was at my desk talking on the phone to Richard Strand, a leading authority in the U.S. on Nuristan and Nuristanis. We had a lengthy conversation on everything from anthropology to linguistics to inter-tribal politics. In the morning call with Strand and a late evening call with Harold Ingram, the State Department's expert on Afghan tribes, I was attempting to reach out beyond the standard military and agency intel that dwelled on the "what" of Nuristan and Korengal, and tried to get to the "why," a better understanding of how historical isolation and a xenophobic culture framed the people's thoughts and actions. I asked both men to form a study group for us and take the lead on producing practical analysis and recommendations that we and those who followed us could use.

The next day was November 11: Veterans Day. I picked up Ambassador Bill Wood at the airfield ramp and we drove over to our Bagram Veterans Day ceremony. In short speeches, we honored America's veterans and those of our allies who served before us and thanked the soldiers, marines, airmen, and sailors who were our audience for their own service. I did not relish ceremonial speeches much more than I did parades, but we finished the event with a naturalization proceeding for seventy-seven troopers who became full-fledged U.S. citizens that day. As they completed the citizenship oath, I looked at the faces—beaming smiles of pride and joy—of this broadly diverse group of all colors and ethnicities and religions who all wore the uniform of an American volunteer warrior, and I had to smile, and be proud of them as well as our country. Our military and our country would be better for these new citizens.

That night, I wrote in my journal that the ceremony had been uplifting. I was a strong supporter of the abbreviated fast track to U.S.

citizenship provided to those who served in our military, especially those who deployed to fight our conflicts. They came to our army, navy, air force, and Marine Corps, and through tough and exacting training learned the profession of arms, but more importantly, learned what it meant to possess and defend the freedoms many Americans gained by birth. I saw America as a nation of immigrants. Patty and I had helped our children research their ancestors from all sides of our family, and we were proud of our German and Irish ancestry that existed on both sides of the family. Our forebears had come to America in the nineteenth century, some fleeing famine or persecution, others seeking land and fortune. They settled in Minnesota and Kansas, and were storekeepers and farmers until the depression and then World War II changed all that. On my father's side, he and his brothers left the family farm outside Jordan, Minnesota, to serve in the post-world war military as teenagers and young men, with a brother eventually in each and every uniformed service: the army, the Marine Corps, the navy, the air force, and the Coast Guard. They were a proud lot, and my father and his older brother Stan made careers out of the military. But none of them returned to the farm, which was sold as my grandfather moved with my grandmother to the city, to Saint Paul, to work in the stockyards.

Patty's father served in the Pacific during World War II, and when the war was over, he too did not return to the family farm outside Saint Joseph, Missouri, instead moving to Leavenworth, Kansas, to work the rest of his career at the Veterans Affairs Center.

Our folks were not wealthy but solid middle class, and our values reflected our immigrant status, even though the families had been in America for generations: hard work at a steady job, church, and a strong if unpretentious education for us kids.

I was proud to be an American, knew from my service and life outside of America just how privileged that made me in 2008, and was happy to help others become citizens.

The next day the Taliban showed the depths of their depravity. A group of young Afghan girls were walking to school near the Mirwais Nika Girls High School in Kandahar when two men on a motorcycle accosted them. Using water pistols or water bottles loaded with battery acid, they sprayed several girls in the face, and then sped away. The Afghanistan National Military Command Center reported that two of the girls were blinded, and two others injured. The Kandahar local government spokesman said up to six girls had been burned.

Later reports indicated a series of coordinated attacks had taken place on girls and their female teachers walking to school that day in Kandahar.

It was a heartless, despicable act, meant to frighten parents and young girls, and to keep them from attending school. It was impossible for the Afghan police to guard every school site and protect the girls as they walked from home to school and back. As an act of terror, it was frightfully simple and yet effective: the Taliban again demonstrated their belief that women should not be educated in schools, and simultaneously showed the weakness of the central or local government and police to prevent such a horrible attack.

Before the American-led invasion of Afghanistan in 2001, less than one million Afghan children attended school, most of them boys. In 2008, some six million kids were in school, including some two million girls. ISAF and other allies spent millions building schools throughout the country, and schoolbooks and supplies flowed in from all over the world. Many conservative Afghan families still kept their girls at home and did not allow them to attend school, and other families were deeply concerned about their daughters' safety when they did attend. Attacks like this would not stop the government or ISAF or the UN from supporting education in Afghanistan, but it was a horrible reminder of the fragility and frailness of our educational development programs. We could build schools in every village in Afghanistan, but we could not force the parents or the children to participate.

And the next day, no girls went to the Mirwais school.

★ ★ ★

The following Monday found Mark Milley and me back in Islamabad. We met with Ambassador Patterson and Rear Admiral LeFever, as well as a senior American intelligence official. We briefed our winter campaign and intelligence sharing with the Pakistanis, as well as how we intended to support their regular army and Frontier Corps in their operations against TTiP, the Pakistani Taliban in Bajaur and Mohmand. We drove over to Rawalpindi to meet with the new DGMO, Major General Javed Iqbal. His predecessor, General Ahmad Shuja Pasha, had been promoted to lieutenant general and taken over the Pakistani intelligence service (ISI). Since April, Pasha and I had developed a working relationship that was hardly warm, but was positive and transactional, and I thought we were making some real progress in leading our troops to cooperation and some limited collaboration along the border. I wanted an even better relationship with Iqbal.

In a joint session with Iqbal and his deputy Brigadier Amjad, Mark and I laid out our winter campaign along the Durand Line and they briefed us on Operation Sherdil in Bajaur, named Lionheart in English. Inspired and planned by Frontier Corps Inspector General Tariq Khan and led by Brigadier Abid Mumtaz, the ongoing operation had killed over 2,700 militants so far, including TTiP and al-Qaida. To secure cleared areas, the Pakistanis were encouraging the tribes to organize armed militias, Lashkars, to keep the militants from returning. Iqbal asked for help in blocking operations now during phase one in Bajaur and soon along the Afghan border of Kunar and Nangarhar and the Pakistani border frontier of Mohmand in phase two. I quickly and enthusiastically agreed.

This was real progress.

I asked for a private session with General Iqbal before our departure. I thanked him for his leadership and openness to work with ISAF and my troops. I then gave him a sealed folder. A target folder. I asked for his help in finding Abdul Wali, aka Omar Khalid Khorasani. The leader of TTiP in Mohmand, Wali was brutal, effective, and slowly gaining power among the insurgents and militants in the FATA.

We wanted Abdul Wali captured or dead, and needed Pakistani help. Iqbal accepted the target folder, making no promises other than to review it. I had not expected much more.

Our departure was cordial and I invited General Iqbal and Amjad to Bagram for more talks, to which they agreed.

As we drove back to the airfield, Mark and I agreed that the day had been more successful than we had hoped. With Tariq Khan running the Frontier Corps and Iqbal as the DGMO, as well as Pasha running the ISI, could we expect an era of closer collaboration along the Durand Line?

On Friday night, I had a video teleconference with Brigadier General Steve Townsend, our new 101st Airborne Division rear commander. He had just arrived at Fort Campbell, joining our rear detachment commander Lieutenant Colonel Tom Kunk and "mayor" Colonel Fred Swope. Steve was a North Georgia College grad with impeccable infantry and Ranger credentials, and had served in just about every fight since joining the army, including Grenada, Operation Urgent Fury; Panama, Operation Just Cause; Haiti, Operation Uphold Democracy; Operation Anaconda in Afghanistan, as well as later on the CJTF-180 staff; and in Iraq.

With our Iraq deployments coming to a close after one year, those units were coming back home to Fort Campbell, and they needed a senior officer in command. Steve was perfect to corral and command those battle-hardened soldiers as they came back from a tough deployment. We had served together on the USS *America* during Haiti and I trusted Steve 100 percent. We didn't know what the aftermath of this deployment would be: more suicides like the last return? Time would tell, but he was already on the hot seat. He told me President Bush was going to visit Fort Campbell on Tuesday, November 25.

We talked about preparations and POTUS. I deeply respected President Bush, knew he would honor our returning soldiers and their families, and also knew his advance team was vastly experienced in setting the stage for a safe and noteworthy visit. I told Steve not to worry, but to prepare.

★ ★ ★

The president's visit four days later went smoothly. Fort Campbell was cold that late in November, but the president warmed the crowds of soldiers and families that packed a huge aircraft hangar to see and hear him speak. He was no stranger to Fort Campbell; he had made several trips our way before, including Thanksgiving 2001, as the 3rd Brigade Combat Team Rakkasans deployed as the first conventional army brigade to Afghanistan. With our returning 101st Airborne brigades, the constantly deploying 160th Special Operations Aviation Regiment, and the quiet professionals of 5th Special Forces Group, the president had plenty of reason to praise soldiers and their families, and did so. I was deeply pleased by Steve Townsend's report after the visit, as well as Patty's thoughts when I talked with her on the phone afterward. Our soldiers and their wives, husbands, and children truly deserved the thanks of their president, which he profusely offered, and his sincerity and concern for them showed.

Years later, I asked Patty to tell me about the president's visit that day. She wrote:

My Morning With President Bush

It was a beautiful sunny morning as I drove to the airfield. I was to meet the other greeters and Ft. Campbell VIP's at the VIP Lounge. On the roads to the airfield there were buses and heavy machinery blocking areas along the road to add extra security. The plane was planned to arrive about 9 am. We were updated every few minutes as to how far out the plane was. The Color Guard was ready. We walked out onto the tarmac. The red carpet was being placed down and the Soldiers from the Color Guard marched out just as Air Force One touched down. The pilot positioned the airplane perfectly and the stairs were rolled in place. There was some delay but soon the door opened. Out came President George W. Bush. I was the first in line to greet the President. He immediately said, "Hi, Patty. I saw Jeff a little while back and he is doing a great job over there." I thought to myself this guy is genuine, warm, and really personable. The President greeted everyone else in line and thanked the Color Guard. He then started toward the waiting limo and turned and asked if I wanted to ride with him. I was flabbergasted and pretty nervous. We got into the car and he faced backward and I faced forward right in front of him. President Bush thanked me for everything I was doing on the "home front" and then asked how the families were doing. I relayed to him that we were doing our best but it was difficult for them especially with the fifteen month expected deployment. We spoke back and forth and then arrived at the Hangar where President Bush was going to speak to the Soldiers.

I remember even more buses, trucks, and fences lining the roads and I felt sorry for all the Soldiers since I knew they had been inside the Hangar since 6 am. That meant they were probably at the units before 4 am so they could either march or be bussed to the Hangar. I did see that several organizations had set up food and coffee tents for the Soldiers.

President Bush did arrive to great applause and gave a wonderful speech. It seemed to me that the Soldiers and family members were thrilled and didn't mind the early arrival and wait. There was a lot of clapping and happy faces. Of course, President Bush thanked them for their sacrifices. He said he prayed for their safety.

The VIP's then went with President Bush and his one aide, who carried a very heavy backpack into a little room at the front of the Hangar. I think there were Brigadier General Townsend, Theresa Vail, Maria McConville, Colonel Tom Kunk and a few others but to be honest I don't remember who else was there. I do remember there were about eleven of us. President Bush went around the room and gave each one of us a coin that his aide handed to him. I was the first to get my coin. As we got to number eleven in line the aide ran out of coins. Both President Bush and the aide seemed a little miffed. I offered to give my coin to the person but the aide sent someone to the plane to get more.

I then got back in the car with President Bush to ride to the mess hall where we were to have lunch. This time President Bush spoke to me about how he worried about the Soldiers, their injuries and deaths. He said that it bothered him very much and hoped the Soldiers and families understood he felt he was doing the right thing. He seemed to have tears in his eyes as he spoke and I did completely believe he was very sad about the Soldiers. We talked about going to Walter Reed and what services were there for the families and Soldiers as they were recovering.

We went into the back door of the mess hall through the kitchen. Attention was called and President Bush stepped in. He shook hands with every Soldier in the room and then we went to the front and through the food line. He shook hands with everyone there and as he walked to the table he shook more hands and spoke with the Soldiers. We all ate a little bit and then he got up to say thank you to the Soldiers.

President Bush then left and he went to the airfield where he took off.

While President Bush visited Fort Campbell, Brigadier General Jim McConville and I flew to Nangarhar. We picked up Colonel John Spiszer at Forward Operating Base Fenty and flew to meet Governor Sherzai at his Nangarhar estate.

We landed in a private soccer field and walked up through gardens still green and lush in spite of the late November date. Governor Sherzai met us outside his home and welcomed us in his loud but genuinely friendly manner.

Gul Agha Sherzai was a bear of a man: tall, stout, an easy laugh, and yet one felt an undercurrent of uneasiness, like he was measuring you as a boxer in the ring, sizing you up, and figuring out his next move to beat you into a pulp.

We were the same age, born in 1954. He was named Mohammad Shafiq at birth. I knew his father had been a shopkeeper in Kandahar, and had fought bravely as a Mujahedeen against the Soviets. When son joined father as a Mujahedeen, he took the name Gul Agha, and added "Sherzai"—"son of the lion" in Pashtu—when his father was killed.

A former governor of Kandahar twice (once before the Taliban and then after the U.S. invasion), Sherzai had a significant reputation: he got things done, often leading from the front like he was still a Mujahedeen commander, but he bulldozed every obstacle and everyone who did not see eye to eye with his policies. And then there was the corruption. I, and most of my key leaders, had read Sarah Chayes' book *The Punishment of Virtue*, and her exposé of Sherzai's business dealings and tribal politics was eye-watering. By this time, I was deeply concerned about our ability to alter in any positive way the seemingly ingrown and rampant Afghan corruption, and I was leery of being seen as close to Sherzai. And yet he got things done, and was one of the most powerful and successful governors of our fourteen provinces.

The governor led us on a lengthy tour of the Sherzai home and estate. He told us that his great-grandfather built it some 130 years ago, which made no sense to me, given his modest birth and family background, but I held my tongue. Maybe something was lost, or added, in our conversation, which was in English. Regardless, the palace and the grounds were a stunningly beautiful display of multicolored mosaics, antique oriental carpets from Iran and Afghanistan, fountains and pools, and expansive public rooms for meeting and entertaining. Sherzai was proud of the place and of Nangarhar, and told us stories of the province's fascinating history over fruit drinks and boiling hot sweet tea. We moved into the dining room, which could seat fifty or so comfortably, and ate a tasty Afghan meal of grilled meats and rice pilaf with pomegranate seeds. After lunch, we went to a sitting room for our meeting.

Jim, John, and I covered our winter campaign and the additional troops we planned to move to Nangarhar Province after January. We told Sherzai about all the resources we were putting into the Afghan Border Police, and he admonished us for allowing regular Afghan National Army officers to be seconded to the border police, saying it caused, not lessened as we thought, further corruption. We talked about the status of Nangarhar Inc., a comprehensive development plan championed by Colonel Chip Preysler and continued by Spiszer. Sherzai was clear: he wanted more CERP investment in Nangarhar, more roads, a civil airport, and a cold storage warehouse for Nangarhar's bountiful fruit crops, which too often spoiled before going to market. From our end, I told him we needed his help with the tribes and specifically the elders, as we added more troops and built new outposts in the province. He agreed. We ended the meeting with Sherzai proudly declaring Nangarhar poppy-free, which I doubted. Nevertheless, he had been awarded $10 million from the U.S. for the clear reduction of poppy fields in the past year, and planned to use the money to build three simple but much-needed earthen dams.

In spite of Sherzai's reputation as a former warlord and current Afghan strongman, it was hard not to like his infectious enthusiasm and bold economic plans for Nangarhar, and I grudgingly had to admit to myself that he was effective. He was an Afghan survivor.

CHAPTER 24

*"It is curious that physical courage should be so common
in the world, and moral courage so rare."*
Mark Twain

Wednesday, December 10, 2008

Winter was finally coming to Bagram and the Shomali Plain. Cold rains
the first week of December were followed by frost, and the dark peaks
to the west of the airfield were capped in snow, which seemed to creep down
the mountain further and further as the nights passed. The low ceilings kept
me Bagram-bound for a couple of days, and so when the sky cleared on
Wednesday morning, I was excited to get back out beyond the walls and wire.

We flew to Forward Operating Base Bostick and picked up Lieutenant
Colonel Jim Markert, and headed into Task Force Raider country. The
Hindu Kush was snowy but not yet so snowbound as to prevent insurgent movement over the trails. But the storms and the deep snows were
coming soon, and I spent as much attention inspecting the preparations
for a harsh winter as the operational plans against the insurgents while
we visited outposts Lowell and Keating.

There was some snow in the passes and ratlines as we approached Combat
Outpost Lowell, but not enough in my mind to be much of an impediment
to the insurgents. There had been many improvements since my last visit. I
was pleased. The camp was still Fort Apache on the frontier, but the defensive

plan was solid, the defenses much improved, and the camp was as ready as we could make it for a brutally cold, windy, and sometimes snowy winter.

The mountains were much more snow covered as we ascended up the river to Keating. The wooden bridge from the river gravel-landing zone to the bank and the outpost had been repaired, but I thought of Captain Rob Yllescas as we crossed, one at a time. He had lost his legs in the command-detonated IED attack on this bridge a little more than forty days earlier. He lost his life on the first day of December, after a last-chance operation to relieve bleeding in his brain. He had fought to live in the intervening days just as he had lived life and fought war, with strength and courage, and survived longer than doctors thought was possible.

The soldiers at Keating had not forgotten Rob, and the news of his recent death was deeply troubling for them. Captain Dan Pecha was now in command, and along with First Sergeant Howard he was keeping the soldiers working, motivated, and sharp, but it was clearly hard to do, and the pale winter sky reflected what felt to me a very somber mood throughout the camp.

The death of someone you respect is hard for anyone to deal with. In combat, in small-unit combat especially, the death of a fellow comrade is especially burdensome, and, sometimes to some, intolerable. Soldiers enlist for a variety of reasons: for some it's the steady paycheck, for others the adventure, and for others, it's out of a sense of duty and honor to be sought. And all have some inkling that it is a patriotic thing to do when the nation is at war. But soldiers endure untold and unfathomable hardships not for their country, but for each other. They fight—and war is brutal and nasty, ugly beyond comprehension for civilian folk who have not experienced it—not for their fellow citizens, but for their fellow soldiers in their dugout and outpost. And when one of them is killed, it is a frightening reminder of their own mortality, but the main thing is the loss of a friend like no other, a bond of hardship endured and unspeakable violence promulgated and shared that is now broken, forever.

I worried about Keating and its soldiers.

I had plenty to worry about that night. The day prior, I met with the U.S. Secret Service and CIA team leads, and the leaders of the special operations task force. President Bush was coming to visit U.S. troops and President Karzai in less than a week. Bagram was more secure than Kabul Airport, and we would host the president for his short stay. He would be flying in on Air Force One, and we would provide the helicopters to get him and his small traveling team to and from Kabul. We talked about every kind of threat, from the monthly random rocket attacks on our airfield to suicide bombers and assassins. The trip would be unannounced and cloaked in secrecy, and he would arrive in darkness. We would strictly limit local workers' access to the base during his entire stay, from landing to final takeoff. We would have extra patrols, both ground and aerial, outside the wire. In flight, Air Force One, the president's massive 747 painted in blue and gold with the "United States of America" on the fuselage, had plenty of defensive countermeasures. But on the ground, parked on our ramp, it was up to us to keep it and its passengers safe.

On Monday, five days later, Command Sergeant Major Vince Camacho and I met General McKiernan and Ambassador Wood at the helipad at 4:20 a.m., and we headed down to the main airfield ramp. In a clamshell hangar lit with high-intensity lighting, soldiers, sailors, marines, airmen, and civilians, some eight hundred of them selected by their commanders to represent their units, waited expectantly. We had yet to tell them who the dignitary they were waiting for was, but the word was out. It was a cold, dark morning, but the 101st Airborne Division Band played rousing songs that kept spirits high.

At precisely 5:30 a.m., Air Force One landed, and quickly taxied to parking near the airfield firehouse and the clamshell. The ambassador, McKiernan, Camacho, and I positioned ourselves at the bottom of the aircraft stairs. The aircraft door opened, and President Bush bounded down the stairs, beaming. He shook our hands, and as we walked towards the clamshell, he told me he had just seen Patty during his Fort Campbell visit, and that she was doing a great job with the families.

The troops gave the president a loud and genuine welcome as he entered. I made a short introduction to the man who needed none, and the president took the podium and spoke from the heart. This was his last trip as commander-in-chief to Afghanistan, a country where he had sent so many Americans to serve, and he was very aware of the human cost.

I had always thought President Bush was far more articulate speaking to small groups rather than large public audiences, but that morning I believe he gave one of the best speeches I had ever heard. He thanked leaders by name, and just about every military unit by their designation. He explained why all of us were fighting in Afghanistan, and what had been accomplished in the past seven years, including getting Afghan children and particularly girls into school. He noted how much further we still needed to go to ensure a more peaceful Afghanistan with a modernizing economy and more robust infrastructure. He said we would build our capability through a "quiet surge." He told us he believed in what we were doing and in us:

> I am confident we will succeed in Afghanistan because our cause is just, our coalition and Afghan partners are determined, and I am confident because I believe freedom is a gift of an Almighty to every man, woman, and child on the face of the Earth. Above all, I know the strength and character of you all. As I conclude this final trip, I have a message to you, and to all who serve our country. Thanks for making the noble choice to serve and protect your fellow Americans.

The president was a family man, and he concluded with a request:

> And finally, we think of your families back home. You've got a loved one wondering what you're doing, how you're doing—I want you to do me a favor. When you get back to wherever you're getting back to, call them, email them, or write them. Tell them you love them, and tell them the Commander-in-Chief thanks them for their

sacrifice, thanks them for loving you like they do, and thanks for—thank them for standing with you as you serve the noble cause of peace.

The troopers' applause and cheers were genuine, and I could not help but feel proud of them, of our president, and of what we were about so far away from America and our loved ones just ten days short of Christmas.

He shook hands and posed for multiple pictures with the troops lucky enough to be in the front ranks. Watching the clock, we eventually got the president to the firehouse. It was one of the few well-made concrete block buildings in Bagram and provided some amount of protection to the president and his party. We talked for thirty minutes while we waited for the weather in Kabul to clear. The president said he wanted to talk with me one-on-one, and asked Steve Hadley and General McKiernan to give us the time. He asked about the conditions on the ground in eastern Afghanistan, and I noted how violent the year had been—a record year for the insurgents—but I said I was optimistic the increase in troops that he granted would help significantly in 2009. I told him the new unit's advance parties were arriving now, with the main bodies arriving soon after Christmas. He asked how the situation with Pakistan was, and I talked about my positive meetings with the Pakistani Army leadership and Frontier Corps. The president was a good listener, and seemed very much interested in what I had to say. He was also genuine. In the several times I had met with or briefed him over the past seven years since 9/11, it was always as commander-in-chief, not as a politician, and while I did not always agree with his policies (especially on Iraq, which I was duty bound to carry out), I always respected him as a leader, as a commander, and as a human being.

At 6:35 a.m., the president boarded a Black Hawk, accompanied by the ambassador and McKiernan, and flew to Kabul. It was a formation of helicopters fitting the commander-in-chief in a combat zone: the several Black Hawks carrying the president and his party were escorted by well-armed Apache and Kiowa Warrior helicopters flying high and low cover, and large CH-47 Chinooks carried security as well as the press.

I was concerned about Kabul's standard winter smoke and ice fog that often reduced visibility to less than a half mile, and so sped back to the CJTF operations center. We had a Warrior UAV, a drone, covering the route and the destination, and I could see that the visibility would be good enough to get the mission done.

The ambassador told me later that the meeting and breakfast with President Karzai went well, that he was a welcoming host and very thankful to President Bush. After a joint news conference, the president and his party reboarded the Black Hawks and flew back to Bagram. I met them on the ramp and led them back into the firehouse. The president was upbeat, and posed for pictures with the special operations task force as well as the 160th Special Operations Aviation Regiment task force, and finally with several of us from the CJTF-101 leadership. The president was in his element, and joked with us all, and lingered until his advance team insisted that he depart. We took him back to Air Force One, said our goodbyes at the bottom of the stairs, and waved back as he paused to look out one last time from the aircraft door. And then he was gone, taking off almost exactly five hours after he had landed. I breathed a sigh of relief as the 747 climbed high into the gray morning sky, out of small arms range.

The next evening was one of the most difficult for me in the entire fifteen months of command in Afghanistan. A young but experienced captain, a former company commander at Forward Operating Base Airborne, stood before me as part of a General Officer Article 15. An Article 15 was an administrative proceeding, not criminal, but when executed by a general officer, it would be career-ending, and sometimes only marginally better than a court martial.

The captain was accused of abusing detainees. In particular, it was alleged he and the company first sergeant had staged mock beatings and mock executions to get the detainees to talk. If true, it was a violation of the Uniform Code of Military Justice, and the laws that civilized nations attempted to follow during war.

I already knew the circumstances and context in which he and his senior non-commissioned officer had acted. Stretched thin by his huge company area of operations in Wardak, with a determined enemy who was achieving some success and killing his soldiers, and little support from his higher headquarters, the captain had acted to gain intelligence and, in his mind, save his troopers' lives.

Up until I learned of these accusations, I believed him to be one of our best company commanders: solid, trustworthy with the lives of over a hundred men, and resourceful. I could understand his despair in the loss of his soldiers to the foe; I felt the same so often that it had become part of me, part of my psyche, and every day I had to force myself when waking to act, talk, and be positive.

But I could not have this action go unpunished. I could not allow my commanders and their soldiers to believe that I would support ends justifying the means, for in combat, that would release demons that lurk below the surface of so many seemingly normal human beings, a hell that I could not condone.

The captain asked me to end the Article 15 proceeding, but admitted to the actions he was accused of.

I asked him to admit to me that what he did was wrong: wrong for the army, wrong for his men, and just plain bad leadership. He could not, and refused.

My general officer Article 15 that evening ended his army career.

Years later, I still think of the young captain, his decisions, and my own. On the battlefield, I knew him to be a brave man, and it was clear his soldiers knew that, and would follow him into hell, if so required. But I saw and experienced something else, a bravery at a different level, and yet found in the very best leaders: courage. In my mind, bravery is tactical: fearless or fearful, it is the willingness to put one's own life at risk for another person, a comrade, or even a group of comrades, such as a squad. It is seen best on the battlefield, but bravery is found in firefighters, police, and many other professions. I see courage differently, and think of it strategically, as a willingness to mortgage your own future, and maybe your family's, for the present betterment of those you lead. Standing firm to your beliefs—especially if those beliefs significantly impact other people—is a form of courage, as is the willingness to "bet one's bars" in a complex and often morally unclear situation. Courage is found on the battlefield, especially among leaders, but it is also found and required in many other walks of life, including among educators, business leaders, politicians, and journalists. We speak about the "courage of convictions," and that is meaningful: courage requires conviction, ideals, and the willingness to sacrifice one's personal reputation for a greater cause.

I disagreed significantly with the captain's actions, yet I understood them, and ultimately, admired his courage.

The following days leading up to Christmas were a blur of visits, including the Chairman of the Joint Chiefs Admiral Mike Mullen, with an accompanying USO show tour, our Army Chief of Staff (and my old boss from the Joint Staff) General George Casey, and the commandant of the Marine Corps, General Jim Conway. I thanked them all for spending these days with us in eastern Afghanistan, and made sure they were able to see as many bases and troopers as possible.

On the 19th we held the transfer of authority between our aviation brigades: Colonel Jim Richardson's 101st Combat Aviation Brigade had completed twelve months on station and was being replaced by Colonel Ron Lewis' 159th Combat Aviation Brigade, also part of our Fort Campbell and 101st Airborne Division team of teams. We had trained both brigades, and I was confident Lewis and his leaders and soldiers would do well in the unforgiving terrain and weather, as had Richardson and the 101st Combat Aviation Brigade.

It meant Chief Warrant Officer Four Dave Draper, my command pilot, and our Black Hawk crew would be heading back to Fort Campbell. Two days before Christmas, we held a small private ceremony for Dave and his crew members, and I presented them medals for their competence, professionalism in combat, and from time to time, bravery. We had flown seven hundred hours together since my arrival, and I had asked them to fly into tough conditions, and they did so superbly. We laughed about our war stories: about picking us up after Camacho, Turk, Andy, White, and I had to "beat feet" after the Independence Day attack in Kabul back in April; and about reluctantly dropping me off on a nine-thousand-foot mountain with a couple of security teammates to decide the fate of the crashed Chinook, not sure if they would see me again. There were plenty of stories, and good laughs. I knew these men well, and they me, and we had spent many, many days outside the wire. In one sense, they were my squad, and I was their squad leader. And perhaps only I knew it would still be that way when we were old, and retired, and sitting around at some reunion in a beat-up hotel convention center telling lies, but remembering the sense of the squad, and of the closeness in combat, that we had felt these past nine months.

The operations center woke me at 3:00 a.m. on Christmas Day to inform me of a potential special ops-versus-ANA fratricide, but there were no reported injuries, and I fell back to sleep quickly. I was up and running at 6:00 a.m. on a dark, crisp morning that soon gave way to clear skies as the sun peeked over the mountains.

Good weather.

Excellent. We were going to need it to get to all the places we wanted to today.

We flew east to Kalagush, then Torkham Gate, then Khogyani, and then Jalalabad, with *Wall Street Journal* reporter Yochi Dreazen along for the ride. Then on to the Zerok outpost, then Forward Operating Base Boris, and finally, Kushamond. At each stop, my message was the same: I was proud of them, thankful for their service, and understood and shared their sacrifices. Even the most remote locations had some Christmas decorations, and every site had some sort of Christmas meal that may not have been exactly like what they might have at home, but was better than the daily chow.

It was well after dark when we landed back at Bagram. I shared a quiet Christmas dinner with my personal staff. The cooks at our mess hall had done a superb job of baking turkey with dressing and mashed potatoes, and we lingered, telling stories of our families and what they might be doing that day.

Later that night I called my own family: Patty and Kelly were together; Ryan and his wife Molly were together; my father and his wife Ina were in St. Louis, and my brother and his wife Jessica were together. They were short calls from a combat zone, just enough to wish them a Merry Christmas and send my love. In January, I was scheduled to go back stateside for two weeks of mid-tour leave after my first ten months in Afghanistan, and I was upbeat.

Later that Christmas night, I laid on my bunk, ate a few pieces of the chocolate fudge my brother had made and sent, and read an outdoor magazine Patty had sent in a Christmas box stuffed with Starbucks coffee and other goodies. The night passed remarkably peacefully.

PART 4

CHAPTER 25

"The ordinary air fighter is an extraordinary man and the extraordinary air fighter stands as one in a million among his fellows."
Theodore Roosevelt

Thursday, January 1, 2009

We had to be the oldest F-15 cockpit crew in the history of that superb fighter and attack aircraft, I mused, as we moved out of parking and down the long taxiway at Bagram. The pilot in the front seat was Brigadier General "Mobile" Holmes, the commander of the 455th Air Expeditionary Wing stationed at Bagram Airfield. I was in the back seat. Together we had more than fifty-five years or so of aviation experience, and over one hundred years of life experiences. But I was an army aviator, a helicopter pilot more accustomed to one hundred knots at one hundred feet, and had never been in a combat jet in my life.

Mobile had extended the invitation to fly the F-15E with him early on in my command of RC-East, but it had taken months for the approvals followed by more months to schedule. I didn't want to interfere with our ongoing close air support to our troops throughout Afghanistan, and our staff settled on New Year's Day as the best time.

I was to get a feel for how the F-15E crews conducted close air support and aerial reconnaissance, and maybe more importantly, their situational awareness based on their onboard systems as well as their view of the terrain and the disposition of our outposts and camps. It was a picture seldom seen by an army division commander, and yet as a joint task force commander who required extensive close air support each and every day of our deployment, it was to prove critical to my understanding of air power.

We asked our close air support crews for a lot: to understand what was happening on the ground throughout the area of responsibility, and to be ready within minutes to intervene in a firefight with a low-level pass if that was the best option, or if not, attack with precision-guided bombs if need be, sometimes in close proximity to our friendly troops. It was easier for me to understand how the A-10 crews could do all this, because they operated closer to the ground and were significantly slower, thus allowing the pilot to grasp the enemy-friendly situation directly, eyes on. And our A-10 crews were awesome, saving the day many a day. But we also had F-15E Strike Eagle squadrons. Maneuvering at altitude, maybe twenty-five thousand feet, "seeing" the target and friendlies with onboard sensors like a high-resolution radar for a look-down/shoot-down capability, as well as a low-altitude navigation and targeting system for night and bad weather (LANTIRN), and then rapidly descending for engagement at about 450 knots, the F-15E crews were operating in an unfamiliar world for soldiers, and I wanted to see it firsthand.

It was a crisp winter day, the midday sun barely warming the surrounding landscape, as we stopped at the end of the runway and our wingman, another F-15E crew from the 391st Expeditionary Fighter Squadron, taxied into position slightly behind and to the side of us. I was comfortable in the stiff and narrow ejection seat, and seriously hoped the detailed instructions I had received on how to actually eject from the jet would not be necessary. The close-fitting pressure suit, meant to help my body sustain high-G maneuvers, and the oxygen mask were new accouterments, but both seemed to fit well and were as comfortable as I imagined they could be.

The tower cleared us for takeoff and Mobile asked if I was ready. "Absolutely. Let's fly."

Engine on afterburner, Mobile released the brakes and we were off. I had been catapulted off an aircraft carrier in a navy C2 turbo-prop transport plane several times before, but that was nothing like the seat-of-the-pants acceleration I felt as we screamed down the two-mile runway and lunged upward at an impossible angle toward the sky. I wanted to say something casual, even nonchalant, to Mobile to show I was a seasoned aviator.

Instead, head slammed back against the seat, face distorted by the Gs, I could barely talk into the intercom.

"Holy shit!" I believe I squeaked. Or maybe nothing came out, and I just thought it.

We climbed above surface-to-air missile range with afterburner, and then Mobile eased the plane over. Suddenly we were upside down, and I was looking through the top of the clear canopy down—down to Bagram's runway, which seemed too distant for the handful of seconds our ascent had taken. The pressure suit squeezed, the view was totally disorienting, and a wave of nausea swept me. I swallowed the urge to vomit and fixed my eyes on the aircraft gauges, as I had learned decades ago in flight school, to avoid disorientation. But the artificial horizon was all out of whack; it was upside down.

We are flying upside down for God's sake, I thought.

So I focused on the moving map, and the urge to barf dispelled.

Mobile righted the jet, and we headed with our wingman to a rendezvous point with the tanker. Climbing with an afterburner used up a huge amount of gas, and we always wanted to be able to react within short minutes to a firefight, so keeping plenty of fuel on board was a critical part of each F-15E mission. En route, Mobile gave me the controls, and I cautiously moved the stick to get a feel for the flight characteristics. I was a lifelong sports car fan, and I was flying the Porsche of the jet fleet.

With the wingman standing off, I did some banks, climbs, and descents. Mobile urged me to do a gentle roll, but I think it was his hand on the stick, backing me up, that got us through those. My stomach was not a believer in flight upside down, even if just a roll, and I was determined to not use the in-flight paper barf bag.

I was gaining a new, and profound, respect for F-15E pilots.

We met up with the tanker, it coming seemingly out of thin air, and we came on the refuel boom with ease. Long ago, I qualified for en route air-to-air refueling in a special ops MH-47E model Chinook helicopter, and the extraordinarily challenging nighttime refueling, done under night-vision goggles, with drogue basket-equipped MC-130s, was some of the hardest flying I had ever done.

Refueling the F-15E in daylight was a cinch, and we were soon off boom and headed towards Kunar and Nuristan.

Mobile let me fly, but I spent more time using the aircraft sensors and my naked eye to look at the ground. Even at around twenty-five thousand feet, I easily made out the key river valleys, the Kunar and the Pech in the east, and rapidly placed the Korengal and some of our larger camps along the Pech. The sensors brought a new and profound situational awareness, and I began to really understand how the F-15E crews were able to accomplish what they did flying at such speed and altitude.

We headed back for another tanking, and then descended out near the flat desert land along Highway 1 well south of Kabul for some simulated gun runs with the F-15E's M61A1 Vulcan 20-mm cannon. I was astounded how well Mobile flew the plane so near the earth, as we discussed the intricacies of a show of force, a low-level fly-by meant to scare or deter the enemy. Mobile gave me the controls and I did a return to target and a low-level run, not nearly as adeptly as I hoped I could do.

It was a quiet day, no troops in contact or need for a low pass, and after a few hours we headed back to Bagram.

After parking, we posed for a picture or two, then went to the ready room for a debrief. I thanked Mobile and his team profusely, and honestly told them how useful, and fun, the flight had been. I also told the pilots—Mobile and our wingman crew, as well as the ops officer debriefing us—of my newfound respect for the physicality and skill of their profession. I was worn out.

I recall walking a bit wobbly the rest of the day, and my inner ear kept reminding my stomach of the odd permutations it had been forced to endure.

In hindsight, I should have requested and insisted on the flight much earlier in our deployment. It gave me a nuanced grasp of the capabilities of the F-15E as a close air support platform, as well as some of its limitations, such as a reliance on air-to-air fuel tankers. It also enhanced my own understanding of the complex terrain of our area of operations, which I frankly had thought was already sophisticated: from twenty thousand feet, it was easy to see how the mountains defined routes of passage, what we call lines of communications, for both friendlies and enemy. Maybe most importantly, I came away with a profound consideration for those who manned and maintained these aircraft, twenty-four hours a day.

★   ★   ★

A couple of days later, the morning featured no dawn: a dense, dark gray, dripping ice fog seized Bagram. We were on a ground delay. By 10:00 a.m. the fog cleared, and Mark Milley, Brian Winski, and I piled into a C-12 airplane and took off to Pakistan.

Peshawar was clear and warm and humid, as if we had flown hours rather than minutes to arrive. We met up with the U.S. consulate's acting director, Mike Via, as Director Lynne Tracy was on leave. Amid heavy security provided by the Pakistani Army, we moved by car from the military airport to the 11th Corps headquarters, the only regular army unit in the frontier region of the Khyber. Lieutenant General Masood Aslam greeted us and led us into his office: I later wrote in my journal his office was "right out of the history books." Masood was a career professional soldier and older than me, having attended the Pakistan Military Academy in 1970. He had been wounded in the Indo-Pakistan War of 1971 as a young lieutenant. Later he commanded troops in the 1987 Siachen glacier fight, and again in the 1999 Kargil War. I had first met him early after our transfer of authority, and knew him to be realistic and pragmatic. He had seen war and its consequences.

Frontier Corps Inspector General Major General Tariq Khan joined us. I admired both men as soldiers and straight shooters, which I deeply valued when working with my fellow commanders from other countries.

Masood opened up by castigating me: *Why has it been ten months since you last visited me?* We laughed together, as we had all been very busy, and many of my trips to Pakistan involved Masood's higher headquarters. I invited him to come to Bagram for our next visit, and he accepted.

We moved to a larger room where the 11th Corps staff briefed us on ongoing operations in Bajaur and Mohmand. They didn't talk much about the ongoing operations in Swat. The "Battle of Swat" had begun in the fall of 2007 and had had early success against the Pakistani Taliban, but I knew of late there had been several setbacks. For our side, Brian briefed our operations east of the Kunar River, which included absorbing an additional battalion, the 1st Battalion, 32nd Infantry from the newly arriving 3rd Brigade Combat Team from Fort Drum. The battalion, well led by then Battalion Commander Lieutenant Colonel Chris Cavoli, had just departed Kunar and Nuristan in June of 2007, had retained many non-commissioned officers with deep Afghan mountain experience, and was well suited to be the buttress to the Pakistani Army and Frontier Corps operations on the other side of the Durand Line.

The 1st Battalion, 32nd Infantry was a proud, seasoned unit, with a long history. My friend and former deputy Major General Mike Oates had once led the battalion, and former Chairman of the Joint Chiefs General Colin Powell was a previous commander. I was convinced their additional firepower and influence would make a significant difference along the Durand Line.

I told Masood and Khan that we would fully support their operations.

Over lunch, we discussed the need to back up combat operations—clearing the insurgents—with economic operations to vastly improve the lot of the local people. Sitting next to me was the Pakistani brigadier general currently running the Battle of Swat. He was evasive to my questions, and I assumed things were not going smoothly. The Pakistani Army had trained for decades to battle Indian conventional forces and had little or no experience fighting insurgents. As a result, they tended to employ firepower ineffectively against enemies that offered only elusive targets while their maneuver columns blundered into repeated ambushes.

I wasn't aware then of the Pakistani political pressure to reach some sort of settlement with the insurgents in the frontier area.

It was an excellent overall meeting from my perspective, and we flew home to Bagram satisfied that we were making progress, albeit slower than we would desire, to slow Taliban and other groups' infiltration and fires along our porous eastern border.

Two days later, on Wednesday the 7th of January, we flew eastward again, this time in my Black Hawk, deep into Nuristan's Hindu Kush, to Parun. I last visited the remote provincial capital in early October, and I remembered the trip as one of the highlights of my time in Afghanistan: it was fall in the high alpine valley, the colors somehow deeper at this high altitude, the evergreens darker and thick with cones, the lush grasses a golden-straw hue, and even the simple homes looked quaint. At least that's how I remembered it as we flew over the crags and into the valley this time.

But in October, the recently appointed provincial governor had been out of the province on travel.

The purpose of this trip was to meet governor Jamaluddin Badr in his capital. Remote in the best of seasons and weather, Parun was impossible to reach in winter by car or even most four-wheel-drive trucks, and I was very interested in seeing how Badr planned on governing from such a location during this time of year.

The afternoon sun was cloud covered and weak, and the landscape seemed to be one of dark grays and greens against a backdrop of white. The snows had blanketed the mountains and the valley, and the tall cedars and pines were almost black, the river an ice-rimmed, roaring, gunmetal gray, and the few homes we could make out near the landing zone snow covered, with the mottled brown stone walls and black timbers the only indication that they were in fact homes.

Chief Warrant Officer Five Brent Driggers, who had taken over as my command pilot, landed in a foot or two of snow, almost up to the belly of the Black Hawk, and we jumped out. The security detachment led us to the rock and mud trail that constituted the main drag, and out of the trees came a squad of Afghan National Police and two Toyota Hilux trucks. We climbed into the bed of the trucks and they drove us into Parun, jostling us and giving us a few hard knocks as they maneuvered through the huge potholes and over the rocks. We had a good laugh; this was indeed an interesting way for the commander of ISAF troops in all of eastern Afghanistan and his team to appear before a local magistrate.

Governor Jamaluddin Badr met us at the gate of his compound and led us into his offices. My first impressions were that he was younger looking than I thought he would be, his black hair and cropped dark beard showing no signs of gray, and his eyes wary, maybe darting, but intelligent behind his aviator-like glasses. Dressed warmly in a winter shawl and a beige pakol to cover his head, the governor led us to a coal stove lit by a lantern in the center of a gloomy room, apologizing about the lack of central heat and electricity on this cold winter day. We huddled around the stove, and an assistant brought steaming cups of strong tea, which we cupped to warm our hands.

He was not a man of small talk: "You must bomb the Paprok Hotel!"

We had indeed considered ways to address the Paprok recently. An alleged insurgent way station and rest stop in the far northern town of Barg-e Matal, the "hotel" was even more remote than Parun: located on the northeastern border of Nuristan, opposite Chitral and Dir, in a small town that was more village than town, and yet of strategic importance to our Afghan allies. Minister Wardak and General Bismillah Khan both continued to lobby me to support their police and army units there.

But it was so remote, in sheer and stark mountains fifteen thousand feet and taller, and with such a small population, that it was hard for us in the CJTF or ISAF to consider any major involvement up there.

I told the governor I would consider attacking the hotel, if we could ensure there were insurgents present and not families.

The governor called for the NDS chief, the local intelligence service director, and the Parun police chief. We discussed the Paprok in more depth, as well as insurgent movements elsewhere in Nuristan. They were deeply concerned about Lashkar-e-Taiba (LeT), and promised to send us more intelligence about the group's local makeup and movements.

We moved out of combat operations and talked about infrastructure, which Nuristan sorely lacked, in spite of what I guessed was $100 million in investments from CERP over the years since the American invasion.

"We need real roads, to and from the Pech River, and to Barg-e Matal. Only after we have roads can we bring clean water and eventually electricity to our region."

I agreed that development here in Parun and Nuristan was critical. I inquired into how he was going to govern from Parun: Did he have transport and communications?

That let loose a torrent. He needed up-armored SUVs, and radios and satellite phones, and of course, security teams.

From the tone and intensity of the conversations between the governor and his police and intelligence service chiefs, which I could not understand and were not translated, I could sense their anxiety.

In truth, living at the edge of such a remote town in a remote province hundreds of miles from Kabul, I could understand their uneasiness. We were their best bet for survival, much less resources to build the roads, and wells, and micro-hydropower facilities that could move Nuristan into the twentieth century, much less the twenty-first.

I wrote in my journal that night that I thought Governor Jamaluddin really did want to help his province and people, and he knew he had to make some inroads against the insurgents in his area. With such a poor history of governance in Nuristan, I was concerned about the governor's ability to make much of a positive impact. I was also concerned that he would survive. I wrote, *Got to keep him from an untimely death.*

★　★　★

The next day was another quarterly commander's assessment brief. All the brigade commanders and command sergeants major joined my senior staff and me at the Bagram Jirga Center for an all-day vigorous exchange of thoughts on our progress, or lack thereof. It was a brutally frank assessment: we were achieving the goals of our winter campaign, and enemy activity was significantly down since November, but many of us were frustrated by the slow pace and the lack of troops, surveillance, and reconnaissance to ensure that our kinetic line of operation (to clear and hold on to areas that had been cleared of insurgents) was successful enough to enable the development and local governance that would actually win over the people.

We had to be patient. Colonel Dave Haight's 3rd Brigade Combat Team was deploying into Logar and Wardak as we were meeting, and more surveillance aircraft were flowing to the CJTF and down to the brigades. Still, for the CJTF staff and my command team, after ten months in command of RC-East, we had expected to be more successful, and we were beginning to understand what was possible in our remaining five months.

It was less than I had hoped.

The next day I packed my backpack and met with Mark Milley and Tom Vail, our chief. I was headed back to the States for mid-tour leave. We had carefully structured our command team's stateside leaves, with Jim McConville and the chief taking their two-week leave earlier, then Milley, and finally me.

Mid-tour leave, otherwise known as rest and relaxation (R and R), was a part of the military I grew up with. I remembered my father's first deployment to Vietnam from 1965 to '66. He had received R and R then too, and my mom and I took a U.S. Navy ship from our home at Schofield Barracks, Hawaii, to meet him in Japan. In his two subsequent Vietnam tours, Dad had come home, usually deeply fatigued but tan and fit, once with a bushy mustache that lasted all of two or three days before my mother insisted that he shave it off.

In my deployments to Haiti, Albania, and Kosovo, no one thought of R and R, and the deployments were overall less than a year anyway. When we deployed the 101st Airborne Division into Iraq in 2003, no one thought we would be there long, and as the fighting intensified in the summer, my boss Major General Petraeus started to push Lieutenant

General Rick Sanchez and the Pentagon brass to start an R and R program for the troops. Some of our troops made it back during that first Iraq tour from 2003 to '04; most of the division command team and the battalion and brigade command teams stayed for the duration, and the months stretched into a very long year apart from our families.

When planning for our fifteen-month combat deployment to Afghanistan, we carefully considered how to maximize the positive effects of a relatively short period out of the constant stress of a combat zone. For the troopers out in the small outposts, Bagram itself was a relative R and R location, with its warm showers, well-stocked PX store, and excellent chow halls. For them, going back to the States and home was incredibly important. Even for the staffer, stuck on shift work in the Bagram-based CJTF operations center, getting away from the stress of conducting war in a faraway place was critical to the ability to sustain high performance and good decision-making over a year or more.

As a commander, I was aware that not all R and Rs worked well for some soldiers. There were plenty of stories about going home to find an empty apartment, or discovering an unknown relationship that was unknown only to the soldier. In other cases, the soldier had no loved ones or a home to return to, and spent the two weeks drinking and partying, often missing the camaraderie of their squad or team back at their outpost.

No doubt the same issues existed for families who waited for their soldiers to come home on R and R. Sometimes the soldier who came home was very different from the soldier who had left them months before. And while even us professional "old-timers" with multiple deployments thought we were the same coming home as when we left, that was usually not the case. War changes us all, for better or worse.

And as the commanding general, Eagle 6, I never really felt I could be away from our war, my war, in the mountains of eastern Afghanistan, even if I was on the opposite side of the planet. I was still responsible.

So, I was a little nervous as I flew out the next day around noon. With me were my admin assistant Sergeant First Class Gail Sims, my enlisted aide Sergeant Russ Sauers, and aide Captain Stan Goligoski.

We stopped in Kandahar for gas, and then flew on to Fujairah, UAE, and then to Kuwait, where we boarded a regular civilian airliner back to the States.

We landed in the U.S. on Sunday morning and Gail and Russ continued back to their homes, while Stan and I flew from Dulles to Augusta, Georgia, and then drove to Fort Gordon. That afternoon I went out for a long run, maybe ten miles or more, and it felt absolutely wonderful to be home in the United States.

On Monday morning, Stan and I drove to the Augusta Veterans Affairs Center hospital and toured their blind vet rehab center, met with the director and many of their patients, some of whom were my soldiers, and talked. I was impressed. We then drove to Eisenhower Army Medical Center, where the commander Brigadier General Don Bradshaw briefed me on the improvements that had been made since Patty's visit in August 2008. We visited our inpatient soldiers and those in the Warrior Transition Battalion, and I came away impressed. We were doing our best as an army and a nation to support those who were wounded, and their families.

The next day, we flew to Reagan National Airport in Washington, D.C., where Patty met us. It had been more than ten months since we had last seen each other in the flesh, and she looked radiant.

We spent the next day at Walter Reed Army Hospital with our wounded and their families, including soldiers, marines, sailors, and airmen, active or Guard or Reserve who served with us. We did an open forum to encourage frank dialogue, and I took back many issues to the hospital chain of command, but everyone agreed the quality of care was really, really good. I was very much relieved. Deployed in Afghanistan and worried about the day-to-day execution of a war, I had little time to worry about or check on the quality of care of our wounded back in the States. I counted on it being professional, supportive, and as successful as any nation could make it be. It was fulfilling to find it so.

Patty and I bid goodbye to Stan, who flew home, and we headed to Carlisle Barracks, Pennsylvania, to see our daughter Kelly, who was the deputy public affairs officer there.

The remaining time went by rapidly.

On the following Tuesday I reversed the movement, and landed at Bagram at 2:00 a.m. on Thursday, where I went immediately to the operations center for a combat update.

I returned from R and R as rested as I could be and resolved to do as much as humanly possible in our remaining months to consolidate our winter campaign gains and set the stage for a successful fighting season in 2009.

CHAPTER 26

*"The United States supports the reintegration of people who
have fought with the Taliban into Afghan society provided
they: one, renounce Al Qaida; two, lay down their arms and
renounce violence; and three, participate in the public political
life of the country, in accordance with the constitution."*
Ambassador Richard Holbrooke

Thursday, February 12, 2009

The day started with a ramp ceremony for a fallen Polish soldier killed
in a military vehicle rollover the day prior. It was the second ceremony
in twenty-four hours: we began Wednesday at 2:30 a.m. with a farewell
to two Company D, 2nd Battalion, 506th Infantry soldiers killed in a
suicide-vehicle IED. The weather too was grim: winter had descended
onto the Shomali Plain and Bagram, and we had intermittent freezing
rain and snow forecast for the next few days.

General McKiernan and Ambassador Wood arrived in the early
afternoon, their helicopter just able to make the trip up from Kabul in
the deteriorating weather. We sat in my office for almost two hours, and
talked a lot about President Karzai's continued denunciations of ISAF
operations.

"He is helping the enemy," I said.

I told them I was hearing that and more on my talks with our troops, even those far from the flagpoles of Bagram or Kabul.

"Sir, the C-17 is on approach," an aide said.

We drove down to the airfield ramp in a cold rain, snowflakes threatening. The C-17 transport plane taxied in, and we walked out to meet our visitor and his delegation.

Down the aircraft stairs bounded Ambassador Richard Holbrooke. He was accompanied by a small delegation, including Deputy CENTCOM Commander Lieutenant General John Allen, the Joint Staff's Deputy J5 Major General Burt Field, and Paul Jones from the NSC. The wind was building, snow was coming, and we kept the greeting short and headed to the headquarters conference room.

Ambassador Holbrooke was President Obama's newly appointed special representative for Afghanistan and Pakistan. From my time in Germany and Kosovo, I knew Holbrooke had been the U.S. ambassador in Germany and the assistant secretary of state for European affairs when he had led the U.S. side of the Dayton Peace Accords, which brought to a negotiated end the Bosnia conflict. In preparing for this visit, I learned Holbrooke had served in the foreign service and USAID in Vietnam about the time of my father's first Vietnam tour. He was the youngest assistant secretary of state for East Asian and Pacific affairs when serving in that position from 1977 to 1981; following his time as the envoy for the Bosnia and the Balkans, he became U.S. ambassador to the United Nations. I knew he was a confidant of Secretary of State Hillary Clinton. I also knew that he had earned a reputation as egotistical, unbending, and extraordinarily strong-willed once he had made up his mind.

This should be interesting, I thought as we got hot coffee and sat down at the conference table.

"I will be coming to Afghanistan every month or two, or I will send Paul here," Holbrooke started. I made a mental note: if that was the case, he would be a visitor about as often as the CENTCOM commander, or slightly more frequent than the chairman of the Joint Chiefs, Admiral Mullen, had been. This was not a "one and done." I needed to establish a cordial working relationship with Holbrooke and his team.

As he spoke, I looked him over. In his mid-sixties, his appearance belied his age. With salt-and-pepper dark hair, a scrubbed and firm face with no hint of fatigue, and the pale blue eyes that stared directly into one's own as he listened or spoke, he looked to be a seasoned world diplomat with a mission and the vitality to pursue it.

We had barely begun briefing a status update when he received a call on his cell phone, which appeared to be a blackberry. I was surprised. Cell towers were spotty in and around Bagram, much less in the rest of Afghanistan outside of Kabul, and I expected that if he received a call, it would be transmitted via his communications team.

It was the secretary of state.

He left the conference room for a quiet spot for a few minutes. When he returned, he apologized, but said he really had needed to talk with Secretary Clinton and could not delay the call.

So much for direct access to decision makers, I thought.

General McKiernan and I gave an overall brief of ISAF and RC-East. Holbrooke was a good listener, and took it all in. He was interested as much in the development side as the combat, and asked many questions about our agricultural development teams and progress to diversify the farmers' crops. We shifted to talking about Pakistan, and I briefed him on the current approach we worked out with Masood and Khan to have us block the Durand Line.

"The hammer and anvil approach. But are the Pakistanis a strong enough hammer?"

I said they had come a long way from even a year ago, when they basically refused to acknowledge they had a Pakistani insurgent problem in their own country.

General McKiernan said he thought we were doing all the right things in RC-East, with partnered combat operations and stronger border security through our line of outposts, but also through a much-strengthened Afghan Border Police that we assisted, increasing development—reaching almost $450 million in CERP this year—and constant meetings with and support to the district and provincial governors. He said he thought we were approaching irreversible momentum. I was a bit surprised, and would normally not have used that phrase. My father's Vietnam experience was buried deep in my psyche, and influenced my own outlook. No matter how much progress we made, it would take years, even decades, of U.S. and NATO commitment to secure a modernizing and democratizing Afghanistan.

All it would take to reverse our progress was a failure to support the troops, equipment, and resources that had to be funneled this way, for an undetermined time frame. If the American people, and the Congress, ended our support for what I knew was seen back home as a most foreign of foreign wars, in a place most Americans had never heard of prior to 9/11 and still could not pick out on a map, then it would be for naught.

"Your success in Afghanistan could lead to more instability in Pakistan," Holbrooke said.

McKiernan didn't think so, and he and Holbrooke had a spirited exchange. Holbrooke said our Predator strikes in the FATA must continue, but we had to mitigate the political cost to the Pakistani leadership.

The talk shifted to Holbrooke's upcoming meeting with President Karzai. I told him just what I had told McKiernan and Wood that afternoon: Karzai's rhetoric was demoralizing to our troops.

General McKiernan was blunt: "Karzai is a horrible president."

Holbrooke mentioned a meeting in Munich between Karzai, General Petraeus, NSC Director retired General Jim Jones, and himself. Karzai displayed bizarre behavior. Jim Jones was deeply disappointed, and likely told President Obama. We discussed the upcoming elections, and a subtle way ahead quietly being voiced by the UK Special Representative Sherard Cowper-Coles of a "one-year option."

After a late working dinner, we walked over to the Bagram Theater Internment Facility (BTIF) next door. It was snowing heavily by then, and the winds kicked up small drifts against the tall chain-link fences of the facility, and the bright white security lights were almost obscured by the heavy snowflakes that came vertically, then horizontally, then vertically again.

I briefed Ambassador Holbrooke on our relationship with the ICRC, which I thought was as strong and collegial as it could be. Holbrooke knew the director of operations, Dr. Pierre Krahenbuhl, personally. As we walked through the BTIF, the ambassador was effusive with his compliments and thanks to our troops. I showed him the plans for the new internment facility being built on the other side of Bagram Airfield. He welcomed the increased capacity as well as the far better infrastructure, noting he was certain the interred population would grow as our operations in RC-South expanded.

It was late when we drove Holbrooke, his delegation, General McKiernan, and Ambassador Wood to a waiting C-130. I was pessimistic about them flying. The snowstorm was closer to a blizzard now, and visibility for takeoff was at minimum for a legal departure. We sat on the C-130 for what seemed an hour in the cold as the crew worked with the tower and departure control and de-ice crews. Meanwhile, I had my security detachment and the CJTF operations center develop another option: drive the high-powered delegation along with the U.S. ambassador to Afghanistan and the ISAF commanding general some forty miles, along snowy narrow roads, in the middle of the night, with no supporting helicopter escort.

With the snow falling stronger than I had ever seen in Bagram and the flight options dwindling, they insisted they could not spend the night at Bagram, and we hustled them to waiting military vehicles, and off they went into the night.

The trip down to Kabul was sporty in the weather, but uneventful. It was early in the morning when I was satisfied they had safely arrived, and went to bed myself.

In spite of the atrocious weather and the tough trip to Kabul, our part of the ambassador's first visit as special envoy had been a success, or so I believed. I hoped he would become a much-needed political interlocutor to the White House, an insider with deep knowledge of conflict resolution, and a voice from the field to the West Wing.

As I thought about our wide-ranging conversation with Holbrooke, I grew increasingly dissatisfied with my own analysis of our progress and future potential for success. It seemed clear that we, the U.S. and NATO, had squandered our early battlefield successes against the enemy as we knew it in late 2001 and early 2002: al-Qaida and the Taliban. Both were essentially removed from Afghanistan, forced to relocate to Pakistan's frontiers or be totally destroyed. But we brought in too few U.S. and NATO troops and government experts to consolidate and hold the country, and as we shifted our counterterror and much of our conventional resources to Iraq, the enemy—in the form of a morphing, often uncoordinated syndicate of similarly motivated and typically like-minded groups—seeped back across the border, fighting when it made good tactical sense for them, hiding back across the Durand Line when it did not. We, the U.S. and NATO, made no serious moves to negotiate a political settlement with the Taliban, who remained committed to returning to Afghanistan, even when we had the preponderance of military power in those early years. And in hindsight, we totally rushed to put an Afghan face on the national and provincial governments; that is how Karzai got to be president over time. Would it not have been better to maintain a U.S./NATO military or civilian-run government as we came to grips with the total disenfranchisement of the typical Afghan from government at any level, and the elephant in the room, a corruption entwined in the culture, civil society (such as it existed), business, and the police? After all, if Afghanistan was truly a primary national interest for the U.S. (and I still believed it was—another 9/11 was clearly not impossible), then we needed in 2002 to face the potential of a generational struggle, or at least decades of commitment not unlike the U.S. roles in Germany and Japan post WWII and Korea after 1953.

Such was the state of my mind as we completed our first twelve months in command of Regional Command-East.

Four days later I flew to Jalalabad to pick up United Kingdom Foreign Secretary David Miliband, UK Special Representative Sir Sherard Cowper-Coles, back again after his tour as ambassador to Afghanistan, and the new UK ambassador to Afghanistan, Mark Sedwill.

Miliband looked like he was right out of college with dapper good looks, but his Oxford credentials, graduate degree from the Massachusetts

Institute of Technology, and decade of high-level public service starting as a Tony Blair protégé belied his youthful looks and enthusiasm.

We flew by Black Hawk up the Kunar River Valley to Asadabad. I pointed out key points of interest including the historic Nawa Pass, as well as the approximate demarcation of the Durand Line. My guests knew their British history, and we chatted about previous foreign excursions, including those Britain had led, into Afghanistan. None had turned out well over the years. I mentioned that I found Churchill's *The Story of the Malakand Field Force* one of my favorite books when preparing for our eastern Afghan deployment, which they found amusing. I also said that two other favorites were Frank Holt's book on Alexander the Great's foray into Afghanistan and the region, *Into the Land of Bones*, as well as Grau's masterpiece on the Soviet invasion twenty-two hundred years later, *The Bear Went Over the Mountain*. It was sobering to think of all the military excursions, invasions, and occupations in this ancient land, and insightful to realize so little good came of them over the centuries.

We met with our Kunar Provincial Reconstruction Team at Asadabad. They gave the delegation a good brief on their campaign to build responsible local governance and increase development in Kunar, and Miliband and the others asked excellent, probing questions. They were no pushovers and clearly Cowper-Coles was deeply experienced and opinionated about the potential for long-term success in Afghanistan, and we had a lively, robust exchange of views.

We piled into several MRAPs and drove out the gates of the base and through the streets to Governor Wahidi's compound. It was hardly ostentatious like Governor Sherzai's palace, but much more comfortable than Nuristan Governor Jamaluddin Badr's spartan offices and abode in the deep Hindu Kush of Parun. Wahidi served us steaming, strong tea and sweets. For an hour, the governor briefed Secretary Miliband and us about the history of the region, the insurgency (he said there were eight hundred insurgents operating in Kunar), and the populations that moved back and forth across the Afghan-Pakistani border through the mountain passes. He said there were some forty thousand displaced men, women, and children that had been pushed out of Bajaur, Pakistan, by the military and insurgent fighting over the past few years, and that they were living with family, tribal affiliates, and friends in Kunar, straining the economy.

When Wahidi had an attentive audience he barely breathed between sentences, and he went on to talk about more local short-term and long-term development projects he had to have. I told him he would soon have a dedicated agricultural development team from the California National Guard in Kunar. He smiled, said not a thank you, and insisted I coordinate for more: more ADTs, more CERP, more rule of law team members.

What a guy, I thought. Was he trying to get the UK to supplement the U.S. PRT in Kunar, or was he just demonstrating his firm grasp of governorship to a famous audience?

After an hour, we packed into the MRAPs and headed back to base. Miliband was impressed with Wahidi, and Cowper-Coles added a bit of color to what I knew of Wahidi's background. It was a good meeting.

We flew south along the Kunar River all the way to Torkham Gate, and carefully made our way almost at a hover up to the border-crossing site at the Khyber Pass. Spellbound, Miliband was taking notes on a Blackberry...or so I thought. We landed short of the actual border crossing at our Border Coordination Center, a small but spanking new-looking base where we hosted a tripartite team of ISAF, Afghan, and Pakistani soldiers whose job it was to coordinate operations in this sector of the border, with a goal of achieving some limited collaboration. Personally, my first objective for this BCC, which was the first of several we were building, was to prevent another Gora Paray-Nawa Pass incident between our forces.

Colonel Lowe from our Joint Coordination Cell met us, and led us into the huge, gleaming steel Quonset hut that sheltered the actual operations center, living areas, gym, and dining facility. Lined up in the ops center was the BCC team: officers and senior non-commissioned officers from the U.S., Afghan Army, Afghan National Police and border police, the Pakistani Army, and the Kurram Scouts from the Pakistani Frontier Corps. It may have looked like a motley group in so many diverse uniforms, but the purpose—to coordinate among all of the units and militaries represented—was profound, and I was proud of what had been accomplished so far. Just getting this group together to live, eat, and work at a common purpose was an important milestone. Now we had to make it real—really coordinate among us all.

Secretary Miliband was complimentary in his remarks to the BCC and Colonel Lowe, and I think he was surprised. Cowper-Coles was not a huge fan of U.S. and ISAF counterinsurgency operations, and I am sure he pre-briefed Miliband to the effect that we were doing nothing new under the sun. The BCC was unexpected, and when I said we were building five more along our 450-mile border with Pakistan, they looked shocked.

Miliband was busy tapping into his Blackberry on the Black Hawk flight back to Jalalabad. I dropped them at the airfield, where they would catch a UK flight. He and the delegation were effusive in thanks for an interesting and insightful day, and I flew back to Bagram satisfied that we had made a positive impression on Secretary Miliband, which could be very helpful in keeping the UK in this war.

It was only after we had parted ways that I found out that he was actually sending his thoughts in almost real time back to the UK and the general public via Blackberry. When I landed at Bagram, my public affairs staff gave me several of Miliband's observations from the day, all positive. It was my turn to be impressed. It was the twenty-first century, and Miliband had strategic communications down cold.

Three days later, we had another political delegation at Bagram. CODEL Pelosi. Congresswoman Nancy Pelosi was speaker of the House, and second in line of succession to the White House behind the vice president. She was leading a high-ranking bipartisan congressional delegation, and we expected tough questioning and, frankly, a jaundiced eye toward our campaign and what we thought we had accomplished so far.

CODEL Pelosi landed at Bagram in the early afternoon and we spent the next three hours with the speaker and the delegation. Several of the congressmen looked beat, but the speaker was alert, talkative, and in charge. As we fed them strong, hot coffee and cookies they all perked up, and we had a passionate, sometimes heated, but always respectful exchange both ways:

"Why not just kill or capture the bad guys, and then get out?"

"Why are we worrying about the Taliban? Why not concentrate only on those that attacked us, al-Qaida?"

"Will the seventeen thousand additional troops the U.S. and ISAF are deploying be enough to do the job?"

"What about NATO's contributions—are they doing their share?"

These and all the rest were excellent questions, and I was duty bound to answer them as truthfully and frankly as I could. Those who had done their homework knew we at CJTF-101 had been in eastern Afghanistan almost a full year by then, and some even knew of my role in starting the "ask" for more troops, surveillance, and reconnaissance capabilities. They all had strong opinions, some of them partisan, but they were all deeply and honestly thankful for what we, and more importantly, our troops, were doing so far from home. Their sincerity was striking, and welcome.

CHAPTER 27

"May God keep you away from the venom of the cobra, the teeth of the tiger, and the revenge of the Afghans."
Alexander the Great

Wednesday, March 4, 2009

The explosion rocked Entry Control Point 3 at Bagram. A black debris-filled dust cloud rose just to the south of the ECP, and the alarm went out to lock down all control points.

Bagram Airfield was under attack.

The natural inclination of first responders is to rush to the point of the blast or attack, in a well-meaning urge to help those who might be injured but still alive.

The trained insurgent or terrorist is counting on just such a move.

As the quick response team approached the blast sites, they could see the vestiges of a car or small truck, blown into pieces, and parts on fire: a SVBIED, a suicide vehicle-borne improvised explosive device. Somewhere amongst the twisted discolored steel and burning rubber were pieces of the driver, smoking hot torn flesh.

Nearby were a damaged vehicle and three wounded Americans. They had been in the way as the suicide driver tried to approach the outer safety ring of the control point, which stretched for some distance, providing standoff for such an attack. They were civilian contractors re-entering the base after a mission.

Watching for reinforcements or first responders, an additional suicide bomber approached the scene. Guards pointed him out, shouting and telling him to stop, or be killed.

Click.

The explosives and metal packed into the bomber's vest ignited, separating head from legs. Bright red mush that was once a torso was scattered about.

He killed only himself.

We got our wounded to the hospital, where all would make a full recovery. We checked the entire area for other bombers or stay-behind explosive devices, and sent a forensics team to examine what was left of the vehicle and vest. We cleaned the site of the two bombers' remains, with a forlorn hope of tracing them back to an explosives factory or neighborhood that we could exploit.

We had had several smaller probes and attacks against our entry control points, and I fully expected the enemy to attack our sprawling base. We had built strong defenses with standoff, and invested in a series of tall watchtowers all along the many miles of perimeter that surrounded the air base itself and the huge logistics support area, as well as the main road that housed the headquarters of our CJTF-101 and many supporting units. Just off the main drag were the troop living quarters, the newest concrete block structures with showers and toilets, the majority beat-up B-huts made of sun-beaten plywood and sporting wires of all natures bringing in power and internet for the lucky. And, for short-timers, there were deployable air-conditioned tents. Blast walls, some small, some the large "Texas" barriers, separated the various structures. If a lucky rocket or mortar shell fell in the living or working areas, the blast walls would contain the damage, and limit the casualties.

We augmented the defenses with constant ground and aerial patrols outside the wire and for miles beyond. OH-58D Kiowa Warrior armed reconnaissance helicopters patrolled far out, examining in detail named areas of interest as well as anything that seemed abnormal. Slightly closer in, mounted and dismounted patrols conducted random stops to search for explosives, talking with the locals and asking who was new to the neighborhood. Other than the small town and souk that had grown up outside of Bagram decades prior, the surrounding countryside was largely rural, and made up of small, often well-irrigated fields and sun-hardened family compounds, with rocky thistle-infested fields for the goats and sheep to graze, under the watchful eye of a child. It was the pilot's curiosity that often led to uncovering an attack before the rocket was laid, just as it was the ground patrol team leader's experience of what was normal and what was not that often prevented the close-in vehicle or suicide vest attack.

But not today. The two bombers had penetrated several lines of our defenses. Both had likely set off their charges before they really planned to, which prevented many more casualties.

I took this attack, like many others that I thought preventable throughout my area of responsibility, personally. After an earlier attack the past year I had decided to use the Kiowa Warriors to extend our outer perimeter at Bagram, at a time when I knew they were needed in several other locations to conduct the type of close-up recon and surveillance that they were so good at. We ensured every helicopter sortie taking off or landing at Bagram knew and watched our named areas of interest (NAIs) and we treated the pilots and crew like adjunct intelligence spotters. I knew that I was trying to stop, or prevent, or better yet deter, those who were often readily willing to die as part of their attack. Some said that you could not deter someone willing to die as part of their mission, as if a suicide bomber was by their very nature beyond deterrence.

I did not agree. I thought suicide bombers were rational, given their screwed-up version of humanity, religion, politics, and armed conflict: they were more than willing to die—in fact their death was one of the mandatory components of a successful attack—but they also sought victims and destruction, without which their death would be meaningless in this life or the hereafter.

We had to make it harder for the "would-be" bomber to get close to our troops, our outposts, and our entry control points. I thought there could be some deterrence value in making it just too hard, too unlikely, for the casual suicide bomber to think he could be successful in killing our troops or destroying our equipment.

As we investigated, cleaned up, and reviewed, I had to break off and meet with officials from a most important ally. Poland.

The Poles were the second-largest troop contributor among the ISAF forces that served and fought side by side in RC-East, the U.S. being first. Task Force White Eagle was a small brigade of well-trained and equipped combat troops, led by a charismatic, battle-hardened brigade commander, Colonel Rajmund Andrzejczak, White Eagle 6. Mark Milley and I had met with Rajmund on the previous weekend to discuss our spring campaign and priorities for Task Force White Eagle, which commanded all of our Ghazni Province. The Poles kept a brigadier general on our CJTF staff, and as they rotated through, my staff and I became increasingly knowledgeable of recent Polish history and their pride in reforming their country and military. We became battle comrades, and friends.

The Polish delegation was led by Minister of Defense Bogdan Klich, supported by General Gagor, the chief of defense forces (CHOD), the ambassador, and several other senior officials, plus several journalists, almost thirty people strong. I hosted the minister, CHOD, and ambassador in a private session in my office, then held a campaign update attended by all the delegation that briefed our previous winter campaign, the upcoming spring operations, and Task Force White Eagle's role.

The minister and CHOD were deeply interested in how we conducted combat and development operations throughout the rest of RC-East, and they asked penetrating, far-reaching questions that probed into how they could best prepare and equip their troops for the tasks at hand. We discussed how the task force needed to work hand in hand with the provincial reconstruction team in Ghazni, and they were aware of the tension between their task force and the reconstruction team leadership, which I was confident Colonel Andrzejczak could resolve. Still, I knew I was asking a lot from the Poles. Unlike the French task force I had in

Kapisa, whose fathers and grandfathers had campaigned in Indochina and northern and central Africa, counterinsurgency was new to the Poles. Their centuries-old martial esprit de corps and willingness to fight were evident daily, and they felt an affinity to the 101st Airborne Division from our World War II exploits that was deeply gratifying to my soldiers from the division, be they privates or generals. And yet I wondered: counterinsurgency required a deft hand, a lightness of touch in combat, and yet a firm approach to the local governance, plus deep pockets, and finally a constancy over years that I wasn't sure the Polish government was ready to sign up for. But then, I wasn't sure my own government fully understood what this was going to take to ultimately prevail. And would we hang in there?

The next day was March 5. Thirty-two years earlier, Patty and I married in the white clapboard Catholic chapel at Fort Benning, two days after she and my father pinned the "butter bars" of a second lieutenant on my shoulders at my OCS commissioning.

I could not call her that day. I simply wrote in my journal: *I love her deeply, and miss her more than words can express.*

Later that day, I was engaged in a secure video teleconference from my desk with Major General Mike "Scap" Scaparrotti, the 82nd Airborne Division commander at Fort Bragg, North Carolina. Mike and his division staff would replace my CJTF-101 at the upcoming transfer of authority, which was now just two months away. In addition to swapping out headquarters elements, the incoming CJTF would bring new brigades along to replace those who had battled the Taliban since early 2008. Pete Johnson's Currahees would hand over to a 5,500-strong airborne brigade combat team from Alaska: Colonel Michael Howard's 4th Brigade, 25th Infantry Division (Task Force Yukon). This transfer of authority would clearly bring more forces, more resources including surveillance and reconnaissance, and more combat capability.

In two weeks, Major General Scaparrotti would arrive for their last predeployment site survey, and I wanted to be sure we supported his visit

100 percent. The two visits I made to Afghanistan with my staff had been critical in my thinking and follow-on decisions, giving me context and even some minor experiences to refer to as the actual deployment played out. I wanted the next team to be equally endowed.

"So how is it going, Jeff?"

"Good, I think we are making progress."

I had barely uttered the words when in came a "whoosh" and deafening scraping sound, apparently right above my head. General Scaparrotti told me later I ducked (he was watching the video) and I must have involuntarily grinned, for there is nothing in the world like a split second of facing death, only to find it missed you, and then there was a loud explosion, but not exactly near. In the distance, I heard several more explosions.

Minutes later, I would be told the rocket had skipped off the top of the old Soviet hangar that enclosed our headquarters, literally over my head, and careened unguided into the detainee internment facility nearby. Thank God no one was injured, my troops or those interned, many of whom were enemy. I had no love lost for those we detained, many I was certain were al-Qaida, Haqqanis, LeT, Taliban, and even the odd TTiP, but I upheld the law of land warfare, and they were mine to protect, even against enemy indirect rocket attacks.

The operations center reported to me quickly with no known casualties, and we set into motion the normal battle drill, except I stayed in the office to finish the teleconference. I wagered the shot at the headquarters was a lucky shot, and the chances of repeating that were nil.

What did bother me was the final report later that evening. At Bagram, we received four likely 107-mm rockets, one that scraped the hangar roof of our headquarters before hitting the detainee facility, and three more hitting the vast expanses of the base, none causing casualties. With radar and aerial and ground patrols we found the point of origin (POO) of the attack to be about six and a half miles south, technically in RC-Capital. And of course we followed up. All a routine part of combat where we were. What was not routine were the twenty other attacks that day in our area of responsibility, a total of twenty-one kinetic events against RC-East on March 5. A full thirty days before the traditional start of the spring fighting season, the annual insurgent "event" was almost always accompanied by a strategic comms fanfare that would have made any public relations firm proud.

The Taliban spring offensive had begun. Thirty days early, snow in the passes be damned.

I went to bed that night pondering the efficacy of our entire winter campaign. We had sought to deny the enemy R and R and sanctuary, to engage them in the dead of winter, to give them no reprieve while rapidly building the Afghan Border Police and border control coordination, and to increase the local governors' reach. And in response, the enemy started its typical spring fighting season a month *early*. Had we failed?

In hindsight, I think I failed to fully understand the result of our own campaign and operations on the enemy. What we did forced them to remain engaged throughout the winter, causing them to improvise in ways we had not seen before, and in one sense, to "match" our own winter campaign with a lower OPTEMPO compared to ours, but still a sustained fight throughout the Afghan winter.

We had acted in a thoughtful, forceful manner, and the enemy had adapted.

A few days later, I flew down to Forward Operating Base Airborne to meet with Dave Haight and his two battalions that had assumed responsibility for Wardak province. Lieutenant Colonel Kimo Gallahue (commanding 2nd Battalion, 87th Infantry) and Lieutenant Colonel Mike Gabel (commanding 4th Battalion, 25th Field Artillery) briefed me on their operations and intelligence rundown. They had been in the country about two full months by then—plenty of time to get their feet on the ground—and I had high expectations.

They told me that 30 percent of their units had previously served in Afghanistan: an astounding figure given the normal turnaround of officers and non-commissioned officers between two ongoing theaters, Iraq and Afghanistan, as well as the usual one tour and out for the younger enlisted soldiers. They shared with me counterinsurgency force ratios—the number of troops, ISAF, allied, and Afghan, compared to the local population—that were some of the very best in all of eastern Afghanistan. Their staff gave me a superbly refined view of the enemy and friendly situation in this difficult province, and we discussed their plans for the next several months as the enemy increased their operations. As I flew back to Bagram, I was satisfied that the troops and resources I had asked for so many months before, almost a year ago, would make a positive difference on the ground.

But I was nagged by thoughts of a different previous decision: I had upheld the UCMJ and our reading of the "law of warfare" against a young captain, who, with a force less than a tenth of the size of the two battalion task forces there now, attempted to do all he could to keep his soldiers alive, and seek out the enemy when he could. My punishment ruined his career, and likely would scar him in some ways for life. We, and I personally, had placed that captain in a situation with not enough of anything except courage, and ordered him to play by a rule book only we played by, not the enemy. It would be all too easy to dismiss my disquiet flying back that afternoon, the valley just beginning to green near the irrigation canals, the dark mountains to the west of us a mottled white from the aging snow. But I pondered the fairness of it all.

I knew war as many things. Fair was not one of them. I was still sometimes startled by the cool cruelty with which we Americans dispatched the enemy, "servicing" a target with 155-mm artillery, a well-aimed .50-caliber sniper round, or a thermobaric Hellfire missile shot from kilometers away. I was guilty of the same, chasing individual insurgents along the Durand Line with 250-pound JDAM precision-guided bombs, unemotionally deciding who would live and who would die. Most of us did not approach the bestial yet calculating brutality of our enemy, who routinely sawed off heads, arms, hands, and more, or calmly sprayed acid into young girls' faces, all in a day's work. And the dilemma: war was also an honorable thing, probably for all sides given our different perspectives, in a world where honor had lost its luster, and how much one earned was more important than what one did for one's nation and citizens.

But fair? Nope. War was not fair, and never would be. Fair fights were for boxers in the ring. In fact, my job as a leader in war was to do everything in my power that I could do within our ethics and morals to make our piece of the war most unfair for our enemy.

We fought to win.

But we expected our soldiers and especially their leaders to uphold the laws of war, such as they were, in spite of it all. And sometimes they were unable to achieve a balance between seeking to create an unfair fight for the enemy and conducting the fight within the bounds of law and convention. And they—we—were held accountable.

CHAPTER 28

"Leadership in the field depends to an important extent on one's legs, and stomach, and nervous system, and one's ability to withstand hardships, and lack of sleep, and still be disposed energetically and aggressively to command men, to dominate men on the battlefield."
General George C. Marshall

Saturday, March 14, 2009

General Scaparrotti and I sat through the morning combat update brief together before he split off for the day to visit some of our outposts and units. He and his team had arrived a few days before and were sharp, focused, and well prepared. Many of his staff had been to RC-East before, having been the CJTF that we relieved the previous year. I was certain this was the best way to ensure continuity of operations as well as relative success in our overall campaign.

I headed one way in a Black Hawk, Scaparrotti another. Colonel Scott Spellmon and I flew north up the Shomali Plain toward the towering Hindu Kush, then entered the narrow Panjshir River canyon as it cut down and out of the high mountains. It was easy to see how the Northern Alliance had delayed and disrupted nine successive Soviet campaigns into the Panjshir during that war, and how the local Tajiks had defended against the feuding warlords and later the Taliban in the following decades. We landed in a rocky riverbed, the roaring river running turbulent and wide in the spring thaw waters.

Governor Bahlol of Panjshir waited by the river's edge, along with our Panjshir Provincial Reconstruction Team commander Air Force Lieutenant Colonel Mark Stratton, one of my favorite reconstruction team commanders. An Air Force RC-135 Rivet Joint navigator who had been serving on the Joint Staff J-5 Asia directorate, he was not, by background, one I would have selected to command a unit of air force, army, and civilians living and working in the Hindu Kush of the Panjshir.

Was I wrong.

Mark was a tall man, big but not heavy, with a close-cropped haircut that masked a slightly retreating hairline. A strong face and easy smile was matched by a people-oriented intellect. His father had been an army officer and served in Vietnam. Mark was an Aggie, having graduated from Texas A&M in 1991 with an ROTC commission. He sometimes spoke to us about his wife Jennifer and their three kids back in Virginia. Mark was the real thing.

The governor deeply respected Mark, and as we later walked along the only paved road in Panjshir, the locals greeted him with smiles.

We flew up the Panjshir Valley inspecting all of the USAID and reconstruction team projects from the air: concrete block schools, irrigated farm fields, a ten-turbine wind farm, micro-hydroelectric dams just a few feet wide that powered the tiny hamlets perched above the river course, and the simple gravel roads that penetrated some of the most remote box canyons. In the Panjshir, a little CERP money went a long way.

We flew further up into the Hindu Kush along a narrow canyon, the rushing stream pushing down glacial till in the milky gray-blue foaming waters. The governor told us about the small-scale mining that these families and hamlets had done for generations: semi-precious stones, emeralds mainly, some jade, but also the world-famous blue Afghan lapis lazuli. Of course, much of this was unregulated, in spite of the laws and regulations from Kabul, and the mining industry played a role, albeit small, in Afghanistan's overall corruption. But what was the local miner to do? He had to feed his family.

Brent ensured we flew no higher than fourteen thousand feet, but the Hindu Kush towered around us. We landed back at the river's edge and walked across the narrow but paved road to Mark's headquarters. We talked about what we had seen, and what else was needed. I promised the governor some $30 million in upcoming CERP, which we felt would build the roads and schools still needed: this was not a plan to move Panjshir into the twenty-first century, just get it out of the eighteenth.

A couple of days later, I hosted Pakistani Frontier Corps Inspector General Major General Tariq Khan and Pakistani 7th Division Commander Major General Naweed Zaman in my office for two hours of intimate back-and-forth on our respective operations on both sides of the border. By now Tariq and I knew each other pretty well, and I had huge respect for him. I trusted his judgment.

We were joined in my office by a handful of senior officers in a robust but healthy give-and-take: *We are making progress in Bajaur, in a series of small actions. We will need your forces higher up along the border in Bajaur in two weeks' time. We aim next to go into Kurram and the Khyber. Yes, Waziristan is definitely still planned for operations, just not now—in the future.*

I led them into our CJTF operations center for a brief by the chief of current operations, Major William "Hank" Taylor, and we showed them our border mapping initiative. After a simple lunch, we boarded Black Hawks and flew to Nangarhar, then up the Kunar Valley to Forward Operating Base Joyce, where Colonel John Spiszer and 1st Battalion, 32nd Infantry Battalion Commander Lieutenant Colonel Mark O'Donnell (detached to Task Force Duke from Dave Haight's brigade) briefed us on their new initiatives to control the border, all much more tangible since the arrival of O'Donnell's troopers in late winter.

We flew further north along the Durand Line, and Khan and Zaman were fascinated by this bird's eye view of the opposite side of their frontier. After circling outposts (OPs) Mace and Hatchet, we headed back south, and we dropped them at the Khyber Border Coordination Center.

All of us were upbeat after the day. If generals could coordinate and plan to collaborate, we thought for sure we could ensure our staff would, and that would enable our troops to work towards mutually supporting goals, if not together.

On Friday, March 20, I ran around the airfield twice, logging sixteen miles. We had the first-ever Bagram Marathon coming soon, and I wanted to be in shape. It was a crazy idea to hold a marathon in a combat zone. And yet we had planned it from the start. It was a way to keep soldiers motivated to keep doing PT, to have something other than work, chow, sleep, and emailing home to do during our fifteen months. We had always described our fifteen-month deployment as a marathon, not a sprint. We had to pace ourselves from day one, or risk the mid-tour exhaustion many of us had experienced before in other deployments, even ones much shorter. But still, I was surprised by the interest and the planned turnout for our marathon.

Several days later, Patty emailed: my stepmother Ina, my father's wife for the past two decades, had died of a heart attack in her sleep. She had been ill for the past few years, and my Dad devoted each and every day to caring for her at their home in Ballwin, Missouri, just outside of St. Louis. I quickly called my father. He was strong, but I could tell he was devastated. Could I come home for the funeral?

I called General McKiernan and he insisted I return for a couple of days to attend the funeral and help my father. I was anxious about leaving my command, even for a few days, but I trusted my deputy commanders and chief, and knew they would do just fine.

The next day was Friday. That afternoon I caught a UC-35 to Kuwait, and then flew commercial home to Nashville. I was back in Bagram the following Friday. The week had been hectic, two days of travel each way, three days with my Dad and our families and his and Ina's friends. But I had been there, and Patty, Kelly, and I did what we could to ease my father's grief.

My own mother had died in her sleep several years before, a few months after I returned from our Iraq deployment. I had not seen my mother in a year, and she was so frail and weak that I knew she could not stay alone in her condo much longer. It was as if she had waited for my return from war, and her health declined so quickly after our first visit with her at her home that she was soon admitted into a hospice facility, where she died peacefully one Sunday morning.

Her death helped me realize all we miss in this profession of arms. My mother died in 2004, and in truth, I had had little time with her for the previous six years, as brigade command in Germany devolved into deployments to Albania and Kosovo, then promotion to brigadier led to assignment in Kuwait, and then 9/11 led to work seven days a week, fifteen hours a day, for almost two years in the Pentagon, until I departed for Iraq. I barely saw my mom in those years and now she was gone. I missed my mother's life in her final years. Just as I missed huge chunks of my kids growing up, and so many anniversaries and birthdays and holidays that would never be something shared between my family and me. War, and preparing for war, disrupts families in untold ways. Back in Bagram that early April, I was back with my troopers, and I knew that was my place. But I knew I had given things up that could never be replaced.

CHAPTER 29

*"It is morale that wins the victory. With it all things
are possible; without it, everything else—planning,
preparation and production, count for nothing."*
General George C. Marshall

Wednesday, April 8, 2009

The morning started with intense rains and low ceilings. By mid-morning the weather cleared enough for us to fly down to Ghazni, the headquarters of Task Force White Eagle, our Polish brigade.

Polish President Lech Kaczynski had arrived in Kabul the day prior with a traveling delegation of forty-five, including a large number of Polish and European journalists. His visit was extremely important to me and to ISAF. We needed his commitment to stay the course in Afghanistan, and I desired even more Polish troops to augment the sixteen hundred Polish soldiers now in Ghazni.

Colonel Rajmund Andrzejczak was the host, and his White Eagle troops looked sharp in formation as we went through the usual speeches and award presentations. I presented the president with a CJTF-101 plaque, and thanked him sincerely for his leadership and the Polish contributions to NATO and ISAF. Kaczynski was not a tall man, but he seemed to me very comfortable surrounded by soldiers and military equipment, with Polish attack helicopters roaring overhead from time to time in a show of force against any insurgents close by, and I admired him as he spoke, thanking his troopers for their sacrifices and wishing them the best Easter possible in a combat zone. He also said he was committed to adding more troops to their numbers. In a small meeting with the president, Rajmund, and our deputy commanding general for coalition operations, Polish Brigadier General Janusz Adamczak, Kaczynski promised he would send four hundred more troops, a full battalion, to join Task Force White Eagle, and soon. We had heard he had promised more troops during his press conference with Karzai in Kabul the day prior, but didn't say how many. We knew there was a big difference between an additional thirty-man platoon and a four hundred-man battalion, and we needed the latter.

The Polish commanders were elated, and I was deeply appreciative. I knew that not everybody back in Poland supported the Polish role in Afghanistan, and knew we would need to make real progress in Ghazni with minimal Polish casualties and very solid communications to the Polish public and politicians.

Early in the morning a few days later, I was woken and told of a major firefight in the Watapur Valley, deep in northern-central Kunar. Something had gone wrong, and there were many civilian casualties. The early morning stretched into day and then into night. We dug deep into the operation: a special operation against a known enemy, an in-stream battle handoff to supporting AH-64 Apaches, a devastated mountain home, and an Afghan family almost completely wiped out. How did this happen?

That evening, I reviewed the video recorder tapes from the Apaches' gun sights as well as the cockpit voice recorder, which recorded not only the pilots' voices but also all of the radio traffic. I was disturbed by what I saw and heard, and what I didn't hear. What I saw was a two-story stone and log home built into the mountain side, dark except for the four-legged white hot spots on the lower floor that looked like goats or sheep, and both tall and short hot spots on the top floor and roof, which would be men, women, and children. After receiving a clearance to fire, the Apaches opened up with their 30-mm guns and the hot spots mostly fell, with just a few running for their lives outside the home.

What had gone wrong? Was this a bad handoff to the wrong house? The special operations task force was confident they had engaged an enemy command and control node, but I was not at all confident that the home the Apaches attacked was that same node, and the procedures to identify and approve the target were less than clear that night. And why did the Spader headquarters, the land-owning battle command, approve the Apaches to engage?

It was a busy fighting day throughout RC-East, and we had multiple enemy contacts as well as deliberate combat operations to track, but I kept coming back to the Apache attack. By late night, we thought we had killed six civilians and wounded fourteen more, some with wounds that would likely prove to be mortal. Many were children.

I called General McKiernan late that night and told him what I knew, and more, what I didn't yet know. He was pissed and chewed me out.

"You have to get control of civilian casualties!"

Didn't I know that.

In the days to come, our investigation would lead me to personally interview the Apache crews as well as Spader 6 Lieutenant Colonel Brett Jenkinson, my best battalion commander that spring. I thought the Apache crews had been sloppy that night, but they attacked a target they were told was legitimate after being cleared to fire. I was deeply concerned about Jenkinson's command post procedures that fateful night, and as we got deeper into it, decided I would have to take some action.

The war continued and our time in it as the CJTF dwindled. April seemed to last forever. Admiral Mullen came for another visit, and we flew out to visit troops. We went to Forward Operating Base Airborne for an overview of the Wardak operations, and then flew down Highway 1 over the small platoon outposts that were already making a substantial difference in highway security since the arrival of battalions from 3rd Brigade, 10th Mountain Division to the province. We split off and flew the Khost-Gardez Pass to Combat Outpost Deysie, where the company team gave a superb briefing and we walked around within the wire, overlooking the KG Pass Road, still under construction, yet more secure than ever, and slowly being widened and paved. He had seen the progress over the past fourteen months and he said so.

During the flight back to Kabul, the chairman said he finally had seen my point about the depth of experience required to be effective in Afghanistan, and said he would ask the army to bring the same battalions, brigades, and divisions back to the same locations in the country, rather than sending them to a different regional command or worse, off to a different war. I had been making that point with my superiors for a year, and was gratified. As we parted, he thanked the CJTF-101 and me for what we had done the previous fourteen months. I had hoped for more progress, but told the chairman I was proud of what had been accomplished.

The chief of staff of the army, General George W. Casey Jr., came the next evening. We had a short one-on-one and Jim McConville took him off to see the special operations task force. Early the next morning the chief and I met for breakfast. We talked about our progress, including some of my frustrations in not achieving all I had hoped and planned. General Casey had seen plenty of that as the commander of Multi-National Force Iraq, and was reflective and positive. We discussed Milley and McConville's future assignments and potential; I thought they both could be very senior leaders, and said so. Casey agreed. He also confirmed that the secretary would nominate me for a third-star and U.S. Army Europe assignment.

JEFFREY SCHLOESSER

Later that night back at Bagram, I saw General Casey off. He was emphatically appreciative of all we had accomplished. It made me wonder if I was being overly tough on my own assessment of our progress.

★ ★ ★

The next morning was Saturday, the 25th of April. Bagram Marathon Day. I got up at 4:30 a.m., and Command Sergeant Major Vince Camacho and I headed to the starting line. Bagram's main drag was lined with non-running well-wishers, and we had several hundred runners ready to go. Spirits were high as the dawn slowly blossomed into pale light over the mountaintops. At 5:30 a.m. we were off, with a circuitous route that required a double lap of the entire air base. Vince and I ran together. It was his first marathon, whereas I had done over thirty, but we ran side by side, talking to fellow runners, encouraging the suffering, and "high fiving" those who watched and cheered. Hot, dusty, and dangerous not because of enemy attack but because of the logistics trucks that had to keep operating, it was an incongruous but spiritually invigorating event for all who ran the 26.2 miles and those who watched. I was worn out the rest of the day, and spent a couple of painful hours in the office in the late afternoon, but mostly I rested and hydrated.

In the days that followed, many soldiers shared their marathon experience with me. Most runners had never run that distance ever before in their lives, and to do so in Afghanistan, during a combat deployment, meant more than I had realized. They trained in the off-hours, read running magazines sent to them by their spouses, and focused on something else beyond our deployment for the short minutes each day they could steal from our focus on the war.

The Bagram Marathon, crazy as it seemed, was a huge success.

I thought that night about the marathon and its role in building and maintaining positive morale. I felt that morale, especially given a lengthy or even indeterminate deployment, was every bit as important as tough training, adequate resupply, and competent leadership in differentiating a cohesive, successful outfit from one that was not. And it seemed clear to me that it was a leader's responsibility to set the conditions for positive

308

morale. Other leaders more gifted than me had written about battlefield morale and its aspects, but I figured that it could be understood, and thus explained to subordinate leaders, when broken into component parts. There was a physical part: starting with building and then maintaining a robust physical fitness that included enough rest or sleep to enable the other components. There was a mental component: discipline first, then a mental toughness that some called resiliency, an approach to combat, and to life, that strived for good outcomes but accepted setbacks as a natural challenge that must not be allowed to derail one's efforts. There was an emotional component, which for many of us had a spiritual side: this was the ability to place into a broader context one's role, be it as a trooper in an outfit, leader, father, or mother, a human being on a brutal battlefield; to have empathy for one's soldiers, as well as those we were trying to protect, and even for the enemy; and most important, to be able to control one's emotions and not have them control you, even in the heat of direct, small arms combat. And finally, there was something harder to define, an awareness that what one was about was a worthy endeavor. For me personally, running, and especially running marathon distances, combined all four components, even the spiritual, and helped prepare me as a leader. And clearly, it had helped many others in my command as well.

Several days later, I met with my legal team to review the AR 15-6 investigation of the Watapur Valley incident where we had inadvertently killed several civilians, including women and children. I had been over the gun tapes and the radio transmissions, and the investigation added to my deep concern, anguish really, about our subordinate headquarters' decision-making that night. I ordered my judge advocate general, our division lawyer, to prepare letters of reprimand, as I continued to think through what I should do.

A letter sounds like nothing in the way of a punishment or admonishment, but receiving a General Officer Memorandum of Reprimand was usually career-ending, especially for those in command.

But was I convinced that was the right thing to do? None of these officers set out to purposely attack civilians that dark night, and none were purposely negligent from what I had seen and read. But something had gone badly wrong in the battle handoff and approval to attack sequence, call it the "fog of war," and the consequences had been horrendous, especially for that one mountain family that had been decimated.

What should I do?

CHAPTER 30

"Only those are fit to live who do not fear to die; and none are fit
to die who have shrunk from the joy of life and the duty of life."
President Theodore Roosevelt

Friday, May 1, 2009

The call from the Bagram operations center came a little before 5:00 a.m. Observation Post Bari Alai was being overrun by a major enemy force.

Bari Alai? Where the heck was that? And who manned the OP?

I rushed to the operations center floor, meeting Mark Milley and Brian Winski there.

The road that paralleled the Kunar River was our major supply route from Jalalabad in the south up to Bostick and Asadabad, and further supported the camps and outposts along the Pech River to the west. There had been periodic ambushes and attacks on our logistics convoys including a major ambush in July 2008, right after Wanat, that had wounded eleven troops from the newly arrived 1st Battalion, 26th Infantry, the Blue Spaders, who were moving north to their area of responsibility. The ambush took place near the Ghaziabad District Center at Nishagam. To improve security along the road and prevent that kind of ambush, the newly arrived battalion responsible for that area, Lieutenant Colonel Jim Markert's 6th Squadron, 4th Cavalry, the Raiders, began to establish a series of observation posts and vehicle patrol bases along the road. Responsible for the Ghaziabad and Naray districts in Kunar, and the Kamdesh and Barg-e Matal districts to the north in Nuristan, the Raiders were seriously undermanned. They had to make the most of partnering with the newly formed Afghan Army units that were completing training and gradually appearing in our area. Most of these Afghan units were only partially manned, unevenly led, and still learning how to conduct platoon-level combat operations. They depended on their ISAF advisory teams for fires and air support, and often logistics support as well.

By January 2009, the Afghans had positioned a company from the 6th Kandak (Battalion), 2nd Brigade, of the Afghan National Army's 201st Corps at the Nishagam District Center, and had placed one of the company's platoons at newly established Observation Post Bari Alai, high above the district center and able to oversee much of the road from south to north, as well as part of the approach to the Helgal Valley. Named for an Afghan soldier killed nearby by an IED, Bari Alai was situated atop a mountain spur outcrop, and was supported by an additional small security detachment of Afghan Army troops that guarded the access to the spur.

As the morning wore on, we found out at CJTF headquarters just how much we didn't know about Bari Alai.

Embedded with the Afghan platoon was a small mentoring and liaison team, an OMLT, made up of four Latvian Army soldiers, an American senior advisor, Staff Sergeant William Vile, plus a two-man signals team from 6th Squadron, 4th Cavalry, Sergeant James Pirtle and Specialist Ryan King.

The Latvians were all from their 1st Battalion, 1st Kajnieku, which supported other advisory teams throughout the region.

I was frankly surprised that we had a four-man Latvian OMLT and the three American soldiers at Bari Alai. I think much of my senior staff was too.

In the military, just like in all big organizations, the ability for higher headquarters to drill down into the minutiae of everyday business was increasing day by day, yet I had always resisted the urge to micromanage small units as I progressed from commanding four-hundred person battalions to brigades, with several thousand soldiers, and finally to division, responsible for over twenty thousand soldiers. The army taught leaders that you had to establish your intent—like I tried to do with the tactical guidance we issued the previous year—then resource, lead, and guide the subordinate leaders and soldiers. And verify, meaning get to as many units as possible to ensure they were resourced and focused on your ultimate priorities. When they sometimes failed, you had to have their back, meaning you had to support that failure, taking ultimate responsibility, as long as it wasn't deliberate or based on negligence. The Germans called this *Auftragstaktik*, or mission-type orders, the American Army called it "mission command," and I called it just plain common-sense leadership.

Wanat and Watapur were defining moments in testing this type of leadership, and judging from my anguish on both, I was still learning to deal with decentralized combat when things went wrong, or the enemy just had a good day.

The downside of mission command for large headquarters was that sometimes you were surprised by what had been deliberately planned below your level, and it slowed you down when trying to help.

Over the course of the morning, while we were sending in F-15Es, Apache attack helicopters, several quick reaction forces that Markert had ready to go, and others, we pieced together what we thought happened.

The enemy was about two hundred insurgents strong, and assembled overnight, coming from the north and west most likely. Some were dressed in Afghan Army camouflage uniforms. They seized the security point on the spur above Bari Alai; it was not clear if the ANA had abandoned it hours or even the day before. The attack began shortly after 4:30 a.m. Heavy machine guns and RPGs firing from west of the observation post immediately fixed and pinned down the troopers at Bari Alai. Staff Sergeant Vile, a veteran of the Korengal in a previous deployment, immediately called for fire support from the heavy 155-mm artillery at Forward Operating Base Bostick and the 120-mm mortar section at a nearby vehicle patrol base at Tsunel Valley. He adjusted the fires as the rounds came in. The CJTF operations center was informed of the attack and two F-15Es were repositioned to support Bari Alai and Vile, if he could pinpoint the enemy locations. Looking out the mountaintop bunker, the dawn slowly breaking, the smoke and airborne debris from the heavy artillery and mortar shells would have made it tough to see the insurgents.

Later, we would learn Vile also was firing the only automatic grenade launcher allocated to the observation post. Latvian Sergeant Ansevics fought alongside Vile. What they didn't see was a small fifteen-man assault force making their way to the wire along the spur left unguarded, as well as up the rocky slope from at least two directions. Ansevics was wounded, treated by a Latvian medic, and returned to fight. He was killed at the bunker entrance by several rounds of machine gun fire. Latvian Private Markusevs took his place, firing upon the assault force that was now within the wire. Inexplicably, the claymore mines meant as final defensive fires were apparently disarmed, their wires cut.

Vile called for final protective fires as the enemy surged over the wire and into the camp. An RPG exploded in their bunker, detonating stockpiled ammo, and the bunker collapsed. Staff Sergeant Vile was killed in the explosion or by an RPG round, and his radio destroyed. The two other American troopers, Pirtle and King, were killed in their small signal annex nearby. Latvian Sergeant Levine was later found alive, buried under the remnants of the bunker. Three Americans and two Latvians were dead, along with five Afghan troops. Some of the Afghan Army platoon ran down the mountain to the company at Nishagam District Center. With a Predator overhead, we saw the enemy pull out of Bari Alai, and move rapidly into the Helgal Valley.

They had taken prisoners.

By 9:00 a.m., Lieutenant Colonel Markert had moved two quick reaction forces to the observation post, one by helicopter that he personally led, the other driving down from the Tsunel Vehicle Patrol Base. The outpost was destroyed, still burning, black smoke rising in the mountains, odd rounds still cooking off from time to time. The insurgents had left quickly, uncharacteristically leaving behind almost twenty dead.

Markert, his boss Colonel John Spiszer, and the aviation task force commander Lieutenant Colonel Jimmy Blackmon did a masterful job of taking the soldiers and aviation we could spare to immediately reoccupy and reinforce Bari Alai, then pursue the enemy and their prisoners into the Helgal. The U.S. Special Forces team at Jalalabad played a critical role by air assaulting later that day and evening deep into the Helgal to block the enemy from exiting the valley over the mountaintop ridgeline. Over the next few days, we would surge two U.S. companies along with two Afghan Army battalions into the mouth of Helgal Valley and slowly work our way up the valley, while the Special Forces and their Afghan Army commandos blocked the upper valley and reported insurgent movements. We worked with the local tribal leaders, asking them to tell the Taliban to give up the Afghan prisoners or face certain death. On the morning of May 6, we added even more troops and surged up the valley. The Taliban released their captives, put them in pickup trucks, and had them drive down to the Nishagam District Center. They were healthy and apparently had been well cared for during their captivity.

By the end of the first day, my staff and I thought that Bari Alai had likely been compromised internally, with some number of Afghan Army soldiers aware of the attack, some disappearing before it started and re-appearing no worse the wear at the district center, and some twelve taken prisoner, to be later returned unharmed. Meanwhile, the Latvians and Americans had fought to the death, with two Latvians surviving, one gravely wounded and the other alive because he was buried under the rubble. Five Afghans were killed. This made me wonder again about the overall commitment of some Afghan Army soldiers to this war: clearly many were fighters and fought well, but equally clearly, some were not fighters, or perhaps were not willing to put their lives at stake for an American or NATO ally, and either fought poorly or not at all.

As is common at this level of war, I had to put on a game face that afternoon and host a visiting high-level Pakistani Army delegation led by DGMO Major General Iqbal. The Pakistani Army would begin their clear-and-hold operations in North and South Waziristan in June, and they wanted us to block the enemy from crossing into Afghanistan along the Durand Line. They confided in us about the very tough fighting they had had against the enemy ("miscreants," they called them) with their Special Services Group the week before in the mountains of Daggar. The enemy had quickly located the special ops team and attacked with nine suicide bombers in six vehicles, two motorcycles, and a lone bomber on foot.

They admitted they had underestimated the resilience of the "miscreants."

I shared with them what we knew so far of the attack at Bari Alai, and once they departed, quickly went back to the joint operations center for a Bari Alai operational update. Later that night, I would record in my journal how much progress we had made in the fourteen months working with the Pakistanis. To confide in us, and ask for specific military operational support to their own upcoming operations in the sensitive Waziristan area meant that they actually trusted us. And we had to trust them enough to deliver on our promises.

I continued to think the Pakistani intelligence service, the ISI, was playing a dual game, and supported multiple sides of our war simultaneously. We had heard of a special section within the ISI with just such a charter. I had begun to understand a bit more clearly the position of the regular Pakistani Army—the DGMO, the 11th Corps, and Khan's Frontier Corps—who seemed to have an uncertain relationship with their own intelligence service. Like us, they could never be certain exactly who the miscreants were: the TTiP, or the Haqqanis, maybe al-Qaida too. But I was certain these groups received support or refuge or both from the ISI.

Along the Durand Line that spring, it was an uncertain war that crisscrossed the international border. With our over-the-border special operation in September, the continuing Predator strikes on al-Qaida targets, the artillery fires and close air support I authorized in hot pursuit, and the Afghan Border Police buildup we were supporting, the Pakistanis were never completely certain what we might do next. And we felt the same about them, less about their army and Frontier Corps, but mainly because of the Taliban and Haqqani moves, which in most cases I believed had some level of covert ISI support.

That night I pondered the day's events. The level of corruption on both sides of the border was mind-boggling. I was certain that some number of Afghans had cut a deal with the enemy, and lived because they had, but that guaranteed that the Latvians and Americans at Bari Alai would thus die or be gravely wounded. I was also certain the ISI would continue to play both or all sides in Pakistan, and that the Pakistani Army and Frontier Corps were facing immense odds, fighting the miscreants as well as their own intelligence service.

Shortly before noon the next day, we held a ramp ceremony for the three U.S. soldiers killed at Bari Alai: Staff Sergeant William Vile, Sergeant James Pirtle, and Specialist Ryan King. After fourteen months of combat and ramp ceremonies to honor the fallen, I found myself steeled emotionally from the searing experience, but this day was different. King's wife was Sergeant Rachel King, and she helped lead the ceremony. She had been working in the CJTF operations center when the attack at Bari Alai began. She suspected the worst as the fighting continued early that morning. I talked to her before and after the ramp. She was a strong woman and soldier, but to hear her story and remain stoic was impossible. She had met her husband while both were serving in Korea. Ryan was a Georgia boy with a mischievous grin and lots of smarts, and was a proud military intelligence specialist. And now their dreams and life together had ended. I wanted to reassure her, and tell her that even this wound would heal over time. I knew my words could not ease her grief, but I tried anyway.

Staff Sergeant Vile would be awarded posthumously the Silver Star for his defense of Bari Alai, and Sergeant Pirtle and Specialist King would receive the Bronze Star. I ordered Bari Alai rebuilt and its defenses enhanced, work which began that day. Weeks later the vehicle patrol base at Tsunel Valley was renamed Combat Outpost Pirtle-King.

The following Monday night we held the ramp ceremony for the two Latvian soldiers killed in action at Bari Alai, Sergeant Ansevics and Private Markusevs. Another Latvian soldier was severely wounded and was medevacked to the U.S. Army hospital at Landstuhl, Germany. Their fourth comrade eventually was flown back to Latvia to recover.

On Tuesday, May 5, Mark Milley, Brian Winski, and I flew back to Peshawar to meet with Major General Tariq Khan and his Frontier Corps staff. The U.S. consulate Principal Officer Lynne Tracy met us at the airport and accompanied us throughout the trip to historic Fort Bala Hisar. We were less than thirty days from our transfer of authority, and I was determined to solidify the huge gains we had made in substantive coordination of combat operations between RC-East and ISAF and Khan's Frontier Corps. I genuinely liked and admired Khan, and by now we were at ease with each other in a manner I found rare with other Pakistani general officers, who tended to be somewhat aloof even when we knew them well: perhaps a holdover from the British staff legacy from generations past.

We reviewed in detail our ongoing operations on both sides of the Durand Line in Bajaur and Kunar, and Khan's expectations on operations in Bunair and into Dir, east of Nuristan. We discussed the tough slog in Swat. He told us he planned to move into South Waziristan and Wana in June or July. Across from Paktika Province and a vast, remote, and highly permeable border area, this was a vulnerable region and his announcement was excellent news.

We decided our staff would meet in two days to make detailed plans, and parted with a promise to meet one more time before our transfer of authority but after Major General Scaparrotti's arrival. I wanted Scap and Khan to continue this relationship.

On Friday, May 8, we hosted Secretary of Defense Gates at Forward Operating Base Airborne. He and about forty staffers, press, and aides were on a two-day whirlwind visit to Afghanistan, and he wanted to see remote forward operating bases in RC-South and RC-East. His time was short, and we had recommended Airborne, not far by helicopter from Kabul or Bagram, but still very much a forward base supporting significant combat operations against an entrenched enemy, as well as a critical component in building local governance in Wardak Province and moving development forward for the people.

The mountains west of Kabul still had snow-covered peaks, but Airborne was dusty, dirty, and illuminated by a brilliant bright sun that morning. Gates got off the Black Hawk in a dark suit and white shirt, looking like he was headed to a meeting with President Karzai at the palace. Instead, he walked over to a large camouflage net set up to ward off the sun's building heat, and sat down on a folding metal chair next to General McKiernan. Gates in his suit and McKiernan in a camouflage uniform with an armor vest and a 9-mm on his chest made for an incongruous pair, but Governor Fadai smiled, welcomed the secretary to Wardak, and began a *shura* with Gates, McKiernan, and tribal elders. Rod Rodriguez, the secretary's senior military assistant, and I sat nearby, along with the Afghan Army and Police chiefs from Wardak and several tribal elders. U.S. Army Special Forces Major Brad Moses joined us. The subject was the Afghan Public Protection Program (AP3).

It was an unusual sight, the gray-bearded elders in robes and pakols, the U.S. military in camouflage, body armor, and armed, and the secretary in a suit and dark tie, neither armed nor armored. And yet the conversation, translated quickly between the Dari and Pashtu and English, flowed. The elders were happy with Moses and the AP3 that his teams had trained, and recommended we do more there in Wardak and elsewhere. They were already making the villages more secure.

"We need jobs. If we have jobs for our men, then the insurgency will wither away."

The secretary was nuanced enough to realize that jobs were in fact important, but understood also that the professional insurgents, comprising many of the Taliban and Haqqanis, were in this fight for ideological, religious, and local governance reasons. Jobs were not the be-all and end-all in Wardak, or throughout RC-East. We had to rid the area of the insurgents or get them to reconcile, as well as provide an honest day's pay for an honest day's work within a local governance structure that was far less corrupt than they were at this point.

The *shura* ended quickly and the secretary and entourage walked along the dirt and gravel road to the motor pool area, where Airborne's vehicles were parked and staged. Along the way, Katie Couric interviewed Gates for *60 Minutes*, and I chatted with Geoff Morrell, the secretary's longtime press secretary. He was looking fresh and was as sharp as ever, after a long overseas visit to several countries.

Neither Rod nor Geoff gave any hint of the coming bombshell, which I found remarkable in hindsight.

The secretary spoke to a large gathering of Airborne's soldiers.

He said the U.S. and others had turned away from Afghanistan after the Soviets departed in 1989, and that "We paid the consequences in 2001. We won't do that again. You are here to make sure we don't do that again."

He told the troopers that he wanted them to be successful and to go home safely, and to do that, he saw his job as providing the proper equipment and assistance to enable their success.

I knew Gates was the primary reason we now had almost 2,500 MRAPs throughout Afghanistan, and more medevac helicopters, and far more surveillance and reconnaissance aircraft. The increase in ISR was significant. When we began our tour, we had the single Predator line, plus the brigade combat teams' indigenous Shadows and small Ravens. Now we had our own Task Force ODIN (observe, detect, identify, and neutralize), plus two Global Hawk sorties a week, five U2 sorties a week, a quick reaction-capability army Warrior UAV, and four Hunter UAVs, as well as the Predator line. It made a huge difference.

Most importantly, with Gates' support, my request for troops had become an Afghan surge, which went far beyond the additional 3,500 troops from 3rd Brigade, 10th Mountain Division. Both General McKiernan and the chairman, Admiral Mullen, played pivotal roles in seeing the need for more U.S. and ISAF troops, and then convincing the French, the Poles, New Zealand, and many others to augment their troops. They also played a major role in getting a Jordanian Ranger battalion, which I had decided to position in Logar to work with Haight's brigade. To the credit of Gates, Mullen, and McKiernan, they saw the situation was worsening in RC-South, and added a substantial U.S. Marine force that would have to turn that around.

All of these additional troops required a major increase in logistics. Armies run on fuel and ammo and food, plus spare parts for everything from helicopter turbine engines to rifle barrels. Getting the troops these things in what was essentially still an Afghan frontier required fleets of trucks, mine-clearing units, and vehicles to secure the convoys, plus fleets of contracted and military aircraft to resupply the more remote and smaller outposts. A substantial amount of our total combat power was absorbed into providing and securing our lines of communications and logistics. It was hugely, insanely expensive, but then all wars are so. A politician may wish to pursue a war, even one limited in scope and goals, cheaply, but the professional soldier knows otherwise.

General McKiernan told me as we were departing that he would call me that night on secure Tandberg.

"I have something important to tell you."

McKiernan and the secretary flew back to Kabul, and the secretary departed Afghanistan soon thereafter.

I worked late that night in the office on paperwork and legal issues while awaiting the call. The previous night I met with Spader 6, and gave him a General Officer Memorandum of Reprimand (GOMR) for his decisions during the Watapur civilian casualty incident. I had decided to give GOMRs to several of those involved, but this one was really, really hard for me to decide what to do. He was likely my finest battalion commander in combat, and certainly led the most combat-engaged unit in the CJTF, in the toughest terrain, against a very determined and clever enemy. He had made a bad decision, which had snowballed into the deaths of six civilians and fourteen more civilians wounded. He admitted so. In my mind, he was clearly not deliberately negligent, and certainly never intended to target innocent civilians.

And yet they were dead, a whole family almost wiped out. I had to respond, to send a clear message to all of our soldiers and leaders and Afghan partners that this was not OK, that this was not another consequence of war, not another collateral damage incident that we would acknowledge, investigate, and forget.

Like the young but strong captain the previous year at Forward Operating Base Airborne, my heart and soul were with the soldiers and the leader making the tough decisions on the ground. I wanted to protect them, to take responsibility myself, for I set the conditions for success as best I could, and shared in failure when it occurred.

GOMRs were filed in one of two places: locally, within the general officer command, or at the Department of the Army, where they became part of the soldier's file. The latter case was essentially cause for most careers to end early. Few officers or NCOs would be promoted with a GOMR in their file. But if filed locally, the GOMR was destroyed when the soldier departed the command, if no further negative proceeding had occurred.

So the previous night I gave him the GOMR, but withheld where I would file it, and this night as I waited for the call from McKiernan, I pondered what was fair, for the army, for my CJTF and division, for the Spaders of 1st Battalion, 26th Infantry, and for their battalion commander.

Before midnight, I decided the call from General McKiernan would not come that night, and went to the operations center and then to my bunk for some sleep. I didn't know what I would do with the GOMR.

I was in the office the next morning, Saturday, May 9, when the secure videophone came alive, and General McKiernan's face came on. He looked tired.

"Jeff, the secretary told me I would be replaced as COMISAF and commander, U.S. Forces Afghanistan. Soon."

Why?

"Seems I have lost the political support back in Washington."

Who will take your place?

"Stan McChrystal is the likely choice."

It was a short call. I was shocked.

Lost political support in Washington.

I knew the Pentagon and White House well enough. The combatant commander, General Petraeus, and the chairman, Admiral Mullen, would have blessed this kind of strategic decision. Both had seen enough of Afghanistan to know that it was not the strategy of our counterinsurgency that was off-kilter, but that the means—the resources—were sadly underfunded, leaving commanders in this theater to do the best they and their troops could do given the limitations of what they had in order to do the mission.

There had been significant increases in the troops, vehicles, and ISR assets, most of which were coming on line now in the country. McKiernan would not have the chance to show what they could do.

I was no fool. Ambassador Holbrooke may have played a role, as may have any number of senators and congressmen who came through our war, as well as the multitude of national security "experts" that visited us, and went home to write tough, sometimes blistering reports.

I also remembered General McNeill's warning, now almost two years past: "Generals will be blamed if we don't win this."

So why was I surprised?

The shock had worn off two days later when Secretary Gates made the formal recommendation and it was released to the press. Stating the need for "fresh leadership" as the U.S. was taking a "new approach" to the war, Gates said Stan McChrystal was his recommendation to the president to replace McKiernan, and that his own military deputy, Rod Rodriguez, would return to assist Stan as deputy commander of U.S. Forces Afghanistan.

I pulled up the Department of Defense news release.

Gates said, "Today we have a new policy set by our president. We have a new strategy, a new mission, and a new ambassador. I believe new military leadership is needed."

After taking office in January, President Obama had ordered an Afghanistan policy review, and quickly accepted the Pentagon's recommendation to send some seventeen thousand additional troops our way. At the end of the review, in late March, the president spoke at the White House, saying that the U.S. now would have a "clear and focused goal: to disrupt, dismantle, and defeat al-Qaida in Pakistan and Afghanistan, and to prevent their return to either country in the future." He announced that an additional four thousand U.S. troops would be deployed, to assist the Afghan Army in training, on top of the seventeen thousand he had previously approved.

We had about 38,000 U.S. troops on the ground in May, with 17,000 to 17,500 on the way, and now this additional 4,000. I thought those numbers seemed satisfactory, but that all depended on how many were sent elsewhere in Afghanistan. I knew RC-South needed many.

The president also spoke about the critical role Pakistan played in the outcome, which was reassuring, since I had spent hours showing Mullen and Petraeus the border region, had talked to then-Senator Obama about it during his Afghanistan visit, and highlighted its importance to every CODEL and VIP visitor.

I had been baffled in March by the way the president explicitly focused on al-Qaida, and did not include the Taliban in his statement. *Was this to be strictly a counterterrorism strategy as we sought to build the Afghan Army to take over?* As time went on, it was clear the Taliban were still a focus, as were infrastructure and governance.

In truth, it was the beginning of a focus on Afghanistan that was long overdue. With the situation in Iraq stabilizing from the surge there, it was high time to turn our attention and resources to Afghanistan. In country, a new U.S. ambassador was sworn in on April 29. Former Lieutenant General Karl Eikenberry was a colleague, someone I respected and had sought advice from prior to deploying, based on his previous command of Combined Forces Command in Afghanistan from 2005 to 2007. I had yet to brief the new ambassador, but knew that he planned to mirror the troop surge with a surge in U.S. civilians at the embassy and USAID workers with our provincial reconstruction teams.

I thought these steps, focusing more on the ways and means, but clearly showing the end state was more narrowly focused, were sound. In fact, I was delighted. We would never make Afghanistan a truly democratic country like the U.S., and it was doubtful they could achieve the democratic governments like in Japan and Germany post World War II. But I was sure we could make it better, and good enough to make it just too hard for al-Qaida to be a really significant future player in Afghanistan.

My biggest concerns were the Taliban, Pakistan as a continuing safe haven, and Afghan corruption. Holbrooke would need strong support in Washington as well as in the region and the Middle East writ large to negotiate a viable and long-lasting settlement with the Taliban, bringing them back into the political system as a minority party in exchange for renouncing arms and violence. I wasn't privy to anything that convinced me this was afoot. And as long as Pakistan allowed a small section within the ISI to support the insurgents with refuge and resources, how could we convince the Taliban to negotiate? And finally, I saw no multi-echelon endeavors to tackle Afghan corruption, if that was even possible from an American or ISAF perspective. All of which boded ill for the ultimate success of this new American strategy and surge.

But I felt then, and still do, that General McKiernan could have led this surge and focused approach. That said, I understood how, half a world away in Washington, D.C., our slow progress looked like a leadership issue that could be solved at the top.

The next day was Sunday, May 10, and we were about three weeks from transfer of authority. Major General Scaparrotti's 82nd Airborne Division staff had been flying in daily, and we had begun the left seat, right seat ride process that ensured we did an in-stride handoff of mission, staff section by staff section. As my staff completed the process, they would start to flow back home to Fort Campbell. On the day of our transfer of authority in early June, when Vince Camacho and I furled our CJTF-101 colors and Scaparrotti and his command sergeant major unfurled the CJTF-82 flag, his staff would be running the show, and some twenty to thirty of the last of my team would board a C-17 with Camacho and me and head home.

That evening began the many award ceremonies and farewells that would occupy much of my time in the remaining days ahead. I started with my own command group and our division special troops battalion, as they would be transitioning soonest, but each and every day until we left, I spent time with a unit, most of them outside the wire of Bagram, thanking them for their role in our campaign; some were coming to the end of their own tours, while others had just begun, but to all I highlighted how important their unit was to our overall efforts and the key role each soldier, marine, airman, and sailor played. In the ensuing days, we flew to almost every major operating base and outpost we still had, sometimes for a visit as short as an hour, to say a sincere thanks, and place their mission and sacrifices in a broader context.

It was worth the effort.

Two days later, the insurgents tried to kill the Khost Governor Asala Jamal at his home. They also attacked the Khost municipal building using an unprecedented number of suicide bombers. Afghan and U.S. forces counterattacked and killed eleven insurgents, and freed four hostages. Several Afghan and U.S. troops were wounded, but none were killed.

This was a directed attack on civilians. Where was the national outrage? Where was Karzai?

Monday morning, May 25: my second Memorial Day in command in eastern Afghanistan. I got up earlier than usual and ran a quick five miles, then cleaned up and prepared for a busy day. Major General Scaparrotti and Command Sergeant Major Chappell had arrived the morning before to start their deployment, and Scaparrotti and I had stayed up the previous evening in my office, one-on-one without staff, talking through each province. Before going to the visiting personnel quarters (I had moved out of my room to make way for Scaparrotti), I told my judge advocate that I wanted to file Spader 6's GOMR locally. It would be destroyed when I, and my command, departed. I was convinced this was the right thing to do.

General Petraeus had flown in, and Mark Milley and Mike Scaparrotti flew with him out to Torkham Gate and the Border Coordination Center. At 9:00 a.m., I stood in front of 106 troops from the U.S. Army, Marines, Navy, and Air Force, and conducted a simple but emotional naturalization ceremony. This was my third such ceremony, and it would be my last. I was honored to officially welcome these men and women into U.S. citizenship. Many had tears running down their faces as they raised their right hands and repeated the oath.

I met Ambassador Eikenberry at the ramp, and we had lunch together with several troopers. Karl Eikenberry had retired from active service to assume the ambassadorship, and he seemed to me to have made the transition from military senior leader to ambassador effortlessly, at least from appearances. We headed to my office and General Scaparrotti joined us, back from Torkham Gate, and I went to a map of eastern Afghanistan and frontier Pakistan that I kept on a tripod in the office. I verbally walked around RC-East and across the Durand Line, and Eikenberry and Scaparrotti asked probing questions. After an hour, General McKiernan arrived and joined us in the office for more give-and-take.

We headed out to the courtyard in front of the hangar doors that made up the CJTF headquarters, the flags of twenty-eight NATO nations that made up ISAF fluttering in the summer breeze. Old Abe, the statue of the 101st Airborne Screaming Eagle, was still perched by the concrete steps near the U.S. flag. He too would soon be gone. The troops and civilians that had assembled for the Memorial Day ceremony were quiet, as the ambassador and General McKiernan spoke. We laid out a wreath of flowers for the fallen of all our partner ISAF nations. There had been too many, over 170 killed in action under my command since last April, at latest count, and so many more wounded.

It was a week until our transfer of authority and departure from Afghanistan. I made a silent prayer at the end of the memorial ceremony that we would lose no one else. No more troopers killed in action. No more ramp ceremonies. No more letters to families. No more nights awake, wondering if it was worth it. No more devastated lives, torn-apart families, young lives ended prematurely.

It was not to be.

CHAPTER 31

"You cannot build character and courage by taking
away man's initiative and independence."
Abraham Lincoln

Tuesday, May 26, 2009

After early morning PT, General Scaparrotti and I met at the Jirga Center with our staff. We spent five hours working through a commander's assessment brief, a detailed status check of our entire CJTF-101 campaign plan, and what we thought we had accomplished in the past fifteen months. We went through the major lines of operations—security, connection, and empowerment of local and regional Afghan governments, development projects to transform the environment, and a proactive approach to information operations to engage with our different audiences while actively countering enemy propaganda—with what I hoped was a modest, realistic review of the facts on the ground as we knew them. It required a detailed, province-by-province discussion.

After the overviews, we focused on the forty or so most challenging and violent districts of our 158 that made up our fourteen provinces. This was where most (about 75 percent) of the violence in RC-East occurred, and with the violence came less ability to enhance local governance or effectively improve economic development. This was where

CJTF-82 would need to focus more resources, or alternatively, consider abandoning.

I wished we had been more successful in withdrawing U.S. and ISAF forces from the really remote, and often very violent, outposts on the edges of our Afghan frontier: Keating, Fritsche, the Korengal camps, maybe Hatchet and Mace—all in the north, and often in sparsely populated areas with unfriendly, historically xenophobic tribes. I thought we could withdraw to the Pech and Kunar rivers, and to the district and provincial centers of Nuristan and Kunar, with little harm to our overall counterinsurgency effort. Of course, Minister of Defense Wardak and General Bismillah Khan did not agree, and worked hard on COMISAF General McKiernan, CENTCOM Commander General Petraeus, and myself to limit our withdrawals in 2009. Still, we had reduced from about one hundred camps and outposts in April 2008 to eighty-two now, in late May 2009.

It was true that in the summer of 2009, the Afghan Army was not yet ready for us to turn many of these camps over to them to command.

I was satisfied with the success we had had solidifying and significantly increasing the ISAF forces in RC-East. We started in spring 2008 with two brigade combat teams, one headquartered in Jalalabad, the other at Salerno. Based in Bagram, we also had an ad hoc brigade-level command responsible for Parwan, Kapisa, and Bamyan. To work the development and governance lines of operation, we had U.S.-led reconstruction teams in ten provinces: Parwan, Panjshir, Kunar, Nangarhar, Laghman, Nuristan, Khost, Gardez, Sharana, and Ghazni. From our allies, we had an augmented Polish battalion in Ghazni, and a French company task force in Kapisa, as well as a Czech PRT in Logar, a Turk PRT in Wardak, and a New Zealand PRT in Bamyan. As our June 2009 transfer of authority approached, we were much larger: a U.S. brigade combat team based in Jalalabad responsible for Nangarhar, Kunar, Nuristan, and Laghman; a U.S. brigade combat team in Salerno responsible for Khost, Paktiya, and Paktika; a new U.S. brigade combat team at Shank responsible for Logar and Wardak; and a U.S. maneuver enhancement brigade in Bagram responsible for Bamyan, Parwan, Panjshir, and Kapisa. There was also a French mountain battalion, the 27th Alpine, working with the Americans in Kapisa, a Polish Brigade responsible for Ghazni, the PRTs as before, and an inbound Jordanian Ranger battalion for Logar. We had maintained an entire combat aviation brigade, a sustainment brigade, and an engineer brigade in RC-East (all U.S.) during our deployment. Not under my command but working closely with CJTF-101 were special forces from several countries who worked with our own U.S. special ops units, many based out of Bagram. Overall American troop strength in Afghanistan, many of whom were stationed in RC-East, had increased from about forty thousand in April 2008 to just under seventy thousand in late May 2009. The other plus-up of American personnel was taking place in RC-South, where many thousands more marines were being deployed.

It had been a slog, starting with working to convince our own U.S. leadership of the need for more troops back in June 2008, then working to convince the Poles and French and Jordanians that they could and should participate in larger numbers, and actually assume responsibility as "land-owning" combat units.

On the support side, we had non-NATO countries that supplied major supporting capabilities to RC-East. We had an outstanding Egyptian military hospital on Bagram that treated many local Afghan each day; a South Korean team that augmented our Parwan and Kapisa reconstruction teams; and other countries that did not want to be recognized as being on the ground in Afghanistan but supplied various resources to us.

The Afghan Public Protection Program (AP3) that we started showed promise in Wardak, and could potentially be replicated in other provinces.

I was disappointed we had not substantially reduced the enemy crossing from Pakistan into Afghanistan, but said that our growing relationships and coordination with the Pakistan Army, the 11th Corps and the Frontier Corps, and their own operations along the Durand Line, if sustained, could significantly help RC-East. We talked about the efforts we had put into increasing the capability of the Afghan Border Police, working with the CSTC-A and the Ministry of Interior, which needed more effort to really achieve the effects we desired.

As we built troop strength, we added considerably to mobility through Secretary Gates' emphasis on MRAPs and medevac. We arrived in April 2008 with no MRAPs, and as we departed, we had fielded about eighteen hundred of the vehicles to our outposts in RC-East. We had added three field hospitals and ten additional medevac helicopters. We had fielded numerous surveillance blimps and towers and enhanced optics. The surveillance and reconnaissance capabilities had expanded significantly, but still lagged behind what we really needed to support this many outposts and troops.

The resulting mix—new capabilities, many more troops, enhanced relationships with the Pakistani military, increasing partnering with the Afghan Army and border police—was, however, too new to result in a really major impact against the insurgents, especially the Haqqanis and HiG. CJTF-82 had their work cut out for them kinetically.

I was proud of our economic development efforts led by Brigadier General Jim McConville and his team. If one measured only inputs, it would look to be a huge success. Our CERP funding for economic development had increased from $480 million to $680 million. But outputs were even more important, and the results were impressive: we had built tens of schools, medical clinics, micro-power units, clean water points, and hundreds of miles of roads. The USAID-funded Khost-Gardez Pass Road was still a work in progress, but it was advancing steadily, in spite of the Haqqani efforts to frighten off the construction crews from the Louis Berger Group. At the provincial level in Nangarhar, Chip Preysler and Mick Nicholson's dream of Nangarhar Inc. had achieved solid progress in improving irrigation, power, and farm support.

I was proud of the Agriculture Development Teams we had brought to Afghanistan, another McConville endeavor. The concept worked, and we now had five teams from five states working with Afghan farmers to produce viable, sustainable, and economically successful crops. That had led to eleven of our fourteen provinces being poppy-free, and we felt we were making true progress in the last three provinces that still had some opium production: Kunar, Kapisa, and Laghman.

I was more subdued on our governance efforts. Between Jim McConville and myself, we met with all fourteen provincial governors often, repetitively, and tried hard to mentor them and provide expert support. We held rule of law symposiums, anti-corruption drives, tutored Afghans on civil society, and insisted on legal oversight of CERP funds disbursement. As when we began, the governors and their administrations were a mixed lot in May 2009. Some were outstanding examples of local leadership: educated, moderate, and visionary. A few were corrupt, collaborating secretly with the enemy, and a plague upon the people they were meant to govern. Most were somewhere in between the best and the worst.

I felt leadership started at the top, and said that President Karzai was not helpful in building a responsible, non-corrupt regional government at our level in RC-East. I did not say what I truly thought: Karzai would never be the strong and responsible national leader Afghanistan now needed. He leaned to the Taliban and al-Qaida when civilian casualties occurred, condemning ISAF and the U.S., while rarely showing outrage when the enemy killed innocent Afghan civilians. And yet I seriously doubted he could or would achieve any kind of reconciliation with the Taliban or Pakistani political leaders. If appearances were everything in leadership, then Karzai—charismatic, dapper, impeccably dressed, and well-spoken—would be a great leader because he looked like the president of the Afghan People. But character matters most in leadership, and actions matter more than talk, and Karzai was weak in both areas.

Character: so hard to define, even harder to develop, especially during war. And yet as I looked at my bosses, my peers, and our followers, as well as those of allied nations and the Afghans, I was continuously struck by the differences between us, and sought to learn from them all. Among the many leadership attributes I had studied and emulated throughout my years in the army I found three preeminent at war: competence, courage, and character. Professional competence was easy to observe, and because war is about life-or-death decisions, we did our best in our formations to weed out the incompetent. In truth, we had been an army at war for several years and had institutionalized rigorous training for the squad and platoon level of counterinsurgency operations that dominated our Afghan war, and so seldom saw real incompetence in our leaders.

Courage, the willingness to bet your stars, was also prevalent on our battlefield among our leaders: they understood responsibility came with the authority granted them by rank and position, and did not shirk from their duty.

But character, that was so much more difficult to plumb, to measure, and to deliberately foster. And yet I would argue it was equally, if not more, important to leadership, especially in the challenging times of a war, as professional competence or courage. Why?

There are boatloads of definitions and lists of attributes for character. In my mind, they can be distilled simply: Character is what you actually do in morally and ethically challenging life dilemmas when no one is watching. A person of character may have many laudable attributes and habits, but they must have integrity, good intentions, honesty that is built upon responsibility, and enough self-discipline to control their actions, and if unable to completely master their wandering thoughts, at least ensure those thoughts do not cause one to violate one's own integrity.

Men and women are not perfect, and all of us have flaws, which we usually try to control, or at least hide from others. We are not born with character: instead, we develop it within ourselves over a lengthy period of time, some through education, some through the school of hard knocks of experience, and most often, through watching and emulating those we admire. The most important facet of character is the act of becoming: we are flawed, yet we strive for self-control and hope that others see us as we would wish to be seen and remembered. And the ultimate test of character is how we act when we know our actions are unseen, not attributable, and yet important.

The assessment brief was a helpful forcing function for the CJTF staff and me. In preparing to brief the CJTF-82 team, we had to review our fourteen months with a sharp pencil, and the result was mixed. We had made gains, suffered many casualties in making those gains, and hopefully set up the next task force to have better success.

In this kind of war, year in and year out, with few clearly articulated and achievable strategic goals that we as a military force could achieve, and strategic constraints on negotiating with the Taliban or more forcefully addressing the Pakistani safe haven, it was about as good as could be expected.

That day, Panjshir Provincial Reconstruction Team Commander Lieutenant Colonel Mark Stratton was on a visit to Bagram with several of his troopers, including his First Sergeant Blue Rowe. They had driven down from the mountains of Panjshir, still snowcapped in late May, to the green fields of the Shomali Plain, and to Bagram. Stratton and his team were in several armored Humvees. We had yet to field MRAPs into his reconstruction team and Panjshir; we considered his area of responsibility to be among our safest locales, along with Bamyan, and so they were not as high a priority as several other PRTs in the fielding process.

When the convoy was about four miles north of Bagram, a Toyota Corolla suddenly pulled alongside. The suicide bomber detonated the massive bomb inside the car. Mark Stratton was killed, along with Blue Rowe and Senior Airman Ashton Goodman. The reconstruction team's legal advisor, an Afghan citizen, was also killed, along with two other civilians.

When the CJTF operations center called to tell me the news, I was stunned. I knew Mark pretty well and admired him greatly. I had talked to First Sergeant Rowe several times. Blue was a well-spoken, superbly fit Army Reserve non-commissioned officer from our 426th Civil Affairs Battalion, and he was a good match to Mark Stratton. I remembered Airman Goodman, who had briefed me on some of their projects: she was smart, articulate, and seemed to be having the time of her life in this unusual assignment, a provincial reconstruction team in a province so remote there was little to reconstruct, but much to build.

That night at 7:00 p.m. we gathered at the airfield, and held a solemn, emotional farewell to Mark, Blue, and Ashton Goodman. The sun was setting, but the dimming orange rays lit the mountain peaks to our west, still snowcapped, and the Hindu Kush to our north looked blue and purple in the fading light. That was their land, their last home, their mountains.

Our grief was unspeakable.

But we were hardened, some may say jaded, or stoic, and with grim faces we went back to headquarters to work. I knew what was happening in their families' homes back in the States, and tried to clear those thoughts from my mind.

In my thirty-three years of service, I had grieved at many a memorial to a fallen comrade, and tried to comfort with words stricken families, and especially spouses. But I had never had to notify a family because I was always deployed, along with the soldier who became the casualty, and so I knew only vicariously what that was like, through my rear detachment commanders and Patty, who had done so many notifications in past wars and operations.

The two-person notification team was usually a senior officer, often the executive officer who stayed behind or rear detachment commander, and the rear detachment chaplain, wearing the army dress uniform. They would ring the doorbell if the family was known to be home, or try to get the spouse to be at home, and their appearance at the doorstep was a calamity for those inside. The team was practiced and nuanced, but one could not predict how a spouse, or mother or father, would take the news. Some fainted, some sat down on the floor and screamed, some were gracious grieving hosts who invited the soldiers in for coffee and tears; one could not tell.

The spouse support team came on the soldiers' heels: friends of the family, commanders' and leaders' wives, trained but deeply caring. They stayed as long as they were wanted, sometimes minutes, sometimes days. Patty had been part of these teams all too often, and had even played a role in a film one special operations unit had made about the notification process, which was widely viewed throughout the army. She was an expert. Sadly.

I was numb that night as I walked back to the hooch.

It was the last eight days before handover from CJTF-101 to CJTF-82. Unlike the staff that did a left seat, right seat ride, with the new staffer taking responsibility during the process, command of the CJTF and RC-East stayed with me until the actual ceremony. But it was also my responsibility to ensure General Scaparrotti had a good feel for the senior leaders I had been working with the past fifteen months, and so our last eight days were jam-packed, with both of us attending all of the routine daily and weekly meetings, but spending the majority of the day out of Bagram.

Mike Scaparrotti joined me for the weekly video teleconference with the COMISAF commanding general, which would be my last, and it looked like it would also be General McKiernan's final session. We spent most of it working on security details for the upcoming presidential and provincial council elections, to be held in August. With almost seven thousand polling centers spread throughout the cities, towns, and remote villages of Afghanistan, movement of ballots, ballot boxes, and the trained polling officials was impossible for the government, and we would assist them. At the polling centers, the Afghan Army and police were responsible for security, and thus ISAF soldiers would not be seen as the face of this election. We would have our normal quick reaction forces ready to respond to violence, should it occur.

The Afghans, along with ISAF, had put enormous effort into planning for both registration and the actual election. I knew there would be violence in some locations. I also thought I knew that the corruption of the society, from its politicians to the tribal elders, who could sway—even demand—their members to vote for their favored candidate, would make for a difficult, maybe contested, outcome. That would be bad for Afghan citizens, but potentially terrible for the coalition of countries from NATO and elsewhere that sought a reliable, legitimate partner as president of Afghanistan.

Late in the morning, Major General Scaparrotti and I boarded Black Hawks and flew to Kabul. At the Ministry of Defense, Minister Wardak and Lieutenant General Karimi met with us in Wardak's office and we again reviewed election security and overall security in RC-East. We had a frank but cordial lunch meeting with General Bismillah Khan, then drove over to meet with Minister of the Interior Atmar, where we had a lively conversation about the progress and planning for the borders.

"We are making great progress with the 'Schloesser Line,' formerly known as the 'Durand Line.'" Atmar smiled as he spoke.

The concept had been relatively simple: place a Persistent Threat Detection System (PTDS), blimps or mobile towers with EO/IR cameras, along the known and likely insurgent infiltration and exfiltration routes along our RC-East border with Pakistan, and locate Afghan Border Police base camps about ten kilometers back from the borders to give the border police reaction time after insurgents were spotted. Use ISAF-partnered units to bolster the border police when necessary, but focus on building the capability of the border police themselves: reliable weapons, including some heavy machine guns, adequate ammunition to actually win a firefight, Hilux pickup trucks and, soon, Humvees for added ground mobility, and a logistics organization to plan for, stock, and resupply the border police in their base camps.

Hardly the most advanced concept in the art and science of border security, but for the Afghans in 2008 to 2009, it was exciting. And challenging.

We made a final stop to talk with Lieutenant General Mangal, chief of the Afghan National Police, and then headed back to Bagram. These five men—Wardak, Bismillah Khan, Karimi, Atmar, and Mangal—controlled the Afghan Security Forces, had been my partners over the past fifteen months, and would be General Scaparrotti's partners as well. They and our CJTF and ISAF troops were the present reality, and future hope, of a secure and stable Afghanistan.

The next day, Major General Scaparrotti and I, with our respective deputy commanders for operations, Mark Milley and Kurt Fuller, flew to Pakistan. At Peshawar, Lieutenant General Masood Aslam hosted us at 11th Corps headquarters. Reserved, somewhat stiff, but welcoming, Masood made little mention of the ongoing tough fight in Swat, but was open and insightful on the operations along our mutual borders. What progress we had made in the past fifteen months! I remembered our very first meeting. Back in mid-May 2008, I had met in Islamabad with the Vice Chief of Staff Lieutenant General Yusuf and then DGMO Major General Pasha, and it had been extremely tense, with both sides accusing the other of not understanding the enemy, or each other. I had then flown to meet Masood in Peshawar that afternoon, and while typically cool, he was readily open to further consultation and collaboration. And now we had liaison officers on each other's staff, a fully manned Border Coordination Center at Torkham Gate, and conducted active planning together.

That was progress.

Tariq Khan from the Frontier Corps joined us, and we had a lively discussion, capped by a gift exchange. We then flew to Islamabad, and met Rear Admiral Mike LeFever and Ambassador Anne Patterson.

I respected them both. I would truly miss Ambassador Patterson: she knew the Pakistani political and military culture well, was strongly supportive of ISAF and especially CJTF-101, and had an iron will. I thought of her as a mentor, and truly sought after and paid attention to her advice.

We left the U.S. embassy and drove to Rawalpindi and the army officer mess, where DGMO Major General Javed Iqbal hosted a late afternoon luncheon in our honor. A cordial and caring host, I think he cared as much as I to continue the close working relationship we had built.

On the C-130 back to Bagram, Mike and I talked about our progress with the Pakistani military and security forces. Just over a year ago, we had had an intense firefight at Gora Paray that ended when I approved bombing individual targets as they scrambled back over the mountain border and into Pakistan. Among those we killed were Pakistani Frontier Corps troops caught between the enemy and our forces. It was the low point of our relationship. But we had built it since then into a robust and layered collaboration: the trilateral meetings between General McKiernan, General Bismillah Khan, and the Pakistani Army chief of staff; the multiple engagements General Milley and I had led to Rawalpindi and Peshawar and Islamabad, and the visits the Pakistanis made to Bagram and Kabul; the border coordination centers (BCCs); and the most important, the routine staff exchanges by our J3 operations and J2 intelligence staffs to their counterparts, as well as the daily liaison by our teams. I recalled our liaison team, led by Colonel Jim Dapore, who almost did not survive the Islamabad Marriott bombing.

We had been lucky.

Late that evening, a Task Force Spartan Humvee was struck by a massive IED, and an immediate quick reaction force was hit by a second IED, targeting first responders. Four of our soldiers from Lieutenant Colonel Kimo Gallahue's 2nd Battalion, 87th Infantry were killed, with another five wounded, some grievously. It was another searing, painful attack, but we worked with the special operations task force on intelligence we had collected immediately after the attacks, and early the next morning, an assault team found Sher Agha, leader of the initial IED attack, and killed him and five of his fellow insurgents. This was a military operation against a known enemy, with intelligence-derived operations to find, fix, and finish that the special operations task force was highly skilled at conducting. If it looked like revenge, so be it. Enemy deaths, even those of the perpetrators, could never bring back the lives they had extinguished.

Tuesday, June 2. Twenty-four hours to our transfer of authority. At 6:15 a.m., General Scaparrotti stood with me as I led the ramp ceremony for the four Bravo Company troopers. Kimo marched with his colors, and knelt by each of the four metal caskets. Scaparrotti and I did the same. The sun had been up for some time, but our mood was dark.

Later that day, one of our military police convoys was targeted at Chamkani by an IED, and a soldier was killed in action.

I was numb.

That night I did my third, and final, Pentagon press briefing via a video teleconference link back to the Pentagon Press Room. I was frank: *Violence in RC-East so far in 2009 is up about twenty-five percent over last year.*

"Unlike last year, most of that violence I attribute to the operations that we're conducting with our Afghan partners, as well as those new forces," I said. "The bottom line is we're in areas that we were not before. We've increased forces sometimes tenfold in those areas, and it's making a difference to the insurgents, and I know it will eventually make a difference to the Afghan people in those areas."

The command has grown from two brigade combat teams to five brigades. The command has worked very hard on the counterinsurgency campaign that has highlighted security and development at the district level.

"We try to do all this with and by and through our Afghan partners," I told them.

I spoke directly to the families and friends of those who had been killed or wounded during our campaign: "There's no way we can bring them back, there's no way that we can express enough grief to their loved ones. But I do want them to know that there's not a day that goes by that we don't think about their sacrifices or the sacrifices of their families."

Later in the evening, as the night turned black, we met at the ramp, and farewelled Specialist Roberto Hernandez, from the 549th Military Police Company, our military police soldier who had been killed that morning. Hernandez, from Queens, New York, had been less than a month from going home.

★ ★ ★

June 3, 2009: Transfer of authority day. I got up early as usual and ran five miles along the airfield perimeter. I stuffed the few remaining uniforms I had in my backpack, grabbed some breakfast, and met with Major General Scaparrotti one last time for a morning update. Senior guests began arriving: governors from eight of our provinces, our subordinate brigade commanders and their command sergeants major, Minister Wardak and Minister Atmar, the corps commanders from the 201st and 203rd Corps, General Bismillah Khan, and General McKiernan, who himself was departing Afghanistan that night.

It was a simple ceremony at 10:00 a.m.: medals pinned on our chests, speeches capped by the furling of the CJTF-101 colors by Command Sergeant Major Vince Camacho and me, and then Major General Mike Scaparrotti and his sergeant major unfurled the CJTF-82 colors.

The transfer of authority was over. The last of the major units from CJTF-101, Colonel John Spiszer's Task Force Duke, would remain in Afghanistan for less than a month before conducting its own transfer of authority with Colonel Randy George's 4th Brigade, 4th Infantry Division.

I was a strong believer that outgoing commanders should quickly get out of the way of the new command, and so I departed for the airfield ramp with the small 101st Division staff that had remained with me to the end. Late that afternoon, we boarded the C-17. Roughly thirty airplane seats for us were up front, our small amount of gear palletized in the back, and in the middle of the plane was Specialist Hernandez, his metal shipping coffin draped in a large American flag. We gathered around the coffin, and said a prayer. We had been together as commander, command team, and senior staff for fifteen months in combat, and many had been with me for a year or more before our deployment. They knew me and I knew them. I spoke from the heart, telling them that Hernandez would have wanted it this way: if he wasn't going home alive, then he was going home surrounded by those who had in some small way shared in his war, and knew his loss, and grieved. But we also honored him as a fellow soldier, a veteran of a foreign war so far removed from America as to be incomprehensible for many of our fellow Americans. None of us were heroes. We had done our duty.

After a ten-hour flight, we landed at Ramstein, Germany, for fuel. We loaded three more shipping coffins, these dead soldiers the result of a non-combat accident in Germany. We took off, bound for Dover.

En route I dozed, but was awakened by my staff.

Would I conduct the ramp ceremony for Specialist Hernandez at Dover? Every returning soldier, sailor, marine, and airman killed in Iraq and Afghanistan was met by an honor guard and a general officer at Dover, regardless of the time of day.

It would be my honor.

We landed at Dover in darkness, and in an early morning cold mist lined up outside the C-17 ramp. An honor guard marched into the plane, and we saluted as Specialist Hernandez was moved out of the cargo hold. A small group watched from the side, and after the ceremony, I met the Hernandez family, and hugged them, and told them what I knew of their son's death, but also of his life at war, in Afghanistan. He had done his duty, and they could be proud.

We reboarded the C-17 and took off for Fort Campbell. It was a short flight, and I remained awake. I pondered the past fifteen months. It truly had been a marathon: hard to adequately train for, excruciating in execution, and when it was all over, you wondered if the pain was worth the gain. Had it all been worth it? We had had 180 killed in action, 810 wounded, some grievously. The dead gone forever; the lives of the living changed forever. No one comes back from war the same.

We had made some progress in eastern Afghanistan, and had set conditions for those that followed us to be more successful, as long as America and NATO persevered. I thought we had done a satisfactory job helping decision makers understand the stakes, and what it would take to hold back the Taliban, the Haqqanis, the HiG, and all the rest.

But win? This counterinsurgency? That would take the Afghans to step up and to bring down the corruption that devoured the soul of the nascent Afghan Republic. And it would take the Pakistanis to decide to give up any illicit or tacit support to the insurgents. Finally, the Taliban had to reconcile, and become part of the legitimate political landscape of Afghanistan.

Would America, and its NATO and ISAF partners, have the will, and the patience, to remain committed while they waited for those things to happen?

The C-17 landed on the long main runway at Campbell Army Airfield, and taxied toward the ramp where we dedicated a hangar for homecomings. I had landed here in March 2004, returning from Iraq. On this morning it was gray, low clouds hiding the dawn, and a gentle drizzle moistened our faces as we bound down the aircraft stairs to the concrete ramp. We formed up, and I marched the staff into the redeployment hangar, where our families and well-wishers were cheering from gym seating along the sides. The staff still in formation, I jumped up on the stage, and in as few words as I could, welcomed them home, and thanked those who were there to greet us. And then I released the soldiers, and their loved ones rushed to them, hugging and kissing and crying.

Patty was there, of course, as she had been for thirty-three years. We hugged, said a few goodbyes to my aides and staff, posed for a picture or two with friends, and drove home to the Farmhouse.

It was over.

AFTERWORD

"A man's character is his fate."
Heraclitus

I learned many things during my fifteen months in command in eastern Afghanistan. Some were lessons of war at the strategic level, others were in the detailed squad-level tactics that made for a successful combat outpost in remote mountains many miles from a company, much less our divisional and CJTF-level headquarters. But in hindsight, the most valuable lessons were personal. I learned the most about me.

Leadership in challenging circumstances is a soul-searching, energy-sapping journey into a daily and nightly unknown. I thought I was prepared mentally, physically, and emotionally for what I knew would be a brutally hard and excruciatingly long test of my will, skills, and inner discipline: a marathon war.

I was wrong.

I came home and did my best to be a man of character, as had been my goal for decades in my life as a leader, a father, and a husband. And I tried, above all, to do the right things, even when I was alone. But my spirit was seared. I was like a big old oak tree, looking fine on the outside, but lightning had burned out my core.

It was ironic: I would feel nothing inside when people should be sad, or empathic. At other times, a simple poem or movie scene would bring back a flood of memories I had purposely packaged up and shelved in my mind, never to be opened on purpose, and I would tear up for no evident reason.

Patty brought me back over the years that followed, in spite of the strain of what came next, after I came home.

I gave up command of the 101st Airborne Division to Major General John C. Campbell about sixty days after we redeployed, on a fine summer day at Fort Campbell, with many thousands of troopers on the divisional parade field. I confess it was one of the saddest days of my life: commanding the Screaming Eagles over the past thirty-three months, and the fifteen months of command of CJTF-101 in Afghanistan, were the most important and most rewarding years of my professional life. I was self-actualized. I knew, internally, I had a lot of repair work to be done spiritually and emotionally, but I felt then, and still do, that the effort had been worthy of the damage.

Patty and I took off for a few weeks' leave, a vacation, as my aides left for Germany and our furniture was packed and sent to Germany. I was to be promoted to lieutenant general, and would be the deputy commanding general in U.S. Army Europe.

It was not to be, and I would retire within the year.

During our vacation, I was informed that a preliminary account by the Combat Studies Institute at Fort Leavenworth, Kansas, of the Wanat battle had found the leadership above platoon sorely lacking, even negligent, and that the civilian historian author blamed the company, battalion, brigade, and CJTF leadership—personally. I had never talked with the author, and did not think my staff or deputy commanders had had the time since we returned to do so. I found the study inaccurate, damning, and so lacking in the context of the war as to be more fairy tale than fact. But it was being circulated by my peers, my fellow army general officers. And the army, and the Department of Defense, would investigate.

Over the coming months, I would be interviewed for a follow-up and official study, as well as several formal investigations by U.S. Central Command. My move and promotion were on hold, of course, and we lived first in a simple one-bedroom apartment behind a generals' quarters at Fort Myer, Virginia, then after some months moved into regular quarters at Fort Belvoir, where we borrowed furniture from our daughter, since ours was awaiting our arrival overseas. My aides and their families had moved to Germany, and found other jobs while waiting for us.

I asked for an interim job, and was appointed yet again as director, army aviation, at the Pentagon.

Late in January 2010, I learned that Mark Milley and I had been cleared of any negligence, and that holds on our promotions were expected to be cleared soon. But I also learned that the army's designated final investigator, General Charles "Hondo" Campbell, commanding general of U.S. Forces Command, had been tasked to review the previous investigations into Wanat. In early March, I learned he had presented general officer letters of reprimand to the company, battalion, and brigade commander for negligence in combat leadership at Wanat.

It had been an emotional winter for Patty and me as we waited and I wrestled internally with the right thing for me to do. I had long ago taken full responsibility for the Wanat Battle, and sincerely believed that if the Department and the army were going to punish anyone, it would and should be me. That weekend I decided I had to act. Patty agreed.

The first letter I wrote was to the chief of staff of the army, requesting to retire almost immediately. The second letter was to General Hondo Campbell.

When the first letter made its way to the chief, General George Casey, he asked to see me. He told me he did not want me to retire, that I would soon be totally cleared from the hold on my promotion, and would be off to serve in Germany. I told him I felt this was a matter of integrity, that the commanders who served under me had done the very best they could with the resources I had available to provide to them, I was certain they were neither negligent nor derelict, and I could not allow them to be punished as I went on with my career. I asked for his understanding, and his approval. I am not sure about the former, but I eventually received the latter.

The second letter to General Campbell laid out our situation in the summer of 2008, the lack of resources, the fierce combat throughout much of RC-East, and the situation I faced as the senior tactical commander. I took total responsibility for the outcome of Wanat, and requested he review the battle and the actions of my subordinate commanders in light of that context.

I will never know if my letter to General Campbell helped my commanders or not, but before my retirement was effective, I learned that he had dropped all charges against my soldiers. I was relieved beyond any words I could express then or now.

I was asked to withdraw my retirement paperwork, but felt I could not. Again, it was a matter of integrity, of character. My character.

I retired from the army in mid-April, in a ceremony at the Pentagon hosted by the army vice chief of staff, General Peter Chiarelli. Patty, our daughter Kelly, our daughter-in-law Molly, and our young grandson Sam attended, along with many old, close friends. Our son Ryan was deployed to Afghanistan. Sam kept what could have been a sad day and ceremony as lighthearted as possible: I will never forget General Chiarelli giving Sam a horsey ride on his knee as I spoke my last words in uniform. I could not help but grin.

I have been asked since my retirement if it was all worth it: the fifteen months of tough combat, the 180 lives lost, the wounded, and the many of us who came home a bit different than when we left. Usually what people really are asking is a different, bigger question: Was this war winnable, and if so, why does victory still seem so far away, years after we began in the cold winter of 2001? And in my mind, the only way to answer the first question is to answer the second.

By the time we left Afghanistan in 2009, I was convinced that our counterinsurgency strategy was sound, as a framework: we had to concentrate on building the Afghans' capacity to provide security, good governance at a local level, and sustainable development that provided jobs and an improved way of life for the vast majority of Afghans. I was prepared and regarded it as part of my leadership responsibilities to determine the required resources, and then to bet my stars on achieving those resources. But I was equally convinced that Afghan corruption was endemic in almost every field of endeavor, that we had supported and continued to support the wrong man for president of Afghanistan, and that we had given the Afghans back their country from the Taliban irresponsibly, well before they were able to govern it.

I was also convinced that the safe haven and resources provided by a special directorate of the Pakistani ISI made any battlefield defeat of the Taliban or Haqqanis, which occurred routinely, a temporary outcome. And if that continued, there was little we could do to bring the Taliban to the negotiating table, which I believed and still do believe is crucial to move beyond a veritable stalemate to actually bring to a close this very long and most foreign of our wars.

So my answer to the second question is this: the Afghan War is a counterinsurgency and will take generations to totally resolve, especially given the lack of strategic attention given to it by the United States during the Iraq surge, as well as the missteps made early on with a too-early Afghan national government, the too-late discovery of the impact of Afghan corruption on everything we did, and the continuing Pakistani sly bet-hedging.

But it can be resolved, if not "won" in a strict combat sense, by seriously addressing Afghan corruption, Pakistani duplicity, and the desire by the Taliban to play a political role in Afghanistan.

I felt then, and still do, that we can turn our backs on Afghanistan, and declare it is no longer in our national interest to commit our treasure and blood in that country, but that Afghanistan will not turn away from America, or Europe. If we let the country go back to those who seek to destroy us and our way of life, it will not be long—certainly not a generation—before they come looking for us yet again.

And so back to the first question: Was it worth it? We were volunteers, called by a nation that had suffered a devastating surprise attack that began in Afghanistan, and our cause was honorable. We fought for many private reasons, and those who gave their lives or were horribly wounded most often were fighting for their comrades right next to them, which in our culture is the most dignified and worthy commitment one human being can make to another. And to this day, there are Afghan children and young adults who would never have been born, schooled, or cared for, without us. They are the future of Afghanistan.

Yes, I think it was worth it.

GLOSSARY

.50 Cal: Browning M2 heavy machine gun made in the U.S. effective against ground targets and can be used against low and slow aerial targets. Effective range is about eighteen hundred meters.

15-6 (Investigation): a commander-directed investigation under the Uniform Code of Military Justice.

AAR: after-action review.

A-Bad: Asadabad, city in Kunar Province.

ABCT: airborne brigade combat team.

ABP: Afghan Border Police.

ACLU: American Civil Liberties Union.

ADT: agricultural development team.

ANA: Afghan National Army.

ANP: Afghan National Police.

AO: area of operation.

AOR: area of responsibility (such as Regional Command-East, Afghanistan).

AP3: Afghan Public Protection Program.

ASAP: as soon as possible.

Auftragstaktik: German for mission-type tactics, also related to mission command in U.S. Army doctrine.

B-1B Bomber: a supersonic heavy bomber manufactured for the USAF by Rockwell.

Battalion: a military unit normally commanded by a lieutenant colonel, from two hundred to six hundred troops.

BCC: border coordination center.

BCT: brigade combat team: a military unit of brigade size, commanded by a colonel, task-organized for combat; often with at least 3,500 troops, usually more.

BDU: battle dress uniform.

Blue on Blue: friendly fire, in this context between U.S., ISAF, or NATO forces.

Brigade: a military unit normally commanded by a colonel, from two thousand to four thousand troops.

BTIF: Bagram Theater Internment Facility.

C2: command and control.

C2 (COD aircraft): Grumman C2 Greyhound "Carrier Onboard Delivery" aircraft used to ferry passengers and cargo to and from U.S. Navy aircraft carriers and the shore.

CA: civil affairs.

CAB: combat aviation brigade; a U.S. Army aviation unit commanded by a colonel, operating more than one hundred aircraft, primarily helicopters, with 2,500 or more troops.

CAOC: Combined Air Operations Center, at Al Udeid, Qatar, responsible for coordinating the air war over Afghanistan and the entire region.

CAS: close air support.

CCA: close combat attack.

CERP: Commander's Emergency Response Program.

CG: commanding general.

CHOD: chief of defense, the highest-ranking military officer in a given country (non-U.S.).

CIA: Central Intelligence Agency.

CJCS: chairman of the Joint Chiefs of Staff (highest-ranking military officer in the U.S.).

CJSOTF: combined joint special operations force.

CJTF: combined joint task force.

CLP: combat logistics patrol; also a lubricating fluid for cleaning weapons.

CMO: civil-military operations.

CNN: Cable News Network.

COAB: commander's assessment brief.

CODEL: congressional delegation.

COIN: counterinsurgency.

COMISAF: commander, International Security Assistance Force.

Company: a military unit commanded by a captain, with fifty to two hundred troops.

COP: combat outpost.

CSA: chief of staff, army. The highest-ranking officer in the U.S. Army.

CSM: command sergeant major. The highest-ranking non-commissioned officer in large units, from battalions, brigades, divisions, corps, and armies.

CSTC-A: Combined Security Transition Command-Afghanistan.

CT: counterterrorism.

CUB: commanders update brief.

DCG (DCG-O; DCG-S): deputy commanding general (for operations or support).

DCM: deputy chief of mission; the second-ranking diplomat in an embassy after the ambassador.

DFAC: dining facility; D-Fac; chow hall; mess hall.

DGMO: director general of military operations (Pakistan Army).

DIA: Defense Intelligence Agency.

Division: a military unit commanded by a major general, with roughly eight thousand to twenty thousand troops, depending on mission configuration.

DShK: a 12.7-mm heavy machine gun made by the Soviets and used against ground and aerial targets, with a max range of almost 7,000 meters (effective range is closer to 1,500 meters against ground targets and 1,000 meters against aerial targets).

DUSTWUN: duty status whereabouts unknown.

ECP: entry control point.

EO/IR: electro-optical and infrared camera and sensor, used for day and night sensing and targeting.

ETT: embedded training team.

FATA: Federally Administered Tribal Area (Pakistan).

FOB: forward operating base.

FUOPS: future operations.

G-staff (G1-9): staff sections within a division, a general officer-led task force, corps, and army. G1 is personnel, G2 is intelligence, G3 is operations, G4 is logistics, and so on.

GBU: guided bomb unit, as in a GBU-12 Paveway II five-hundred-pound bomb with a laser guidance kit. Manufactured in the United States.

GHQ: general headquarters.

Global Hawk: a high-flying, long-endurance unmanned surveillance and reconnaissance aircraft manufactured in the United States by Northrop Grumman. Designated the RQ-4.

GOMR: General Officer Memorandum of Reprimand.

Green on Blue: Friendly fire involving attacks on U.S., ISAF, and NATO forces by Afghan police, army, or other security forces. Blue on green is the opposite: U.S., ISAF, and NATO forces attacking friendly Afghan security forces.

GTMO: Guantanamo Bay, Cuba (site of U.S. internment facility for those suspected of terrorism).

GWOT: global war on terrorism.

HESCO bastion: a defensive barrier or gabion made of a wire mesh container with a heavy-duty fabric liner, which is filled on-site by sand, dirt, or rocks.

HIMARS: a light, truck-mounted, high-mobility artillery rocket system, made in the U.S by Lockheed Martin. Capable of precision targeting with up to six missiles out to almost three hundred miles.

HMMWV: high-mobility multipurpose wheeled vehicle, often lightly armored and made in the U.S.

Hind Helicopter: Mi-24 Hind attack helicopter, Russian manufacture, heavily armed and capable of also carrying up to eight passengers.

HTT: Human Terrain Team.

Hunter (UAV): The Hunter RQ-5A UAV (unmanned aerial vehicle) is a dual-engine intelligence, surveillance, and reconnaissance platform fielded in 1996, and has seen service in Kosovo, Iraq, and Afghanistan.

HVI: high-value individual.

HVT: high-value target.

ICRC: International Committee of the Red Cross.

IDF: indirect fire.

IDLG: Independent Directorate of Local Governance.

IED: improvised explosive device.

Iftar: meal in Islam during Ramadan (Ramazan in Afghanistan) breaking the daylong fast, eaten after sunset.

Interagency: within the Department of Defense, the U.S. government departments and agencies that support national security, including intelligence.

IO: information operations. Also international organization.

ISAF: International Security Assistance Force.

ISI: Pakistani Inter-Services Intelligence organization.

ISR: intelligence, surveillance, and reconnaissance.

ITAS: Improved Target Acquisition System.

J-Bad: Jalalabad.

JCS: Joint Chiefs of Staff (United States military staff from all services headed by the chairman of the Joint Chiefs (CJCS), the senior military officer in the U.S. Armed Forces).

JDAM: joint direct attack munition.

JOC: joint operations center. A jointly manned facility of a joint force commander's headquarters established for planning, monitoring, and guiding the execution of the commander's decisions.

JRTC: Joint Readiness Training Center, a U.S. military training center at Fort Polk, Louisiana.

JSOC: Joint Special Operations Command.

JTF: joint task force (military unit made up of more than one service).

Kandak: a battalion in the Afghan National Army.

KFOR: The Kosovo Force is a NATO-led international peacekeeping force responsible for establishing a secure environment in Kosovo. KFOR entered Kosovo on June 11, 1999, two days after the adoption of UN Security Council Resolution 1244.

KGB: Komitet Gosudarstvennoy Bezopasnosti, the main security agency of the Soviet Union.

KG Pass: Khost-Gardez Pass, the main route connecting the Afghan cities of Khost and Gardez, and historically, Kabul to India.

KHAD: The Afghan government's secret police prior to and during the Soviet invasion, patterned after the Soviet KGB.

KIA: killed in action.

KPF: Khost Protective Force.

KW (Kiowa Warrior Helicopter, OH-58D): an armed reconnaissance helicopter manufactured in the United States by Bell Helicopter.

LANTIRN: Low-altitude navigation and targeting infrared for night combination navigation and targeting pod used on F-15E and F-16 aircraft.

Lapis Lazuli: a deep blue semi-precious stone mined since antiquity in Afghanistan.

LLVI: Low Level Voice Intercept, operating the AN/MLQ-40 Prophet, which scans airwaves searching and homing on enemy radio and cell phone signals.

LNO: liaison officer.

LOC: lines of communications.

LRAS3: Long Range Advanced Scout Surveillance System.

LT: lieutenant, lowest-ranking commissioned officer in the U.S. Army, Air Force, and Marine Corps.

LZ: landing zone.

MASH: mobile army surgical hospital.

Medevac: medical evacuation, commonly a helicopter or ground vehicle specifically outfitted for en route medical care.

MI-8/17: Soviet and Russian-made military transport helicopters widely exported throughout the world. Can also be armed.

MIA: missing in action.

MIG: A variety of Soviet and later Russian-made military jets produced by the Mikoyan and Gurevich Design Bureau, widely exported.

MINDEF: minister of defense.

MININT: minister of interior.

MLA: military liaison assistant. In the U.S. Congress, a staff assistant that handles the senator's or congressman/woman's military portfolio.

MRAP: A mine-resistant, ambush-protected military wheeled vehicle.

MRE: meals, ready to eat: individual combat rations for U.S. military troops.

NAI: named area of interest.

NATO: North Atlantic Treaty Organization.

NCTC: National Counterterrorism Center.

NDS: National Directorate of Security, the primary intelligence organization in Afghanistan.

NGO: non-governmental organization.

NSC: National Security Council.

NSE: national support element.

NSTR: nothing significant to report.

NTC: National Training Center located at Fort Irwin, California.

NVG: night-vision goggles.

OCS: Officer Candidate School.

ODA: Operational Detachment Alpha. A U.S. Special Forces unit of twelve soldiers, commanded by a captain.

ODIN: A U.S. Army task force organized to observe, detect, identify, and neutralize the improvised explosive device threat.

ODNI: Office of the Director, National Intelligence (U.S. intelligence organization responsible for integrating intelligence and leading the intelligence community).

ODRP: Office, Defense Representative, Pakistan (U.S. senior military officer in Pakistan).

OEF: Operation Enduring Freedom, refers to the U.S. combat missions of the global war on terrorism. In Afghanistan, refers to the U.S.-led combat operations from 2001 to 2014 focused primarily on counterterrorism.

OGA: other government agency; can be a euphemism for the Central Intelligence Agency.

OMC: Office of Military Cooperation. Also sometimes seen as OSC: office of security cooperation.

OMLT: operational mentoring and liaison team, a NATO small unit assigned to advise and assist Afghan Army units.

OP: observation post.

OPTEMPO: operations tempo. The pace of an operation or operations; may also include all unit activities over a period of time, or a series of operations.

OSD: the U.S. Office of the Secretary of Defense.

PA: public affairs; also physician's assistant.

PAO: public affairs officer.

PAX: passengers.

PCC: provincial capital center; also pre-command course.

PDSS: predeployment site survey.

POAC: formerly the Pentagon Officers Athletic Club, the gym at the Pentagon for all military ranks and civilians who work at the Pentagon and join the club. Now known as the PAC, Pentagon Athletic Center.

POLAD: political advisor, in the U.S. context refers to State Department foreign policy advisors assigned to advise military commanders.

POO: point of origin, as in location from which a mortar, rocket, or artillery was fired.

Predator (UAV) also "Pred": The MQ-1B Predator is manufactured in the U.S. by General Atomics and is a long-endurance, medium-range unmanned aerial vehicle with infrared sensor and potential to be armed with Hellfire missiles.

PRT: provincial reconstruction team.

PSD: personal security detachment.

PT: physical training.

PTDS: persistent threat detection system. A lighter-than-air blimp outfitted for intelligence, surveillance, and reconnaissance as well as combat outpost security, outfitted with an electro-optical infrared camera, small tactical radar, and communications radios, and normally tethered to a ground location.

PTSD: post-traumatic stress disorder.

PX: post-exchange.

QRF: quick reaction force.

Raven (UAV): a small, hand-launched, low-altitude unmanned aerial vehicle, normally used by platoons and companies. Manufactured in the United States.

RC: regional command, within NATO's ISAF Afghanistan.

RC-East (south, west, north, capital): NATO subdivided regional responsibilities within Afghanistan into five regions, with lead nations responsible for coordinating each. The United States was responsible for RC-East during my command tour.

RCP: route clearance patrol.

RFF: request for forces.

RON: remain overnight.

RPG: rocket-propelled grenade: normally referring to the RPG-7, a Soviet-manufactured anti-tank weapon that fires a shaped charge rocket, effective to about three hundred meters.

R and R: rest and recuperation; in the U.S. military, usually a two-week stint out of the combat zone.

S-staff (S1-5): As in G-staff, but in units not commanded by a general officer, such as a battalion, squadron, brigade, or BCT. S-1 is personnel, S-2 is intelligence, S-3 is operations, S-4 logistics, S-5 is planning, S-6 is signals/communications, and so on.

SATCOM: satellite communications.

Seabee: U.S. Navy construction engineer battalion (CB).

SEAL: Sea, Air, Land: a U.S. Navy special operations unit and operator.

SF: special forces. In the U.S. Army, refers to specifically trained soldiers and their unique units, sized in ODAs, companies, battalions, and groups.

SFOR: stabilization force(s): NATO term for member nation units providing security operations in Bosnia.

Shadow (UAV): the RQ-7, a medium unmanned vehicle manufactured in the U.S. by AAI, usually positioned at the brigade/BCT level.

Shura: Arabic for "consultation." In the Afghan context, refers to gatherings of tribal or regional elders and notables to discuss key events or political and security issues.

SIGINT: signals intelligence.

SOAR: Special Operations Aviation Regiment; in the U.S. context, refers to the 160th Special Operations Aviation Regiment, a specially trained and unique army aviation unit supporting special operations units.

SOCOM: U.S. Special Operations Command.

STOL: aircraft for short-field takeoff and landing.

SUV: sport utility vehicle. When used by U.S. forces in a combat zone, normally armored.

SVBIED: suicide vehicle-borne improvised explosive device.

SVTC: secure video teleconference, meaning classified subjects can be discussed.

Swat: an administrative district within Pakistan's Khyber Pakhtunkhwa Province, known for high, snowcapped mountains, and scene of intense fighting between the Taliban and Pakistani security forces; commonly referred to as the First and Second Battles of Swat.

TAC: tactical command post.

TACSAT: tactical satellite (as in radio).

Tandberg: a desktop video teleconference system used primarily by senior commanders to confer one-on-one with each other.

T-rations: tray rations. U.S. military field meals prepared to serve units.

TF: task force.

TIC: troops in contact.

TOA: transfer of authority, in this context normally conducted between units departing and arriving in a specific area of responsibility.

TOLO: TOLO news channel in Afghanistan; one of the first TV stations in post-Taliban Afghanistan.

TOW: the BGM-71, a tube-launched, optically tracked, wire-guided missile: a U.S. anti-tank missile capable of ground or air launch.

TTP: tactics, techniques, and procedures.

U2: Lockheed U-2 "Dragon Lady" ultra high-altitude reconnaissance aircraft operated by the United States.

UAE: United Arab Emirates.

UCMJ: Uniform Code of Military Justice.

UK: United Kingdom.

USA: United States of America; also, United States Army.

USAF: United States Air Force.

USAID: United States Agency for International Development.

USMC: United States Marine Corps.

USN: United States Navy.

USO: United Service Organizations: provides entertainment to deployed U.S. military forces, plus a wide-ranging series of services for troops.

VAB: Véhicule de l'avant blindé, French-made lightly armored personnel carrier.

VCSA: Vice chief of staff of the army (United States); second-most senior officer in the U.S. Army.

VIP: very important person.

VTC: video teleconference.

WIA: wounded in action.

XO: executive officer (second-ranking officer in a military unit from company, battalion, and brigade).

INSURGENT AND TERRORIST GROUPS IN REGIONAL COMMAND-EAST 2008-2009

AQ: al-Qaida
Haqqani Group: the Haqqani network led by Jalaluddin Haqqani's son
   Siraj
HIG: Gulbuddin Hekmatyar's Hezb-e-Islami Gulbuddin group
HIK/TBF: Hezb-i-Islami Khalis, led by Younas Khalis
IJU: Islamic Jihad Union
IMU: Islamic Movement of Uzbekistan
JeM: Jaish-e-Mohammed
LeT: Lashkar-e-Taiba
Sipah-e-Sahaba
Taliban: the Afghan-oriented insurgents often referred to as the Quetta
   Shura, led by Mullah Omar
TNSM: Tehreek-e-Nafaz-e-Shariat-e-Mohammadi
TTiP: Tehrik-e-Taliban-i-Pakistan, the Taliban insurgents oriented
   against Pakistan and led by Baitullah Mehsud

UNITS IN THE FIELD
(CJTF-101, 2008–2009)

The 173rd Airborne Brigade Combat Team, Task Force Bayonet, served in RC-East from May 2007 until July 2008. The brigade commander was Colonel "Chip" Preysler. In the northeast, Lieutenant Colonel Christopher D. Kolenda's 1st Squadron, 91st Cavalry (TF SABER) established a position at Operating Base Bostick. Lieutenant Colonel William B. Ostlund's 2nd Battalion, 503rd Infantry (TF Rock) established itself at Camp Blessing in the Pech River Valley in Kunar Province. Farther to the west, Lieutenant Colonel Stephen J. Maranian's 4th Battalion, 319th Field Artillery (TF King) had been transformed into a hybrid organization composed of artillery and light infantry before being sent to Forward Operating Base Kalagush.

The 4th Brigade, 101st Airborne Division (Air Assault), Task Force CURRAHEE, served in RC-East from April 2008 until April 2009. Commanded by Colonel John P. "Pete" Johnson, it consisted of six organic units: Lieutenant Colonel Anthony DeMartino's 1st Battalion, 506th Infantry (TF Red Currahee); Lieutenant Colonel John Allred's 2nd Battalion, 506th Infantry (TF White Currahee); 1st Squadron, 61st Cavalry (TF Panther) led by Lieutenant Colonel Tom W. O'Steen; Lieutenant Colonel David J. Ell's 4th Battalion, 320th Field Artillery (TF Glory); Lieutenant Colonel Anthony K. "Kirk" Whitson's 801st Brigade Support Battalion (TF Mountaineer); and the 4th Special Troops Battalion (TF Strength).

Colonel John Spiszer's 3rd Brigade Combat Team, 1st Infantry Division, Task Force DUKE, served in RC-East from July 2008 until July 2009, and consisted of Lieutenant Colonel Daniel S. Hurlbut's 2nd Battalion, 2nd Infantry (TF Ramrod); Lieutenant Colonel Brett Jenkinson's 1st Battalion, 26th Infantry (TF Blue Spader); Lieutenant Colonel James Markert's 6th Squadron, 4th Cavalry (TF Raider); 1st Battalion, 6th Field Artillery (TF Centaur) led by Lieutenant Colonel Salvatore Petrovia; Lieutenant Colonel Patrick Daniel's 3rd Brigade Special Troops Battalion (TF Valiant); and Lieutenant Colonel Bradley A. White's 201st Brigade Support Battalion (TF Thor). TF Duke also had assigned Lieutenant Colonel Stephen M. Radulski's 3rd Battalion, 103rd Armor from the Pennsylvania National Guard, which we deployed to Laghman Province.

Colonel David Haight's 3rd Brigade Combat Team, 10th Mountain Division, Task Force SPARTAN, served in RC-East from January 2009 to January 2010. Lt. Col. Kimo C. Gallahue's 2nd Battalion, 87th Infantry was based in Wardak Province and Lt. Col. Daniel P. Goldthorpe's 3rd Squadron, 71st Cavalry in Logar Province. Haight detached the third maneuver battalion, Lt. Col. Frederick M. McDonnell's 1st Battalion, 32nd Infantry, to Colonel Spiszer's Task Force DUKE in Kunar Province. The rest of TF SPARTAN, to include Lt. Col. Michael P. Gabel's 4th Battalion, 25th Field Artillery, Lt. Col. Eugene A. Shearer's 710th Brigade Support Battalion, and Lt. Col. Steve Pitts' 3rd Brigade Special Troops Battalion, remained assigned to Haight.

Colonel Michael Howard's 4th Brigade, 25th Infantry Division (Task Force Yukon) served in RC-East from April 2009 to April 2010. TF YUKON was composed of Lieutenant Colonel Robert Campbell's 1st Squadron, 40th Cavalry (Task Force Denali); Lieutenant Colonel Clinton Baker's 1st Battalion, 501st Infantry (Task Force 1 Geronimo); Lieutenant Colonel Peter Minalga's 3rd Battalion, 509th Infantry (Task Force 3 Geronimo); Lieutenant Colonel Stephen Smith's 2nd Battalion, 377th Field Artillery (Task Force Steel); Lieutenant Colonel Brian Scott's

4th Battalion, 25th Brigade Special Troops (Task Force WARRIOR); Lieutenant Colonel Erin Martin's 725th Brigade Support Battalion (Task Force CENTURION); and Lieutenant Colonel Matthew D. Smith's 1st Battalion, 121st Infantry (Task Force Dahlonega)—a Georgia Army National Guard unit whose parent brigade also had responsibility for training the Afghan Army.

TF Cincinnatus, commanded by Colonel Jonathan Ives, served in RC-East from January 2007 to June 2008. The task force had a unique lineage, having been originally created by U.S. Army Forces Command using officers and non-commissioned officers stripped from the 23rd Chemical Battalion at Fort Lewis, Washington.

The 1st Maneuver Enhancement Brigade, TF Warrior, commanded by Colonel Scott A. Spellmon, served in RC-East from June 2008 to September 2009. Task Force WARRIOR was composed of a variety of assigned and attached units during this deployment.

The 101st Combat Aviation Brigade, 101st Airborne Division (Air Assault), Task Force DESTINY, commanded by Colonel Jim Richardson, served in RC-East from December 2007 until December 2008. Task Force DESTINY was composed of aviation task forces formed around the following units: Lieutenant Colonel John Lynch's 2nd Squadron, 17th Cavalry 1st Battalion, 101st CAB; Lieutenant Colonel Timothy Healy's 6th Battalion, 101st CAB; Lieutenant Colonel Tom Stauss' 5th Battalion, 101st CAB; and Lieutenant Colonel Christopher Wolfe's 96th Aviation Support Battalion.

The 159th Combat Aviation Brigade, 101st Airborne Division (Air Assault), Task Force THUNDER, commanded by Colonel Ronald Lewis, served in RC-East from December 2008 until December 2009. Task Force THUNDER was composed of aviation task forces formed around the following units: Lieutenant Colonel Paul Bontrager's 7th Squadron, 17th Cavalry; Lieutenant Colonel John White's 3rd Battalion, 101st CAB; Lieutenant Colonel James Benson's 4th Battalion, 101st

CAB; Lieutenant Colonel Rob Dickerson's 7th Battalion, 101st CAB; and Lieutenant Colonel Brett Bonnell's 563rd Aviation Support Battalion.

The 101st Sustainment Brigade, 101st Airborne Division (Air Assault), Task Force LIFELINER, commanded by Colonel Jeffrey Kelley, served in RC-East from January 2008 until February 2009. The sustainment brigade was responsible for support for all U.S. forces in Afghanistan, and had many attached support elements stationed through Afghanistan attached, assigned, or reporting to it.

The 420th Engineer Brigade, Task Force CASTLE, commanded by Brigadier General Paul Crandall, served in RC-East from May 2008 until May 2009; the brigade was composed of Lieutenant Colonel Ferguson's 201st Combat Engineer Battalion; Lieutenant Colonel Zimmerman's 62nd Engineer Battalion (Construction); Lieutenant Colonel Lloyd's 766th Explosive Hazard Coordination Center; and Lieutenant Colonel Uptmor's 802nd Facility Engineer Detachment.

The 189th Engineer Brigade, Task Force STORM, commanded by Brigadier General "Larry" Harrington, served in RC-East from May 2009 until May 2010.

The Polish Task Force WHITE EAGLE, commanded by Colonel Raymond Andrzejczak, served in RC-East from October 2008 until October 2009, and was composed of elements of the 12th Mechanized Division and 6th Brigade.

The French 27th Mountain Battalion (Alpine), Task Force TIGER, commanded by Colonel Nicholas Le Nen, served in RC-East from December 2008 until June 2009.

ACKNOWLEDGMENTS

Without the love and support of my best friend and wife of more than four decades, Patty Schloesser, this book could not have been written. Our children, Ryan, an Army officer, and daughter Kelly, a former Army civilian and current consultant, have been and continue to be inspirations to me, and so many others.

I must thank the officers and non-commissioned officers who served with me in Afghanistan, including General's Milley, McConville, Holmes, Adrzejczak (now Chief of General Staff, Polish Army), Le Nen (a Brigadier in the French Army), Richardson, Winski, Johnson, Taylor, Spellmon, Howard, Crandall, Harrington, and many others, as well as Colonel Tom Vail and Command Sergeant Major Vince Camacho.

I owe a special thanks to General Jim McConville, who allowed me unrestricted use of his war-time journals from Afghanistan. He as well as General Mike Holmes allowed me access to their deployment photo collections.

To my readers who corrected my errors and provided cogent advice, I salute you and offer my sincere gratitude: General Jim McConville, Lieutenant General Jim Richardson, Heather Hopkins, Major General (Retired) Barbara Fast, Major General Erik Peterson, Colonel (retired) Bill Ostlund, Colonel (retired) Jimmy Blackmon, Colonel (retired) Mike McCormick, Colonel (retired) Jeremy Martin, and Lieutenant Colonel Matt Myer. A special thanks to E.J. Deegan and Mark Reardon from the Chief of Staff of the Army's Operation Enduring Freedom Study Group for their guidance, patience, and access to military plans and studies. Last but likely most important, I thank Bill Depuy, who opened the Depuy family estate and family military library on more than one occasion, and whose encouragement kept me going on this project over the years.

This book was reviewed and cleared by the Defense Office of Prepublication and Security Review (under its working draft title, *Leadership 101*), and for that I owe thanks to Michael Russo.

A final but very sincere "thanks!" to my agent Roger Williams, of the Roger Williams Agency. Without his belief in this book and the value of military history and memoirs, these words would never have been printed.

INDEX

COP Malakshay, 242-243
COP Morales Frazier, 123
COP Najil, 162, 165-167
COP Ranch House, 34, 83-84, 99, 109-110
COP Wanat, 83-85, 88- 89, 96, 99-116, 134, 196, 197, 199, 203, 204, 311, 313, 346, 347, 348,
COP Wilderness, 78, 158-162, 171, 175
COP Zerok, 135-136, 262
COP Zormat, 78,
courage, 52, 82, 126, 254-255, 260-261, 297, 329, 333-334
Couric, Katie, 320
Cowper-Coles, Sir Sherard, 6, 283, 285-288
Craddock, Brigadier General / General Bantz, 163, 237
Craig Joint Theater Hospital, 228
Combined Security Transition Team – Afghanistan (CSTC-A), 79, 82, 151, 216, 331
Cuda, Captain Amanda, 234
Currahee 6, 80, 136, 151
Czech, 55, 178, 216-217, 330

D

Dapore, Colonel James, 177-178, 340
Davis, Captain Mark, 170

de Kruif, Major General Mart, 240
Dell, Deputy Charge of Mission Christopher, 87, 183-184
DeMartino, Lieutenant Colonel Anthony, 54, 237
Dempsey, Lieutenant General Martin, 48, 62-63, 81, 143, 171, 211
Destiny 6, 93
DGMO, 64, 67, 247-248, 315-316, 339
Distinguished Flying Cross, 93, 108
Dover, 343
Draper, CW3 David, 73-74, 261
Dreazen, Yochi, 262
Driggers, CW5 Brent, 273, 301
Durand Line, 46-47, 57, 60, 62, 64, 69, 80, 95, 148, 157, 201, 231, 235, 247-248, 272, 282, 285-286, 297, 301, 316, 318, 327, 331, 338
Durrani, King Timur Shah, 149
Dustoff 34, 101
DUSTWUN, 79
Dwight, Commander David, 31, 170, 174
Dzwik, Sergeant First Class David, 108

E

Eagle 6, ix, 74, 81, 211, 213, 277, 293

Karimi, Lieutenant General Sher
Mohammad, 137, 151, 230,
232, 338
Karzai, President Hamid, 5, 7-9,
42-43, 48, 51, 87-88, 123, 133,
171, 173, 183-186, 191, 198,
205, 207, 223, 226-230, 232-
233, 256, 259, 280, 283, 285,
305, 319, 326, 333
Keane, Major General Jack,
155, 157
Kearney, Captain Danial, 93, 95,
102
Kearney, Lieutenant Colonel/
Lieutenant General Frank, 93
Kline, Lieutenant Colonel
John, 72
Kosovo Force (KFOR), 23
Khan, General Bismillah
Mohammedi (BK), 49, 151,
168-171, 196, 274, 330, 338,
340, 342
Khan, Major General Tariq, 149-
150, 235-236, 247-248, 271,
301, 318, 339
Khan, Genghis, 126, 165,
221, 238
Khan, Emir Abdul Rahman, 196
Khattak, Major General Alam
Khan, 149
Khost-Gardez Pass Road, 154,
159, 332
Khyber Border Coordination
Center (BCC), 92, 95, 301

killed in action (KIA), 76
Kilbride, Captain Thomas, 78,
158-159, 171
King, Sergeant Rachel, 317
King, Specialist Ryan, 312, 317
Kipling, Rudyard, 6, 196
Klich, Minister of Defense
Bogdan, 237, 293
Kline, Lieutenant Colonel
John, 72
Kolenda, Lieutenant Colonel
Christopher, 45, 91-92
Korengal, 4, 46, 93-95, 111,
145, 152, 201, 220, 244, 270,
313, 330
Kosovo, 23, 29, 163, 180, 276,
281, 303
Kote Ashrow, 217-218
Kristensen, Lieutenant
Commander Erik, 164
Kunar Province, 34, 45-46, 54,
70, 73, 91-93, 95, 153, 164-
165, 168-170, 174, 183, 187,
201, 210, 247, 270, 272, 286-
287, 301, 305, 311-312, 318,
330, 332
Kunk, Lieutenant Colonel
Thomas, 248, 250

L

Laghman Province, 84, 123, 143,
162, 165
Larocco, Ambassador James, 24
Lashkar, 56-57, 207, 247, 275